Stephen Parkinson, Marjan Marandi Parkinson
Recognising and Dealing with Business Distress

Stephen Parkinson, Marjan Marandi Parkinson

Recognising and Dealing with Business Distress

Building Resilient Companies

DE GRUYTER

ISBN 978-3-11-068945-7
e-ISBN (PDF) 978-3-11-068949-5
e-ISBN (EPUB) 978-3-11-068953-2

Library of Congress Control Number: 2022942284

Bibliographic information published by the Deutsche Nationalbibliothek
The Deutsche Nationalbibliothek lists this publication in the Deutsche Nationalbibliografie;
detailed bibliographic data are available on the internet at http://dnb.dnb.de.

© 2023 Walter de Gruyter GmbH, Berlin/Boston
Cover image: manusapon kasosod/iStock/Getty Images Plus
Typesetting: Integra Software Services Pvt. Ltd.
Printing and binding: CPI books GmbH, Leck

www.degruyter.com

Contents

Preface

Three events, originating in different continents and linked to completely different circumstances across a period of 15 years, have highlighted the importance of building and sustaining business resilience. The impact of the global financial crisis of 2008 was felt through most of the following decade. It was followed by reductions in economic growth, large numbers of business failures and a renewed and increasing focus on corporate governance. The outbreak of a global pandemic in 2020 was an entirely different matter. Coronavirus knew no political, geographic or business boundaries. As it spread through society, employees were laid off and companies closed, some permanently, and there was a massive downturn in consumer optimism and expenditure. Most recently, the Russian escalation of its invasion of Ukraine in 2022 led to rapid increases in the costs of many raw materials, massive disruption to international supply chains and damage to consumer confidence and investment planning. Companies were suddenly forced to make economic and societal choices about continuing to operate in a market that was subject to major international economic sanctions, with increasing evidence of abuse of human rights.

Resilience never appeared on the module lists of MBA programmes in the 1980s and 1990s in the business schools where one of the authors worked. Presentations focused on worlds where growth, market development and innovation featured far more extensively than restructuring or reorganisation. If the subject was covered at all it was included as part of a strategy module linked to a discussion of organisational change. Company programmes were typically focused on developing the skill set of directors and senior managers to take businesses forward rather than on consolidation or closure. Personal consultancy assignments addressed areas such as market assessment, product development, writing business plans for new start-ups, developing the skills of board directors or occasionally helping with recruitment processes for senior managers.

Looking back, it was a time when there was an inbuilt assumption that business success could be built by applying the most recent techniques to specific situations. In the early 1970s, much of the focus was on customer orientation as a key driver. Coming from a marketing background one of us spent a great deal of time designing and running consumer surveys, panels and focus groups for a wide range of different private and public sector clients. By the 1980s, attention had turned to broader questions linked to the capacity of an organisation to react to its broader commercial environment. The agenda shifted to competitive strategy linked primarily to a series of different core ideas such as portfolio planning and competitive positioning.

There was an implied link between planning and business success. Careful analysis of the situation was followed by choice of strategies and the production of a business plan. This plan was then communicated to others and performance monitored against specific targets. This was the era of total quality management and the

https://doi.org/10.1515/9783110689495-203

period when financial management moved out of its traditional gatekeeping role to a greater strategic role in forward planning and scenario building. Attention turned to the role of effective leadership and the creation of positive organisational cultures reflected in case studies of chief executive officers (CEOs) who had turned companies around or built new business empires. The notorious expression "Fix, Sell or Close" was widely cited when discussing the alternative strategies for businesses that had run into problems.[1] Dealing with business distress and building organisational resilience was an afterthought that was frequently neglected in the rush to build positions in new emerging markets.

Over the last 20 years in the first two decades of the twenty-first century, this position has changed dramatically, and sustainability and business recovery have become major agenda items for many businesses. *It's OK to be OK* is now as important as *we want to be the best* as a driving philosophy in many companies. *Getting past OK* may be the business model for many in the future. In this climate, leading global business consultancies have focused on a rapidly growing demand for business turnaround and restructuring services. An increasing number of business schools and law schools now offer a range of courses and training at different levels in related areas, underpinned by a substantial and growing body of academic research. Regulators have focused increasing attention on the role of directors and their fiduciary duties to companies in periods of distress.

This is not another book about business turnaround, although we do focus on some aspects of this in later chapters, particularly when considering alternative strategies to respond to deteriorating business situations, and the responsibilities of directors in such circumstances. Business turnaround has been very effectively covered by a wide range of different authors. We focus instead on building business resilience—the characteristics of a company that make it better prepared to deal with different challenges and respond effectively. Building new business is an exciting process. Making sure that the existing business is resilient and capable of dealing with potential business distress may seem initially less critical, but in reality the problems that directors face on a day-to-day basis are equally important.

We have approached this area from a range of different perspectives. This book combines elements of commercial practice with insights from a wide range of academic research in related areas. We have looked at different case studies of businesses that demonstrate best practice. We have also included in-depth case studies of five high-profile business failures that document how those businesses attempted to deal with business distress, in some cases over a period of more than 10 years. We have included a legal perspective to reflect the realities that many directors need to address in such circumstances. This book includes a benchmarking framework that can be used to assess different aspects of business resilience. The framework reflects

---

1 Widely attributed to Jack Welch, former Chairman and CEO of General Electric.

the discussion in each of the chapters in what we hope is a practical format that can be used to review different aspects of business resilience.

We hope that this will be a useful resource for those seeking to improve their performance in this critical area and contribute to the overall discussion of business resilience that is now taking place in academic, commercial and legal circles.

Stephen Parkinson
Marjan Marandi Parkinson

Acknowledgements

Firstly and most importantly a big vote of thanks to our family and friends who have given us their encouragement and support whilst we have been writing this book.

When we wrote the original proposal for the book Steve Hardman at de Gruyter responded enthusiastically and has consistently supported this project as it has evolved. We have also benefitted from the encouragement and enthusiasm of Kenny McKay, Managing Director, Interpath Advisory. Kenny was in at the start when we were finalising the original concept, gave his time freely during different stages as the book came together and encouraged us to continue to develop the ideas. Many thanks to both Steve and Kenny for their support at different times.

We would also like to acknowledge the help we have received from Lucy Jarman also at de Gruyter who has helped us through the various stages of the design and production process.

Many of the events described in this book have occurred relatively recently and there will inevitably be new developments to come in many cases. We will monitor such changes, with a view to updating the contents at some point in the future. In the meantime we remain solely responsible for any errors or omissions in the current text.

https://doi.org/10.1515/9783110689495-204

1 Building resilient companies

If you can meet with Triumph and Disaster
And treat those two imposters just the same;
Yours is the Earth and everything that's in it!
(Rudyard Kipling, 1910)

Resilient companies are effectively led, have a business purpose that is clearly articulated, a well-developed business model and performance indicators that give early warning of potential problems and risks to business continuity. They have contingency plans in place to manage funds flow problems including the extension of borrowings, potential asset sale or equity issue. Most importantly when problems do arise that threaten long-term business continuity members of the board are prepared to make the call that change is needed and react quickly to bring the business back in line. They meet triumph and disaster in the business world and treat these two imposters just the same, to paraphrase Kipling.

News that a business has failed or is in serious distress may come as a surprise, even to its own employees. When long-established companies announce that major trading difficulties have led to business insolvency, their difficulties may not have been fully apparent to an external observer or indeed to company employees beyond company directors prior to any public disclosure. Such information may not be shared widely, particularly in smaller companies where disclosure rules do not require detailed external reporting of the company's financial position. In many companies the extent of problems may only become apparent when that company enters a formal insolvency process.

Detailed review of board decision-making by one of the authors confirms that the actions of directors in such circumstances are frequently ad hoc, reflecting a response to an immediate crisis rather than part of a well-reasoned turnaround plan designed to address the fundamental causes of business decline (Parkinson, 2018). Case studies of businesses in distress, including those featured in this book show that many of these companies lose sight of the need to build in business resilience as they pursue plans for growth. Her analysis reveals how directors may ultimately lose control as third parties, particularly secured creditors become involved in the direction of the business and reduce the discretion of directors. Shareholders and unsecured creditors are frequently forced to take a back seat in subsequent negotiations. Conventional models of governance may no longer apply or can be drastically compromised.

By contrast in resilient companies directors constantly check that their product/service offering remains competitive. They compare their business's performance with best practice and seek improvements where problems are identified. They build and restore business resilience in a range of different ways, looking for new opportunities to take the business forward and are prepared to change what

https://doi.org/10.1515/9783110689495-001

the company does to fit new emerging realities. They take employees and other stakeholders with them as they shape the future. Resilience is part of their DNA as the history of Kongo-Gumi, one of the oldest companies in the world illustrates.

Kongo-Gumi: Resilience is in the DNA

Kongo-Gumi dates back to 578 AD when a group of craftsmen were invited to Japan to work on the construction of the first government-sponsored temple. If long life is one definition of business resilience then this relatively small Japanese company may be well qualified for the title of the most resilient company in the world.

At the time of writing this book (2022) Kongo-Gumi is still in business special-ising in the design, construction and maintenance of temples and shrines. The com-pany has survived massive political and economic changes, wars and natural disasters throughout its history. An independent company for most of its life, Kongo-Gumi finally succumbed to the financial crisis that afflicted many companies in Japan in the first decade of the twenty-first century (Kensuke, 2017) and was bought by the Takamatsu Construction Group Company Ltd in 2008 (Takamatsu Construction Group, ND). Abstracts from its annual report for 2019 shed some in-sight into an enduring vision. [The original quotations were in Japanese and have been paraphrased by the authors where a direct translation may be potentially con-fusing or difficult to follow].

> Kongo-Gumi has been alive for more than 1400 years. We have been involved in the construc-tion of religious architecture that fosters the beliefs and hearts of the people of that era. What I have always remembered over the course of that long history is the sense of mission to pass on the traditional techniques based on the awareness of the pioneers to future generations. With an overwhelming sense of solemnity, the realization of a paradise of pure paradise, the purity of all people in front of the gods and Buddhas, the pioneers have worked hard to improve their skills and train their minds [. . .] That kind of feeling is the driving force that has contin-ued for 1400 years in shrine and temple architecture. We will continue to be a leading com-pany that always pursues new technology while respecting tradition. (Kongo-Gumi, 2013-a)

> Always think from the customer's perspective. By earnestly addressing such obvious things, we can become a company that continues to survive as a genuine company by refining tech-nology that can withstand hundreds of years and weather [different challenges]. We take that very seriously. We will be more familiar with traditional styles and technologies than anyone else, yet never lose sight of what they should be, and an aftercare system that responds quickly to customer requests, always realizing good things at a lower price. Corporate efforts, all of which are for the customer. (Kongo-Gumi, 2013-b)

Phrases such as "the sense of mission to pass on the traditional techniques" and an almost spiritual ambition expressed in the use of "an overwhelming sense of solem-nity" give some sense of the company's vision of how they intend to operate. Al-ways thinking "from the customer's perspective" and being "more familiar with traditional styles and technologies than anyone else" conveys a sense of strategic direction. Irrespective of the precise meaning and potential variations in the exact words depending on different translations this enduring sense of what the company stands for and how it should operate seems to have served Kongo-Gumi well over the past 1400 years.

Resilience matters

Company life cycles are getting shorter. A company listed on the US stock exchange in the 1960s had more than a 90% chance of surviving for at least five years compared to just 63% for a company listed in the 2000s (George, 2016). One hundred and forty-seven global companies with turnovers over €50 m entered insolvency in the second quarter of 2020 when the effects of the Covid-19 pandemic were beginning to impact on company performance (Lemerle, 2020). The largest numbers of these insolvencies were in Western Europe and North America with retail, services and energy sectors showing major increases on the same quarter in the previous year (pre-Covid-19). Chemicals, computer/telecom and pharmaceuticals were more resilient with fewer insolvencies, although as the authors pointed out such companies were typically two to three times the average size of the rest of the sample. The collapse of Thomas Cook, Bhs, Carillion, Woolworths and Waterford Wedgewood in the UK, and Enron, Lehman Brothers and Toys R Us in the United States are specific examples of a more general trend.

Whilst the collapse of large well-known companies continues to attract most attention, the failure of a large number of small and medium-sized companies continues to have significant consequences in terms of loss of employment, cash-flow problems for suppliers facing unpaid debts, loss of investor capital and impact on local communities and services. These problems are understandably highlighted in extreme situations such as the Covid-19 pandemic, but as the statistics testify, business failure is an unfortunate if common feature of commercial life.

Business distress can be a life-changing event for those who are caught up in its impact. Behind the statistics there is a human element that should not be ignored. Whilst it is possible to talk about a business as a commercial entity with its own separate existence, the typical business, unless it is run by a single owner-entrepreneur will employ a range of people with different skills, values, assumptions and most importantly capacity to deal with the changes that business distress can bring. Business failure is likely to have negative personal consequences for many of those involved. More positively many other businesses in financial distress facing fundamental changes in the environment in which they operate have implemented strategies to turn such businesses around, halting business decline and restoring competitiveness. Resilience matters.

Business distress has been widely analysed

A wide ranging analysis of the academic literature on financial distress and business turnaround published in 2017 identified 276 separate publications that have addressed the topic from a range of different perspectives including general management, accounting, economics sociology and finance (Schweizer and Nienhaus, 2017). One hundred and fifty-four of the studies identified focused exclusively on companies based in the USA, 36 on European markets of which the UK was the largest with 14 studies, followed by 6 German and 3 Swedish examples. Unsurprisingly perhaps, the authors identify a link between increases in the volume of publication on turnaround and restructuring and periods of economic and business decline in the years immediately preceding publication. According to their analysis previous research can be categorised into content, process (retrenchment or recovery), context and outcomes (turnaround success measurements). Content includes operational decisions in areas such as organisational processes, changes to product/service mix, workforce planning and capital expenditure, managerial decisions such as CEO and top management team changes, portfolio decisions such as divestments and investments, and financial decisions including debt restructuring and liquidity improvement. The breadth and depth of the existing research revealed by the review indicates the level of interest in the general area and the diversity of the potential academic research agenda. In the following chapters we draw on these different research traditions as we explore different elements of our framework.

Focus of the book

Building resilience is a business philosophy (the way that we do business here). It is an active process evident in a systematic and long-term focus on a series of critical issues, that seeks to anticipate and mitigate potential negative impacts on performance and ensure that a company can continue to achieve its purpose, whatever that might ultimately be. The following chapters describe a benchmarking framework that can be used by those responsible for the direction of the company to check their approach against best practice and identify alternative strategies to build a resilient company. This framework is based around a series of benchmarking framework questions (BFQs).

The elements of the framework are set out in Figure 1.1.

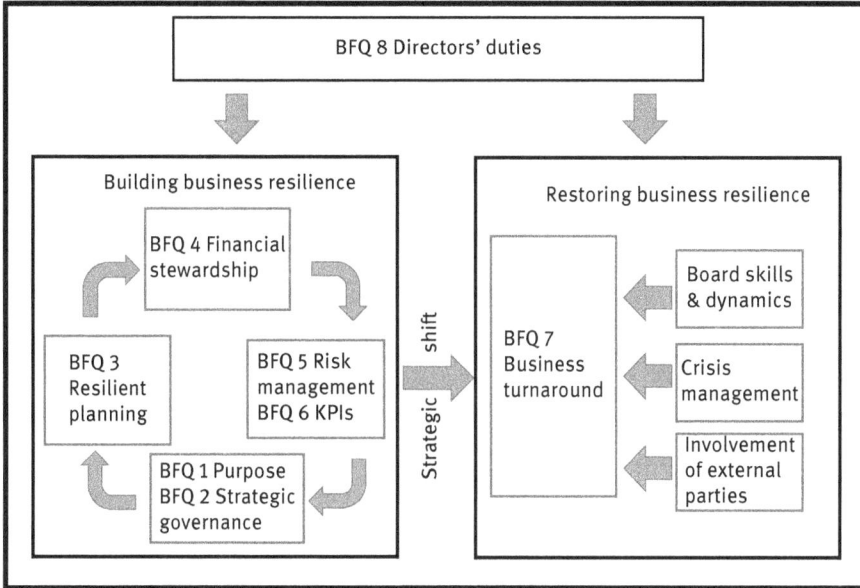

Figure 1.1: Building and restoring business resilience.

Figure 1.1 distinguishes between the ongoing process of building a resilient business and the actions needed to restore resilience. The ability of a company to respond effectively to changes in its environment (its resilience) is driven by its purpose (BFQ 1), taken forward by an effective board that is prepared to check its performance on an ongoing basis against a series of key indicators - a process we describe as strategic governance (BFQ 2). Resilient companies constantly review and update their business plans in line with changing market and competitive positions creating sustainable value for their key stakeholders (BFQ 3). Successful implementation of the business plan depends on good financial stewardship (BFQ 4), appropriate risk management strategies (BFQ 5) and the effective use of key performance indicators or KPIs (BFQ 6). In resilient companies these latter elements provide a feedback loop that leads to changes in direction where necessary.

At some point businesses may be forced to make fundamental changes when the existing model is no longer delivering the expected results (BFQ 7). This strategic shift may be linked to long-term trends including a declining financial performance that shows no sign of improvement, increasingly vocal shareholders demanding better returns on investment, or private equity takeover. When a company identifies that there is a potential threat to business solvency, the situation may become urgent requiring an aggressive and immediate reaction. Cash flow becomes the main priority. Strategies to improve liquidity may include employee redundancies, introducing delays in payment to suppliers and freezing of unnecessary expenditure. Secured creditors may be asked to agree to a temporary freeze on debt repayments, pending a medium-term re-negotiation of funding arrangements.

Each of these changes requires an increasing amount of support and collaboration from outside parties. Whilst directors may retain overall control, they may also rely increasingly on professional advice to support any business turnaround or financial restructuring strategy. Their focus shifts away from existing shareholder interests to creditor interests. Whilst these processes may ultimately lead to proposals for taking the business forward, typically with a different and modified business model, frequently directors will have no option but to put the company into a formal rescue process, at which point they no longer retain control. The company may be liquidated, following the sale of any residual assets which are deemed to have value such as its brands.

Directors have specific legal duties to the company as they seek to deal with situations of financial distress (BFQ 8). These legal duties constrain the actions that they can take in response to specific situations and may limit the options that they have when seeking to take the company forward. These constraints apply to areas such as the treatment of secured and unsecured creditors, employee contracts and ultimately staff redundancies.

Boards and Directors

This book focuses on the actions of those who are ultimately responsible for leading a business. They may carry the title director or non-executive director in a large company. Alternatively they may be an owner-manager of a small or medium-sized company. They may be called the CEO or chair. For the sake of simplicity, in the following chapters we will use board or directors as appropriate in different situations to refer to those responsible for the control and direction of a business. We also acknowledge that in many cases such people may be owner-managers of businesses that do not have limited company status and are not formally registered as directors. As one important caveat, the role of director also typically carries with it a series of obligations that are subject to specific legal requirements. We will look at this distinction in greater detail in Chapter 7.

Benchmarking framework questions (BFQs)

Our benchmarking framework is based on a series of questions for the board that are set out in Table 1.1. The questions reflect close observation of the behaviour of a wide range of companies that have built resilient business models and/or dealt with situations of business distress. The chapters which follow address each of these areas in turn.

When designing this book, we wanted to cover issues that were relevant to as many different types and sizes of businesses as possible. Whilst many of the basic messages may be the same, in practice many of the actions described in the book will be radically different in companies of different sizes and in different sectors (for example, in a small family business running a restaurant in a popular tourist destination in Portugal, compared with an international airline operating out of Heathrow Airport, London, or a major retail chain in the US). This inevitably leads to a generic high level set of messages in the areas that we cover, although we have used a wide range of examples and applications to illustrate our approach. However, the subject coverage in each chapter and the accompanying benchmarking framework with its questions for review are written in a way that we hope is sufficiently inclusive and should allow readers to apply the ideas to their chosen business in a practical way.

Table 1.1 has two separate sections, reflecting the strategic shift we described in Figure 1.1. The first 6 BFQs relate to the process of building and sustaining a resilient business. BFQs 7 and 8 relate specifically to restoring business resilience. Some of the questions will be less relevant to some business situations than others.

Table 1.1 sets out an introductory top-level analysis of all of the framework questions. The following chapters discuss each of these eight areas in detail. In each of the following chapters, we include a table(s) which is similar in format to Table 1.1. Each of these subsequent tables sets out the evidence that might be reviewed when addressing specific benchmarking questions. In the final chapter, we describe how the overall framework could be used in a specific setting to identify areas of strength and areas for improvement.

Readers who are interested in applying the benchmarking approach to their own business and getting a general idea about how the framework could be used might want to begin by reading the case study of Flybe Group plc at the end of Chapter 2 and then go to Chapter 8 where we use the questions set out in Table 1.1 to guide our review of that case (Table 8.1).

Other readers may prefer to start with the discussion of specific topics in each chapter and read the associated case studies as they progress through the book. The overall organisation is designed to take the reader through each of the areas of the framework, providing a review of relevant academic contributions in each area, commercial advice and relevant regulatory initiatives.

Extended case studies

We have included a series of extended case studies at the end of Chapters 2 to 6. Each of the companies featured in these case studies had a series of specific problems that ultimately led to their closure. We have chosen five recent high profile examples to illustrate our discussion. These cases are Flybe Group plc, (Chapter 2), Arcadia Group Ltd (Chapter 3), Carillion plc (Chapter 4), NMC Health Plc (Chapter 5) and Thomas Cook Group plc (Chapter 6).

At an early stage in developing this book, we debated whether to focus on businesses that had run into significant problems. The alternative was to select companies that were apparently successful. We would have then run into the writer's curse

Table 1.1: Resilience benchmarking questions for the Board.

Benchmarking Questions	Commentary (Evidence)	Score
	Building business resilience	
BFQ 1 **Purpose Purpose** **Does the board actively consider business purpose and update to reflect changing stakeholder expectations and the external environment?**	BFQ 1.1 What are the assumptions about why we are in business? How do we define business success? BFQ 1.2 Have we got an explicit statement of purpose and do we communicate this to relevant stakeholders? BFQ 1.3 When did we last check these assumptions about purpose? How did we do this? How do others see us? BFQ 1.4 Is purpose evident in brands and broader corporate reputation?	
BFQ 2 **Strategic governance** **Does the board regularly and systematically review its own competences and performance?**	BFQ 2.1 Do formal reporting systems and structures provide sufficient up-to-date information on key performance areas that is used as part of the board decision-making process? BFQ 2.2 To what extent is there an open atmosphere of information sharing and collective decision-making? BFQ 2.3 How does the board ensure that it has a sufficiently diverse and experienced membership capable of identifying and responding to emerging challenges?	
BFQ 3 **Resilient planning** **How effective is the board in setting the overall direction of the business and monitoring how well plans are implemented?**	BFQ 3.1 Do members of the board and business as a whole believe that the business plan and/or business planning adds value? BFQ 3.2 Does the business have the right range of knowledge skills and experience to put in place and implement a resilient planning process? BFQ 3.3 Is there an explicit process where the major assumptions in the business plan are regularly revisited and modified to reflect changes to the market place and competitive behaviour?	
BFQ 4 **Financial Stewardship** **To what extent do directors give careful long-term consideration to the financial and broader commercial**	BFQ 4.1 Is there a conscious and strategic recognition of accountancy and finance roles, and the impact of effective performance on business outcomes? BFQ 4.2 Has the company consciously recognized the contribution that this area can make to business resilience and put in place effective systems to establish standards and monitor performance?	

Table 1.1 (continued)

resilience of the company?	BFQ 4.3 How does the board reach its conclusions about the going concern status of the business, beyond considering the immediate reporting requirements required to comply with legislation?
	BFQ 4.4 Is there an explicit plan for long-term management of funds that establishes alternative strategies to deal with potential future periods of business distress?
BFQ 5 **Risk management** **How well does the board assess and manage potential risks to the business?**	BFQ 5.1 Is risk assessment recognised as an explicit responsibility for members of the board?
	BFQ 5.2 To what extent are business risks regularly identified, prioritised and monitored and mitigating actions specified?
BFQ 6 Performance Indicators **How effectively does the board monitor key performance dimensions?**	BFQ 6.1 Is there an effective internal system that provides up-to-date information for the board on performance against financial and strategic objectives?
	BFQ 6.2 Do published KPIs meet external expectations?
	Restoring business resilience
BFQ 7 **Business Turnaround** **How effectively does the board implement strategies to restore resilience where appropriate and deal with crisis situations as they emerge?**	BFQ 7.1 Is the board willing to accept that the business may face challenges to business continuity that require a step change in planning?
	BFQ 7.2 Does the company have the necessary knowledge, skills and experience (particularly at board level) to identify and address emerging strategic problems?
	BFQ 7.3 Does the business have the right leadership to take it through the changes that might be required?
	BFQ 7.4 Is there a well thought through long-term plan to reset the financial position when it becomes evident that the current model is unsustainable?
	BFQ 7.5 Is there a well-structured plan to deal with crisis situations?

Table 1.1 (continued)

BFQ 8 Directors' Duties To what extent do directors have an effective and relevant understanding of their general duties in situations of business distress?	BFQ 8.1 To what extent are directors aware of and meet their formal legal obligations (duties) to shareholders, lenders and other stakeholders? BFQ 8.2 How does the board monitor and safeguard itself against possible wrongful or fraudulent trading, misfeasance and preferential treatment?

that having apparently praised such companies one or more of them would hit major problems. In any case, the analysis of successful businesses has already been done very effectively by many other authors. More fundamentally, this is a book about building resilience, specifically the capacity to deal with different setbacks and cope with adversity.

Our failing companies did not ultimately survive but as the cases demonstrate each of them found solutions that kept their business going over an extended period prior to their ultimate closure. In four of the cases, the companies' brands outlived the original business and were sold on to other companies as part of the formal process of administration. In these cases, the brand proved to be more resilient than the original company. These included Topshop and Burton formerly owned by Arcadia Group Ltd, Flybe and Thomas Cook Travel. NMC Health Plc was also relaunched in a new restructured form. In Carillion plc, the business closed as the business model became increasingly unsustainable and the brand had no legacy value.

We believe that there is much to learn from such cases. We have chosen companies that have occupied the attention of the media and in some cases regulatory bodies. From a case writer's point of view, the advantage of looking at such significant cases is that there is a large amount of published information in the public domain. By their very nature, such companies are required to publish regular statutory reports and updates on their performance. They also typically publish a range of different updates for investors, whilst also being subject to scrutiny by the media and investment analysts. We have provided a number of endnotes to each of these cases that should help readers look back at the original sources if you want to explore the cases in greater depth.

Whilst our main case studies describe companies that have encountered significant periods of business distress, we have also included a range of other examples where companies have implemented different strategies to enhance or restore resilience. Again there is a danger that subsequent changes to the circumstances of each company may make the example redundant or no longer appropriate, but this is an unavoidable aspect of trying to address current issues. It is inevitable that future events will influence or change the position of many of these companies in the months and years following publication of this book.

Disclaimer
Each of the cases presented in this book has been prepared from publicly available sources of information. The cases are designed to provide a basis for discussion of the main issues in each chapter and should not be read in any way as being critical of the administrative decisions taken by those involved in each situation.

PLC, Plc or plc
Readers will note a variability in the way in which the designation plc (public limited company) is presented in different cases. Some companies use PLC (all capitals). In others it can be Plc or plc. This format can also change for the same company depending on the context of individual reports. We have tried as far as possible to reflect the most common usage in each company.

Organisation

Chapter 1: Building resilient companies

Rationale and overview.

Chapter 2: Purpose and the effective board

Resilient companies have a strong sense of purpose not only in defining the reasons why they are in business but also in identifying the needs of various stakeholders. The original concept of business purpose which focuses on maximising returns for shareholders by anticipating and satisfying customer needs more effectively than the competition remains a valid long-term objective. However, in order to achieve this purpose, companies are increasingly recognising the importance of broader environmental, social and governance issues that impact on business development. Chapter 2 begins by looking at how businesses might develop an explicit statement of purpose that provides a clear sense of direction that motivates employees and builds competitive advantage in terms of customer, supplier and other stakeholder perceptions. The chapter then looks at the characteristics of an effective board that appear to create a positive organisational climate that is less vulnerable to external threats and more responsive to new emerging opportunities.

Case study: Flybe Group plc

Our first case study Flybe Group plc, describes how one company grew from a regional airline serving local destinations in the UK to one of the largest European operators serving a wide range of different destinations. It looks at the difficulties that the business faced as it struggled to deal with a legacy of high levels of investment in its early years that created a continuous drain on cash flow. The business was under pressure over most of its existence from low margins and changing attitudes to travel, with competition from surface transport, and an increase in online meetings that substituted for business travel. The case looks at the decisions made by three different CEOs who each attempted to turn the business around with their own alternative interpretations of strategy and purpose.

Chapter 3: Resilient planning

Chapter 3 looks at the potential impact of the business model on resilience. Business planning can take a variety of different forms ranging from the implicit assumptions about the future that guide the actions of the smallest company to extensive planning processes in many larger companies. Our discussion covers the basics of strategic planning and the importance of key areas including customer focus and developing and sustaining distinctive competences. It also considers the role of the board in monitoring performance against business plans and the problems that can be created by formalised approaches that do not allow for unexpected changes to the competitive environment.

Case study: Arcadia Group Ltd

The case study of Arcadia Group Ltd describes the evolution of a business, Burton from its original conception, its integration into a broader trading company and ultimately into an online business as it passed through three different ownerships. The case reflects the evolution of retailing from a traditional model based on physical outlets to a multi-mode market place where online presence has become critical to reaching markets and building demand. It also discusses the importance of building and sustaining a credible and differentiated position in the minds of target customers through effective branding strategies.

Chapter 4: Financial stewardship

Chapter 4 begins with a review of directors' financial responsibilities, and the contribution that effective financial stewardship can make in companies of different sizes. Company directors are obliged to ensure that their company can continue to operate as a going concern, made explicit in the requirement to produce such a statement in the annual report and accounts. In Chapter 4, we consider the process of preparing going concern statements, not just in terms of compliance with external accountancy standards but also as part of a long-term assessment of business viability. The third part of the chapter looks specifically at strategic cash management. This includes ensuring that the company's current cash position is sufficient to meet immediate demands. It also includes consideration of the long-term management of cash flow and being pro-active about the sources and application of funds.

Case study: Carillion plc

The Carillion case study looks at the problems which emerged as Carillion (a major UK-based construction company) failed to generate sufficient finance to sustain its business model in an increasingly competitive market. Its position was worsened by significant changes in the procurement policies of one of its major customers (the UK government) and project overruns on several major international projects. The combined effects caused the company major problems leading ultimately to entry into liquidation and the loss of thousands of jobs.

Chapter 5: Risk management and KPIs

Chapter 5 examines alternative approaches to identifying and assessing the impact of risk on business continuity. It considers the contribution of stress testing business assumptions against alternative scenarios and the role of directors in prioritising potential risks to business continuity. The chapter considers the development and use of a range of KPIs, and the role of monitoring systems, in particular internal audit committees and external auditors.

Case study: NMC Health Plc

Chapter 5's case study examines how an apparently successful company, NMC Health Plc, was thrown into turmoil after an independent analyst suggested that the company was not operating as effectively as its directors had suggested in external reports. Detailed investigation lead to rapid entry into administration. The case describes how the administrator appointed to deal with the situation developed a new scenario for the business's future.

Chapter 6: Business turnaround

Chapter 6 examines the range of strategies that are available to directors seeking to avoid the potential problems that distress might create or at least mitigate its worst effects. The chapter begins by considering where the momentum for change may come from. It then discusses who might make the first call that a significant problem is emerging. The chapter then examines alternative approaches to resolving business distress, including challenging the existing business model and financial re-engineering. A final section of the chapter considers the situations that may arise when a sudden financial crisis hits the company that requires immediate attention.

Case study: Thomas Cook Group plc

Our final extended case study examines how a long-established business failed to come to terms with fundamental changes in its market place that made its existing business model increasingly less relevant. It examines how the company accumulated a significant amount of debt in its attempts to build its business. This decision burdened the company with a series of acquisitions that were increasingly less relevant to the needs of new customers as they moved to online booking to assemble and buy their preferred holiday packages.

Chapter 7: Directors' duties

Chapter 7 discusses the current legal frameworks that set out director responsibilities, focusing specifically on the issue of commercial judgement and the capacity of those responsible to make effective decisions in distress situations.

Chapter 8: Benchmarking strategic governance

Chapter 8 sets out an investigatory toolkit that can be used by directors to develop a practical benchmarking framework for their own company.

2 Purpose and the effective board

> If you have built castles in the air, your work need not be lost; that is where they should be. Now put the foundations under them. (Henry David Thoreau, 1854)

Clarity about purpose, specifically the answer to the question "why is the company in business?" is an important driver of business resilience. Highly creative small businesses frequently find a unique position in the market and survive or grow with no apparent underlying logic or explicit business plan. They have a sense of purpose that is intuitive: finding a market opportunity, creating a distinctive position and exploiting it in constantly changing ways that continue to bring customers to the door. Members of the business are motivated by the same values and can clearly articulate how the work that they do impacts on others in the business, the customers they serve and broader society. Kongo-Gumi, the case study that features at the beginning of Chapter 1, is such a company. Many larger businesses also appear to have a clear sense of purpose. We look at several examples of such companies in this chapter including Impossible Foods Inc. and Nestlé Group S.A.

Chapter 2 begins by examining alternative interpretations of business purpose and the potential impact of a clear and distinctive understanding of purpose on performance. The chapter then looks at alternative practical ways of exploring how the purpose of a business is currently seen by different stakeholders. In the third part of the chapter we look at how purpose is reflected in the corporate brand. The final section of the chapter looks at the characteristics of an effective board and its role in creating a meaningful and sustainable business direction.

Purpose

Table 2.1 sets out the specific benchmarking questions that we suggest are included in a review of business purpose. Table 2.2 later on in this chapter contains a series of questions relating to board effectiveness. These are the first two of eight such tables that will appear at the beginning of relevant sections of this book. Each of these tables contains a series of questions that a board might consider when evaluating their performance against the overall benchmarking framework question. We have included areas that might be considered when reviewing each of these questions (evidence used to form a judgement). Those of you who are reading this book with the intention of applying this process to your own organisation might want to make some notes under the commentary section in each table as you read the chapter. We discuss this benchmarking process including scoring each element in more detail in Chapter 8.

https://doi.org/10.1515/9783110689495-002

Table 2.1: BFQ 1 Purpose: Does the board actively consider business purpose and update to reflect changing stakeholder expectations and the external environment?

Benchmarking questions	Commentary (Evidence)	Score
Purpose has several dimensions **BFQ 1.1 What are the assumptions about why we are in business? How do we define business success?**	Relative perceived importance of profitability and financial stability Focus on customer satisfaction Long-term commitment to employees Long-term supply chain partnerships Contribution to broader social and environmental goals Trade-offs between each of the above elements	
Purpose in practice **BFQ 1.2 Have we got an explicit statement of purpose and do we communicate this to relevant stakeholders?**	Nature and content of purpose statement Extent to which purpose is evident in company messaging and branding Independent media commentary on progress and direction of business	
Recognising and defining purpose **BFQ 1.3 When did we last check these assumptions about purpose? How did we do this? How do others see us?**	Key performance indicators that relate to different elements of business purpose Specific consideration of purpose on the board's agenda on a regular basis Ad hoc reviews of different aspects of business purpose Explicit reference to purpose in a formal business plan	
Seeing the business as a brand **BFQ 1.4 Is purpose evident in brands and broader corporate reputation?**	Deliberate attempts to create and sustain customer involvement with purpose embedded in branding and corporate communications and the degree of passion and commitment that customers have for the company and its brands Extent to which actions appear to be driven by fundamental sense of broader purpose rather than paying 'lip-service' to such concerns Reaction of current and prospective employees to business purpose and its reflection of broader social and environmental concerns	

Purpose has several dimensions

BFQ 1.1 What are the assumptions about why we are in business? How do we define business success?

When asked to define the purpose of their business many people will focus on the primary objective of making a profit. They may even be surprised that the question needs to be asked. A widely cited article by Friedman over 50 years ago summarised this point of view (Friedman, 1970). Friedman said:

> There is one and only one social responsibility of business–to use its resources and engage in activities designed to increase its profits so long as it stays within the rules of the game, which is to say, engages in open and free competition without deception or fraud.

This orientation is reflected in the attention given to financial results in most annual reports. It reflects the primary responsibility of directors to serve the interests of shareholders. Shareholders quite reasonably want to know how well their investment is doing and what future prospects look like. Satisfying customers is an enabling purpose that drives financial return. Successful businesses meet customer needs more effectively than the competition. They continue to do this over time, anticipating changes in customer requirements and preferences and adjusting as appropriate. Back in 1960 Levitt's original article on marketing orientation focused attention on this fundamental proposition (Levitt, 1960).

A broader concept of purpose has emerged in the first 20 years of the new millennium. Companies with a purpose that also takes account of other broader corporate social responsibility considerations may ultimately prove to be more resilient in the long term than those driven solely by a focus on financial return (Al-Hadi, Chatterjee, Yaftian, Taylor, and Hasan, 2019; Boubaker, Cellier, Manita, and Saeed, 2020). Examples of this broader purpose might include the extent to which a business can demonstrate its contribution to CO_2 reduction or its focus on sustainability and recycling. In many markets customers identify positively with those businesses that reflect such broader considerations in their apparent purpose. Employees appear to be more committed and work more effectively in such organisations.

Back in the 1980s Freeman was one of the first to give explicit consideration to different stakeholder interests (Freeman, 1984). Sisodia, Sheth and Wolfe's more recent book (2014) explores this area in detail. The authors describe a humanistic company as follows:

> A humanistic company one is run in such a way that its stakeholders–customers, employees, suppliers, business partners, society and many investors–develop an emotional connection with it [. . .] Humanistic companies–or firms of endearment–seek to maximise their value to society as a whole, not just to their shareholders. They are the ultimate value creators. They create emotional, spiritual, social, cultural, intellectual, ecological and of course financial value. People who interact with such companies feel safe, secure, and fulfilled in their dealings. They enjoy working with or for the company, buying from it, investing in it, and having it as a neighbour.

Many observers appear to be less convinced seeing this focus as a form of cynical behaviour designed to meet a new challenge rather than add real business value.

In August 2019 181 CEO's of some of the leading companies in America signed a commitment to redefining business purpose that included the interests of all stakeholders (Business Roundtable, 2019). The statement included a fundamental commitment to observe the interests of customers, employees, suppliers, communities and shareholders in the actions of the firm. Gast, Illanes, Probst, Schaninger and Simpson (2020) suggest that this perspective has yet to gain traction in many companies. Despite all the positive statements about the benefits of a broader sense of purpose, they found that many companies were having difficulties in coming to terms with the concept and incorporating it into practical planning decisions. They cite a survey of more than 1,000 participants from US companies, where 82% said that purpose was important but only 42% reported that their company's stated purpose had made a difference. The authors blamed this lack of impact on the generic nature of most purpose statements.

Gast et al. set out an extensive checklist to consider when determining the impact of purpose. Questions that they ask directors to consider include the capacity of the company to make a distinctive contribution both in its current markets and the broader environment in which its operates. Directors should also assess the impact of company activity on shareholders, workforce, suppliers, communities and the mechanisms by which trade-offs are made between conflicting stakeholder interests. This situation could be improved in the words of the authors by "deep reflection on your corporate identity–what you really stand for–which may well lead to material changes in your strategy and even your governance".

Purpose in practice

BFQ 1.2 Have we got an explicit statement of purpose and do we communicate this to relevant stakeholders?

The two case studies which follow illustrate how two different companies, Impossible Foods Inc. a new business start-up in the food industry and Nestlé Group, a long-established and diversified consumer products business have reflected a range of different considerations in their own definitions of purpose. Both of these businesses have addressed similar concerns about the environment and their broader vision in the way in which they describe purpose.

Impossible Foods Inc.: Turning back the clock on climate change

In December 2020 Pat Brown, the CEO and founder of Impossible Foods Inc. published the following statement:

To the outside world, Impossible Foods is a food company–but at its heart is an audacious yet realistic strategy to turn back the clock on climate change and stop the global collapse of biodiversity.

Here's how:

If we could wave a magic wand and instantly make the animal-based food industry disappear, two game-changing, natural pathways for greenhouse gas reduction would turn on–Methane Decay and Biomass Recovery. [. . .]

Our planet needs that magic wand.

So Impossible Foods is inventing it–a new technology platform for transforming plants into delicious, nutritious, affordable meat, fish and dairy foods, replacing the old animal-based technology in the global food system.

To succeed in our mission, it's not enough for the foods we create to be more sustainable (that's easy). We only succeed if we make meat, fish and dairy lovers happier, by doing a better job of delivering everything that matters to consumers–deliciousness, nutritional value, convenience and affordability (the hard but doable part). And we need to scale up, to make better choices easily available to every current consumer of meat, fish or dairy foods, around the world. We accelerated on both fronts in 2020.

The devastating health and economic impact of COVID-19 shaped 2020 for Impossible Foods as it did for the whole world. As this report describes, we prioritized the health and welfare of our colleagues and communities, adjusted our business plan to adapt to the impact of the global pandemic, and blasted ahead on our essential mission.

Impossible foods Inc. is one of an increasing number of companies that have targeted the plant-based meat and dairy market, seeking to reflect customer demand for meat substitutes in traditional hamburger and other meat based meals. In 2021, the market was still relatively small (less than 1% of the total meat market) but rapidly growing (Terazono, 2021). The company was betting on a future where meat consumption would become an important dietary and ecological concern. The CEO's statement provided a clear sense of direction that could be used by external investors and those involved directly with the company (customers, suppliers and employees) to understand its purpose and the criteria against which decisions were being made.

Nestlé Group: Building on purpose

The Nestlé Group, a large multi-divisional company with headquarters in Switzerland, manufactures and distributes a wide range of market leading brands in countries throughout the world. The company's product line includes bottled water, breakfast cereals, chocolate and confectionery, coffee, dairy products, drinks and food. The company dates back to 1866 when the Anglo-Swiss Milk Company opened its first European condensed milk factory in Switzerland. Its history reveals a continuous series of changes, driven by mergers, product innovation and overseas development, acquisitions and diversification into new businesses (Nestlé Group, 2016). External pressures on the Group over time have included calls from consumer groups questioning baby food marketing strategies to boycott its products in the 1970s, an increasing trend to health consciousness amongst consumers developing initially in the 1980s, and more recently growing concerns about the sourcing of raw materials and its impact on local indigenous communities.

In his annual report to shareholders in April 2020 the company's chair described Nestlé's approach as follows:

> It is based on a fundamental understanding of what the food and beverage industry must deliver today–namely high-quality food and nutritional products for all. Food and nutrition must be available, accessible and affordable for all, and must be produced in a sustainable manner that ensures resilient livelihoods and that respects nature and the planet's resources.
> It is inspired by Nestlé's purpose: "enhancing quality of life and contributing to a healthier future." And it is put into practice through Creating Shared Value–the fundamental principle that determines how Nestlé conducts its business that makes Nestlé a force for good in society.
> It is Nestlé's long-standing belief that a company can only survive and be successful over time if it simultaneously creates value for all stakeholders in society: our shareholders, our employees, our consumers, our customers, our suppliers and our communities. Creating Shared Value–the 'how'–is closely linked to our business strategy–the 'what'–and to our purpose–the 'why'. (Nestlé Group 2020)

It is instructive to compare the formal mechanisms of consultation, discussion and communication that would be necessary to create an enduring statement of purpose in a large multi-national company like Nestlé with the natural embedded sense of purpose in a smaller business as Impossible Foods Inc. was in its early days. In the larger company any process is likely to be formalised with a number of different stages and different levels of discussion across the business. In a smaller company, the values of directors are likely to be implicit assumptions that may never be formally articulated, only becoming obvious as the business changes direction to meet new challenges.

European Super League: An own goal

When a new executive team attempt to put in place changes that could erode confidence in the core product or service that they offer or alienate employees then they may face a backlash that forces them to reassess their proposals, whether or not there is a clear business logic in the changes that are put forward. A strong existing purpose may be a major barrier to change. Pushing through a new vision of what that purpose might be can become a major challenge.

In 2021 12 of the largest and best-known football clubs in Europe announced that they were forming a new super league competition (The Super League, 2021). The proposals included setting up a series of mid-week fixtures with an end of season knock-out competition to find the ultimate winners. Supporters argued that the proposals would create a new funding structure that would benefit clubs at all levels in different leagues throughout Europe. The original founders would receive a payment of €3.5bn. The announcement generated a major negative reaction from those clubs which had not been included in the original proposals and more generally from the clubs' own fans who felt that the proposed format did not reflect the original ethos of competitive football.

The new proposed league would feature a series of high-profile competitive matches between a self-selected group of teams. Many critics pointed out that clubs which were promoting the super league appeared to have lost touch with their local fan base. The adverse reaction from fans, many of whom organised protests outside the gates of their home clubs led to a rapid withdrawal of the proposals with apologies from the chairs of several of the clubs involved.

Recognising and defining purpose

BFQ 1.3 When did we last check these assumptions about purpose? How did we do this? How do others see us?

Purpose is often revisited at specific moments in a company's development. For example, it is reasonable to expect that an appointment panel for a new CEO would select the candidate who sets out the most appropriate sense of direction with a clear plan on how this might be implemented. Typically, a board might expect the new CEO to have his/her own diagnosis of the situation already complete and plans in place to implement appropriate changes following their appointment. The candidate responded to the brief set out by the board and described a vision of how the business could evolve which was compelling. This is why he/she was appointed. The first few months under new leadership typically then involves a degree of adjustment and reorientation. In such circumstances, plans are likely to be revisited, updated or discarded as a new direction is brought to the business. Such changes are likely to continue over several years with a range of different potential impacts through the typical CEO life cycle.

Citrin, Hildebrand and Stark (2019) tracked the financial performance of 747 S&P 500 chief executives and conducted interviews with CEOs and other directors about their experiences. They describe the first few months in office as the honeymoon period when most CEOs achieve above-average performance with a new vision that energises staff. After the initial excitement performance often dips as a result of unexpected negative events that have an impact on external investor confidence. The authors describe this as "the sophomore slump" where full transparency is required with the rest of the board and investors to take the business forward. At this stage the boards of effective companies can play an active role in supporting the CEO and colleagues as they build a new business model.

If they survive this slump then CEOs may enter a "recovery stage" that can last for several years as they build the confidence of the senior team and investors, put in place a lasting and meaningful strategic plan and experiment with new ideas. As this recovery stage extends the CEO may become overconfident in the strategies that are being pursued. The authors describe this as the "complacency trap". CEOs that outperform during this stage are likely to have reinvented the organisation and begun to explore new opportunities for the company. The few CEOs that ultimately survive may enter a period that the authors term the "golden years" where the CEO is trusted by the board to deliver, new projects that were initiated in previous years are coming to fruition and they are often motivated by the idea of building a legacy.

One quick way to get some sense of the way in which companies see their purpose can be to look at the titles that are frequently given to annual reports. The Flybe Group plc case study reported in detail at the end of this chapter describes how three different CEOs at different times in the company's history introduced alternative views of purpose designed to reflect changing circumstances. The titles of successive annual reports for Flybe between 2010 and 2017 included: "UK Leadership–European Growth", "Building Europe's Leading Regional Aviation Group", "Fit to Compete", "Transforming Flybe", "Continuing Our Transformation", "Delivering our Transformation" and "Close to You".

The first two reports reflect a period of planned expansion when the Group was seeking to build its presence as a leading European operator. The second group of reports was produced during a period when the senior team was addressing the challenges that it faced in an increasingly competitive market place with very narrow margins. During this period they were seeking to make major improvements in productivity and reduce costs. The final report produced just ahead of the sale of the company in 2018 refers to a change of focus towards greater customer orientation that stressed two customer focused aspects of Flybe, its local routes which were accessible in a number of different locations in the UK and its customer service.

On a different scale, in many small companies where a business may be passed from one generation to the next the absence of any explicit discussion about where the business is going and why it does certain things may cause significant problems, particularly if the new generation lacks the original founder's vision or does not share the same assumptions about the future. This problem is frequently brought into focus when such a business is asked to produce a formal business plan for the first time when applying for a bank loan, or to attract external investment, or when the owners decide to sell the business.

Putting purpose on the agenda

Practical steps to put purpose on the agenda can include holding board meetings on local sites rather than in head office and inviting staff in customer-facing roles, suppliers and investors to discuss their experiences directly with the board. Where CEOs and other members of the board also get involved with the business at the sharp end, for example by spending time with those closest to the customer this can enhance this understanding and connectivity. This is where those running small businesses should have an advantage as they are constantly in touch with different stakeholders.

In a previous role one of the authors was responsible for the design and delivery of workshop sessions for specific corporate clients that were designed to support business planning. In such a setting the general question "Why are you in business?" predictably generated a series of answers around the general theme of making money for shareholders or keeping employees in a job. A request to describe a specific customer's experience, the benefits that a company's products or services provide over competing alternatives and the way this was conveyed in the company's branding and broader communications often led to a more varied response.

From experience, participants in such sessions do not necessarily share the same view of their company's relationships with customers, the unique advantages that their products and services have over competitive alternatives and how they sustain this advantage over time. When participants were asked to describe the company's relationships with different stakeholders such as shareholders, potential investors, suppliers, employees and society more generally (particularly its focus on environmental or other broader societal issues) this typically elicited a range of alternative views. Broader questions such as "do you enjoy working here?" or "what parts of your job do like best?" were often unasked for obvious reasons but the answers could typically be inferred from the range of replies and the enthusiasm shown by participants when they discussed the first three questions.

This process can be perceived as useful and interesting by those involved and generate some key insights into the current direction of the business. However, unless these insights are turned into practical actions the process itself is ultimately flawed. In the situations described above, participants were typically invited to reflect on their reaction to the discussion and contribute to the design of a roadmap to inform planning in a practical way. The chances of achieving any real change depended on how far members of the board engaged with the process and were able to reflect on the outcome of the discussions. Consultation and review need to be turned into a sense of direction that is well set out and evident to all members of the company and its different stakeholders.

Burberry Group Plc

Burberry Group Plc is a global luxury fashion brand, operating in apparel, handbag and small leather goods, and shoes and jewelry markets. Burberry's annual report for 2019/2020 details how the company undertook a major review to "articulate the existing belief that guides the business". The process involved research into the Burberry archives, surveys and focus groups. Further inputs came from global retail conferences, town-hall meetings and the business's intranet. A "purpose box" was circulated within the company, and over 2,000 suggestions cards from employees were submitted. The report describes how the board was involved at the beginning of the process and participated in a final session that reviewed the findings and produced an updated summary of Burberry's purpose statement – Creativity Opens Spaces. Burberry explained this statement more fully in its annual report:

> 'Creativity Opens Spaces' is the perfect way to express Burberry's longstanding commitment to innovative thinking and the endless possibilities offered by that mindset. Our purpose is our North Star which connects all our employees around the world. We know that companies with a strong sense of purpose perform better, uniting everyone in common values.

This statement of purpose was based on the original vision for the brand set out by the company's founder in the 1930s. The review process identified four distinctive values that the company stated "are intrinsic to Burberry's DNA and express who we are when we are at our best". The values were "creatively driven", "open and caring", "proud of our heritage" and "forward thinking". These were set out for the business as a series of expectations about the behaviours that members of the business should exhibit when fulfilling their different roles. As one example, under the creatively driven heading Burberry included finding beauty in every detail, putting passion and creativity into everything the company did and a commitment to excellence. The company's 2020/2021 annual report described how these different elements were reflected in its communications strategy as follows "We will inspire customers and strengthen the emotional connection with purposeful, authentic luxury storytelling, while leveraging our strong network of communities and influencers to amplify our brand".

Seeing the business as a brand

BFQ 1.4 Is purpose evident in brands and broader corporate reputation?

Purpose is directly linked to how different stakeholders see the business, and it is worth reflecting on the relationship between purpose and the business as a brand. A company's corporate brand or reputation provides a lens through which stakeholders interpret purpose. In some areas the corporate brand will be more important, for example in communication with shareholders, investors or lenders. In other instances individual brands become more important particularly with final consumers who are likely to have little concern about which company has made a product or supplied the service. This relationship is illustrated in Chocolats Camille Bloch SA.

Chocolats Camille Bloch SA

In 2021 Chocolats Camille Bloch SA, a Swiss chocolate maker, described a range of different strategies that it believed underpinned its business success and longevity. The company was founded in Bern, Switzerland in 1929. At the time of writing this book it was directed by Daniel Bloch, the third generation of the family to run the company. The company's statement of purpose provides a narrative on how the company had reached its current position and its perception of the evolution of its brand over time.

> OUR VALUES
> Chocolats Camille Bloch SA. is a family business steeped in tradition, headquartered in Courtelary in the Bernese Jura region of Switzerland. It was founded in Bern by Camille Bloch in 1929. Today the third generation, represented by Daniel Bloch, presides over the destiny of this Swiss chocolate maker. Sustainability is one of our guiding principles, and influences how we run the company, in economic, social and environmental terms. [. . .]
>
> OUR CORPORATE CULTURE
> Although much has changed since Chocolats Camille Bloch SA was founded back in 1929 our values have remained the same. A respect for our family traditions, a passion for chocolate, high quality standards, a sense of social and environmental responsibility – from harvesting the cocoa bean to the finished product – and, of course, our passion for Swiss chocolate and our valley here in the Bernese Jura region of Switzerland. [. . .]
>
> We have been making the finest chocolate specialties for over 80 years and have proven ourselves to be unique due to the high standards we apply to all areas of our business. Our master chocolate-makers use the very latest technology to perfect their recipes, but in a way that respects our traditional values. We also strive to produce authentic and unique creations. [. . .]
>
> Chocolats Camille Bloch SA takes a long-term approach. For us, thinking and acting sustainably is no mere fad, but a guiding – and constantly evolving – principle.

This statement reflects the passion that the business has developed for its role and its focus on the needs of a specific market and the importance that it has given to sustainability as a major source of long-term business resilience.

Waterford Wedgwood Plc

Many brands live on whilst the companies that may have originally developed them have long since disappeared. The sense of purpose that has been embedded in the brand remains long after the original company disappears. This is evident in the case of Waterford Wedgwood Plc.

Waterford Wedgwood Plc, first came to the attention of one of the authors when she was investigating governance in several mega-insolvency cases (Parkinson, 2018). Waterford Wedgwood Plc was the Irish parent company of a group of associated companies in Ireland and the UK, operating as a manufacturer, retailer and distributor of ceramics, crystalware and pottery. Wedgwood could trace its origins in England back to 1759, whilst Waterford was established in Ireland in 1783. The company's products were synonymous with high quality products with a long-established heritage and a distinguished line of customers including Empress Catherine II of Russia and the US president Theodore Roosevelt (Kollewe, 2009).

Longstanding financial problems linked to an over-ambitious expansion strategy, coupled with a decline in demand in 2007 in both the USA and the UK, and the subsequent financial crisis of 2008 which had a major impact on the purchase of luxury brands generally, led to the company entering receivership in January 2009. During its final year of operation the company pursued aggressive strategies of cost reduction including large-scale redundancies at its German subsidiary Rosenthal and at Waterford Crystal in Ireland.

When the company entered liquidation in late April 2011, parts of the company had already been sold to KPS Capital Partners, LP. The brands were subsequently transferred to a new company WWRD (Waterford, Wedgwood, Royal Doulton) Holdings Limited. Following a period of transformation and turnaround, the company was sold on to Fiskars, a Finnish consumer goods company in July 2015 (KPS Capital Partners LP, 2015). The brands survived and are still actively promoted today, demonstrating greater resilience than the companies where they originated (Fiskars Corporation ND).

The new owners appear to have the same sense of purpose as the original creators. Fiskars states: "Established in 1649 as an ironworks in a small Finnish village, Fiskars has grown to be a leading consumer goods company with globally recognised brands including Fiskars, Iittala, Gerber, Royal Copenhagen, Wedgwood and Waterford [. . .].We are proud of the fact that our products are relied upon from one generation to the next and that the centuries-old tradition of craftsmanship stemming from the village where the company's story began, is still with us today".

In Waterford Wedgwood's case although the original company has gone, the broad purpose of the business lives on in the statement of the ultimate owner as a company with "a centuries-old tradition of craftsmanship". Fiskars' website still celebrates its original roots and the tradition that has guided the company.

As both Chocolats Camille Bloch SA and Waterford Wedgwood illustrate creating and sustaining customer involvement with the corporate brand is underpinned by a clear understanding and articulation of organisational purpose. Customers relate positively or negatively to purpose, and their perception of the brand is formed by the cumulative actions of the company over time. Specific purchases mark particular moments in time when these relationships turn into financial transactions that drive business results.

Strategic governance

The second half of this chapter focuses on board effectiveness. Table 2.2 identifies three important indicators of the board's willingness to review and improve its own performance – a process which we term strategic governance.

Table 2.2: BFQ 2 Strategic governance: Does the board regularly and systematically review its own competences and performance?.

Benchmarking questions	Commentary (Evidence)	Score
Informed decision-making BFQ 2.1 Do formal reporting systems and structures provide up-to-date information on key performance areas that is used as part of the board decision-making process?	Use of KPIs (Key Performance Indicators) in a systematic and consistent way to monitor key lag and leading indicators Presentation and review of key strategic issues and scenario testing with appropriate levels of risk analysis Explicit strategies for future funds management and stress testing of the impact of different outcomes on financial planning Regular and consistent feedback to the board on customer experience and competitive activities Regular and consistent use of feedback from employee surveys and review of attrition rates Supplier performance measurement and review as an explicit and continuous process	
Information exchange and problem solving BFQ 2.2 To what extent is there an open atmosphere of information sharing and collective decision-making?	Extent which all members of the board play an active role in shaping discussion and content and share responsibility for outcome of decisions Engagement of those who are not formal members of the board in presentation and review of specific issues as and where required and willingness of board to take account of views Willingness of board to review and debate sufficiently on key issues prior to moving to decisions about implementation The extent to which the quality of board decision-making is regularly reviewed, compared with best practice and improved where appropriate	

Table 2.2 (continued)

Diversity and experienced membership BFQ 2.3 How does the board ensure that it has a sufficiently diverse and experienced membership capable of identifying and responding to emerging challenges?	Spread of talent and experience relevant to decisions that the board faces
	Willingness to regularly review the range of talent and experience that the board may need and refresh when required rather than waiting for director resignation or the expiry of office
	Recognition of the need for specific expertise in emerging areas such as AI and international partnerships/ collaborations and supply chain relationships
	Explicit strategies to enhance the understanding and awareness of existing members of the board in key areas such as funds management, employee relationships and risk assessment
	Multi-cultural awareness and diversity of representation in key roles

Informed decision-making

BFQ 2.1 Do formal reporting systems and structures provide up-to-date information on key performance areas that is used as part of the board decision-making process?

BFQ 2.1 is designed to explore the extent to which there is a culture of informed decision-making that guides the actions of the board. Over the next five chapters we will consider a range of specific questions for members of the board to consider as they examine different dimensions of business resilience, including the systematic use of KPIs (key performance indicators), risk analysis and scenario planning and the strategic management of funds. If there is little or no evidence that decision-making is informed by the systematic use of such information this is a significant indicator of potential problems. The willingness to acknowledge and learn from mistakes is a crucial element of informed board decision-making.

Information exchange and problem-solving

BFQ 2.2 To what extent is there an open atmosphere of information sharing and collective decision-making?

Directors typically make decisions on a wide range of issues, some short term and others linked to broader strategic development. Much of the time of executive members of a board is taken up with immediate problems. Far less time is typically taken up with longer-term issues that might feature in the majority of management text-books or the websites of commercial advisors. We will have more to say about this in Chapter 3 when we consider alternative approaches to business planning. Non-executive directors have less direct involvement in day-to-day business and are more likely to focus on specific areas linked to their own area of expertise. Their involvement is frequently linked to specific roles such as membership of an audit committee or remuneration committee. The time which they have available to focus on broader issues is limited by the time available, their motivation and the quality of information that they receive.

Looking in from the outside it is difficult to interpret the process and outcomes of board decision-making given that board minutes are typically not made public or if so frequently in a redacted form. Books written about inspirational CEOs remain very popular and provide some insight into the workings of the board, each with a different take on the nature of leadership in specific circumstances with different role models for example Goffee and Jones (2006). Far less attention has been given to the way in which different members of a board work effectively as members of a team to address specific business decisions. Two significant exceptions are Garratt (2010) and Cross and Lawrence (2021). Garratt's book in particular is a very readable account of boardroom behaviour and the need for effective better trained directors. Cross and Lawrence put forward a broadly based model of corporate governance based on four main characteristics: board structures, board demographics, board attributes and board dynamics. The key questions according to the authors are "Does the board and its committees have [an] appropriate configuration and is the board compliant [with governance codes]?", "Do directors have capacity, capability and are they well connected?", "Do directors display competence, commitment and character?" and "Does the board model a culture of cohesion and challenge?".

The way in which a board operates, the skills which each member brings to decision-making and the influence of different parties is likely to have a major impact on boardroom discussions. This process can be affected by biases of members of the board that influence the final outcome of discussions. Moats, DeNicola and Malone (2021) identify four such biases. These include deference to authority, groupthink, bias towards the status quo and confirmation bias. Signs of an authority bias problem may include deference to the authority figure either because of their subject knowledge or board leadership role where other members of the board are reluctant to contribute their own opinion to the discussion. This may be a particular problem where the roles of CEO and chair are combined. The authors also identify the role of a tendency towards groupthink as a potential problem where boards move quickly to the same conclusion and are reluctant to challenge the overall consensus. They comment on how the use of virtual board meetings following the pandemic may have accelerated this process, particularly where the materials for the meeting have been distributed at the last possible moment with little time for assessment.

Bias towards the status quo is one of the most critical factors that we have observed in many of the examples of business distress that feature in this book, with companies continuing to operate in the same way despite increasing evidence that the existing business model is no longer working. Evidence can include a failure to eliminate areas of the business that no longer add value, avoidance of long-term succession planning decisions or a reluctance to review and enhance board competences through effective training.

Confirmation bias is the tendency of the board to use evidence of past experience to justify decisions that they take, frequently without testing whether that experience remains relevant to changing circumstances. The challenges that companies have faced over the first two decades of the new millenium have created an environment where past experience is increasingly irrelevant, with companies requiring new talents and skills as well as a different mindset. New board members are frequently needed to bring new perspectives to the problem.

By contrast in a small business there is typically little or no extended deliberation of alternatives beyond the discussions that may take place with employees or members of the family who are involved in the business. A professional advisor (typically the company's accountant) may provide a broader perspective. Individual skills and judgement are paramount. This is a recurrent theme in the following chapters. Formal board meetings to discuss and confirm decisions are unlikely to figure in such companies.

Diversity and experienced membership

BFQ 2.3 How does the board ensure that it has a sufficiently diverse and experienced membership capable of identifying and responding to emerging challenges?
Later chapters of this book identify a diverse range of skills that can contribute to building and supporting business resilience. Small businesses frequently lack such skills, relying as they do on the expertise of the owner-manager or entrepreneur. This position does not appear to have changed substantially over the years with surveys continuing to confirm that small businesses lack basic skills in key areas such as finance, strategy and HR. Whilst targeted help from professional bodies such as the Institute of Directors in the UK or other professional advisors/business schools may offer specific formal guidance and support, the reality is that most directors of small and medium-sized companies could still benefit from external support that is closer to the business and in touch with the problems that such businesses face on a day-to-day basis.

In the early 2020s businesses have been confronted with a range of new challenges in areas such as AI and sustaining supply chain continuity. Sustainability has become an increasingly important issue for boards to confront. Funds and risk management and employee relations continue to be critical performance dimensions. Each development requires a new skills set and potentially a different orientation to inform board decision-making. Whilst a diverse range of skills can enhance the overall performance of the board, unless members recognise that they are part of a team with a collective responsibility to promote the success of the business as a whole then the potential contribution of the board can be considerably reduced. Effective boards recognise the relative strengths of each member, identify any gaps and seek to build the skills of existing members or recruit new members where needed. Such boards work collectively to discuss how to take the business forward, guided by a common sense of purpose.

Flybe Group plc

Readers are now invited to read the extended case study of Flybe Group plc. The case is based on information which is in the public domain. You may want to look back at some of the questions that we raise in Tables 2.1 and 2.2 as you review the case.

The case illustrates specific aspects of purpose and the role of the board that we have discussed in this chapter. Readers may want to consider:

- Flybe's original ambition to be an alternative to land based travel in the UK and more broadly across Europe
- How the company's purpose, business objectives and strategies changed during the tenure of different CEOs
- The changes that took place to the membership and roles of board directors over time.

Case study: Flybe Group plc

Overview

Flybe Group plc (Flybe) took off for the first time in 1979 under the banner of Jersey European Airways. It was renamed British European Airways in 2000 and relaunched as Flybe in 2002. Flybe grew to become one of the largest regional airlines in Europe, focusing on the demand for regional flights, predominantly within the UK, with connections to other European and international routes through partnerships (code sharing) with legacy airlines. In 2006 the company bought British Airways' BA Connect business for £521m, adding more than 50 routes and doubling the number of customers. By 2010 the company was operating more domestic routes than any other UK carrier with a 27% share of the UK domestic market.

In December 2010 the company, seeking to strengthen its financial base, launched a successful IPO (initial public offering), obtaining a listing on the London Stock Exchange. The company stated:

> Flybe believes that Admission and the Global Offer will provide the Company with capital to assist in the expansion of its operations within continental Europe, provide the company with a platform for future growth through acquisitions using the company's listed securities as consideration, assist the Group in recruiting, retaining and incentivising key management and employees and improve the Group's profile, brand recognition and credibility with its customers and employees.[1]

The offer was oversubscribed with Flybe shares fixed at 295p.

Fast forward to 5 March 2020. Having made a net profit in only two of the 10 years since its IPO, Flybe was placed into administration. Four different CEOs with four different business strategies had been unable to resolve the problems created by two fundamentally flawed assumptions: first that there was a sustainable domestic market for a regional carrier that could compete profitably with road and rail alternatives over relatively short distances on a large number of routes and second that business growth could be accelerated through the development of a strong European network, in which Flybe would play a (the) leading role.

Growth ambitions

In July 2010 the company announced an order for 35 regional jets from the Brazilian manufacturer Embraer with options on a further 105, a decision that was to overshadow much of the company's future development. Designed to operate primarily on European rather than domestic routes and restricted to longer runways than those of many regional airports, these aircraft would prove to be a recurring drag on Flybe

https://doi.org/10.1515/9783110689495-003

cash flow for the next ten years. In their strategic report in 2011 directors included amongst key risks the failure to implement the company's growth strategy, particularly in terms of its expansion into Europe, the increasing costs of developing new routes and the prospect of new routes not being profitable. The mitigating factor was "the management team is experienced in identifying business opportunities and developing them profitably".[2]

The company reported a loss before tax - unadjusted of £4.3m for 2010–2011 on total revenues of £595.5m. Part of this loss was attributed to disruption from a volcanic eruption in Iceland as the report commented "Ash cloud resulting from the eruption of the Eyjafjallajökull volcano in Iceland during April and May 2010 shut down airspace across northern Europe and, in particular, our main operations in the UK. This led to Flybe cancelling 3,177 flights, representing approximately 2.2% of our planned flying programme for the year".

The directors reported that in August 2011 the business had been restructured into three divisions, Flybe UK, FlybeEurope and Flybe Aviation support, each with its own managing director appointed from the main board to provide "a clear direction and focus and drive for the implementation of the company's growth strategy". The annual report for 2011–2012 reported a loss before tax of £6.2m, on total revenues of £678.8m citing a significant reduction in consumer disposable income, issues of high oil prices and increases in Airline Passenger Duty (APD). APD was a tax on all flights originating in the UK which effectively created a double charge for Flybe passengers on domestic return flights since both legs of the journey originated in the UK. Flybe executives continued to cite APD as a major problem, right up to the time when the company was put into administration. Expansion into Europe was cited as a continuing pressure on resources with £3.7m share of losses in the first year of a joint venture with Finnair.[3]

In January 2013 the company announced a turnaround plan for the Flybe UK business that involved a 20% cut in management headcount and a further 10% cut in overhead and production headcount (approximately 300 roles in the business). The combined effect was expected to be £35m of cost savings by 2014/2015.[4] In its annual report for 2012–2013 the company reported pre-tax losses of £40.7m, on total revenues of £781m, attributing this to restructuring charges and higher staff and fuel costs (fuel costs increased from £106m in 2011–2012 to £122m in 2012–2013). The company's share price fell to 41p on the announcement. The chairman and CEO in his annual review stated "There's no doubt that the last few years have been tough for Flybe. The business has not progressed the way I, or any of the Board would have wanted". He described "very serious headwinds the industry has been battling" citing austerity measures introduced by the UK government following the financial crash in 2008, the disproportionate impact of APD on a domestic airline operating mainly in the UK, and high fuel costs made even more acute by the depreciation of the pound against the dollar.[5] The titles of annual reports for 2010–2011, 2011–2012 and 2012–2013, respectively, summarise the main strategic routes that the company had followed for the first three years since its IPO, "UK Leadership–European Growth", "Building Europe's Leading Regional Aviation Group" and "Fit to Compete".

Change of direction

A press release in August 2013 announced the separation of the role of chairman and CEO and the appointment of a new CEO. The press release also confirmed that the company's Chief Financial Officer (CFO), in post since 2007, had decided to step down.[6] A further re-organisation followed. In a press announcement in September 2013, the new CEO confirmed that the divisional structure would be disbanded and all of the company's operations would be integrated back into a single operating unit. He commented:

> It has quickly become clear to me that Flybe's prospects will be significantly enhanced by disbanding the existing divisional structure and integrating all operations into a single, simpler and lower cost operating unit. Today's announcement facilitates that move and will form an important part of the strategic review of the business which I expect to conclude in November. I look forward to sharing its full conclusions.[7]

The former divisional managing directors left the company on September 13, 2013. Looking back on the company in an interview reported in the Financial Times in 2015, the incoming CEO described the business before he arrived as "mayhem ...a real dysfunctional business in terms of its processes and structure". Management decisions were "seat of the pants" and route selection was done by "voodoo" while relationships between senior management were described as "fraught". "You had three guys on the main board plus the CEO-chairman and it was like they were at war with each other."[8]

A new independent non-executive chair was appointed in November. Rosedale Holdings, the company's biggest shareholder at the time with 48% of the equity, sold its shares.[9]

Planning to raise capital for development and reinforce its balance sheet, the company announced a rights issue in February 2014.[10] The issue successfully raised £155.7m approximately doubling its capitalisation and introducing several new institutional shareholders. In June 2014 the annual report for 2013–2014 showed that management attempts to turn the business around were having some effect. The company announced a pre-tax profit of £8.1m on total revenues of £868.4m. The new CEO's first annual report focused on a major relaunch of Flybe, stressing the competitive advantages of Flybe over other airlines in terms of the broad regional coverage of its routes and the advantages of Flybe in terms of speed and convenience over rail and road transport.[11]

Focusing on its strategy to realign its operations in line with regional domestic routes in September 2014 Flybe announced its intention to cancel most of the forward order placed at the time of its IPO in 2010 for Embraer jets and lease smaller Bombardier turboprop aircraft.[12] The company's non-executive chairman explained the logic:

> At the heart of this was identifying that Flybe could occupy a distinctive niche in regional aviation. There is a need for relatively short flights (up to around 90 min) from regional airports. Many of these routes are too thin (i.e. they have too few passengers) for the standard jet aircraft format, such as an A320 or B737, and some use runways that are too short for these aircraft to operate effectively. This makes these routes less attractive to a flag-carrying or low-cost airline. However, they are well suited to the turboprop fleet of Flybe. As such, we play a vital part in providing regional connectivity in the UK and to the near continent.[13]

The comments also reflected an increasing concern with the viability of European expansion. The company's major European venture at the time, Flybe Finland, posted a loss of £800k for financial year 2013–2014 and was sold for €1 in November 2014.[14]

In February 2015 CAPA (Centre for Aviation) published a SWOT analysis (strengths, weaknesses, opportunities and threats) of the company's position. Whilst recognising the potential of Flybe under new leadership to move forward, the analysis also acknowledged the challenges to the management of change that the new management team faced, stating:

> There is a transformation taking place in all aspects of Flybe's business, including its culture and branding. The successful management of change on this scale, especially in a highly competitive and fast paced sector such as aviation, presents huge challenges. The largely new executive team under [CEO] appears to be moving Flybe in the right direction, but it is not yet certain that its considerable strengths can be converted into sustainable profitability.[15]

In June 2015 Flybe announced a loss of £35.7m for financial year 2014–2015 on total revenues of £574.14m. This included £12m costs associated with discontinued operations associated with the divestment of its joint venture with Finnair.[16] The report referred to the resolution of the company's legacy issues including completion of its strategies for cost reduction and improved aircraft utilisation, and exit from a $892m obligation to buy additional E175 jets from Embraer.

Progress on implementation of the company's strategy was reflected in an improvement in the company's position for financial year 2015–2016 with an adjusted profit before tax of £5.5m on total revenues of £623.8m. In his report the CEO said "We have returned to growth and made a profit following losses in every year since Flybe's stock exchange flotation in 2010".[17]

The company's strategic report described improved performance against a series of 13 key indicators including employee satisfaction, customer satisfaction, total passenger revenue, cost reduction, adjusted profit before tax and cash generation. It also set out the principal risks to strategy including the threat to margins of fuel price increases, reductions in domestic and regional air travel, particularly in the UK, and exchange rate movements, factors that were to create strong headwinds in the next three years of the company's trading history. The titles of the annual reports for 2013–2014 to 2015–2016 reflect the main focus of management during this period, namely "Transforming Flybe", "Continuing Our Transformation" and "Delivering our Transformation".

A customer and employee-focused perspective

On 26 October 2016 the CEO left the company "by mutual agreement". In his report on the events surrounding this departure the non-executive chairman referred to an acknowledgement that "the company needed a fresh look at its future and a different culture". He added "The Board decided that the command and control culture that had been prevalent in Flybe had to change. We need to listen more to our customers and, and importantly listen to our own employees who work with customers every day".[18]

Commenting on the CEO's departure, CAPA referred to the apparently high rate of expansion in Flybe's capacity in 2016 at a time when demand was declining because of uncertainties such as Brexit.[19] CAPA commented "Significant strategic change may be unlikely in the interim, but a key question for the next CEO will be whether to continue with such aggressive capacity growth in the face of falling fares".

The incoming CEO addressed both of these issues in a new "sustainable business improvement plan" described in the annual report for 2016–17. The plan was presented to staff described as the "key leaders and influencers" in Flybe. It focused on six main pillars, putting the customer at the centre of the business through an enhanced digital e-commerce system, optimising the network based on customer and financial analysis, operational excellence with reliability and on-time performance, organisational excellence with "clear and aligned KPI's cascaded and embedded in every role profile", performance measurement and technology improvement particularly in the IT platform and finally cost reduction. The range of issues facing the company as the new CEO took charge reflected the scale of the problems to be resolved. The approach differed from the business expansion model of the period immediately following the IPO and the cost reduction/business growth route pursued during the tenure of the previous CEO. The fundamental strategic question was whether this was going to be a case of too much, too late.

In June 2017 the Group reported a loss before tax of £19.9m on Group revenues of £707.4m. The annual report also reported a reduction in cash from £171m in 2015–2016 to £124m in 2016–2017 and a change from net funds of £62.2m in 2016 to a net debt for 2016–17 of £64m.[20]

Commenting on the company's position in June 2017, CAPA noted that Flybe had returned to a greater focus on UK operations, reversing the trend of the previous two years. In a succinct summary, it also highlighted the main problems that Flybe had faced since its inception as a regional airline noting that:

> In spite of operating a network that faces no competition from other airlines on the majority of its routes, and in spite of being comfortably Europe's largest regional airline–Flybe has regularly struggled to make a profit. Its thin/negative margins are evidence that, in fact, it faces significant competition, but from surface transport. They are also evidence that its unit cost is too high relative to the unit revenue that it is able to generate. This has been exacerbated by excess capacity growth, but also partly reflects the high unit cost that is inherent in the regional airline model.[21]

Problems continued in 2018. An offer in March from the Stobart Group to buy the company was rejected.[22] A trading update from Flybe in April cited "extremely poor weather in February and March that led to airport closures and flight cancellations, a weaker pound and higher fuel prices" as major impacts on full year results. The company's annual report and accounts for 2017–2018 reflected this warning. Pretax losses for the year to end March were £9m on Group revenue of £753m. Total cash had fallen to £95m, and borrowings were £154m. Following the discovery of an accounting error for financial year 2016–2017, related to the leasing costs of nine Embraer aircraft, the loss before tax was adjusted retrospectively from £19.9m to £48.5m.[23] The business model was beginning to look increasingly unsustainable.

In the 2017/2018 Annual Report the CEO referred to the introduction of a new balanced scorecard approach "to keep our focus on delivery and to measure the 5 key success factors behind our business model". The report also identified three specific key performance indicators, continuously improving revenue, a sustainable cost position and a stable and reliable operation. A new strap-line "close-to-you" was used to emphasise the company's focus on providing regional airline services at locations around the country that were convenient and easy to use, with high levels of customer service and responsiveness.

In its interim report on financial year 2018/2019 in November 2018 the company indicated that it was still facing pressures from the weakness of sterling and higher fuel prices which had driven up cost-per-seat.[24] When combined with overcapacity in the European short haul airline market and a reduction in demand for airline services generally, this had led to continuing pressure on profitability. A net decrease in cash and cash equivalents in the first half of the year was reported as £32.5m, leaving cash and cash equivalents at the end of the period at £54.2m. Significantly a further £16.4m of cash was held as security by credit card acquirers acting as intermediaries between Flybe and the credit card companies used by customers to book flights. As doubts about Flybe's ability to continue to provide its service to customers grew, the acquirers, who were responsible for any defaults in service, had begun to demand increasingly higher levels of security in terms of retained payments. An interview with the CEO in 2019 reported by the Financial Times commented on the financial difficulties that this had created for the business.[25]

The board said in its interim report that it was reviewing a number of options, including capacity and cost saving measures, as well as other initiatives to strengthen the balance sheet. Other possible changes included a move to an LSE standard listing from a premium listing which would allow the company greater freedom to divest assets to raise cash.[26] Cash generation was becoming a critical issue as reflected in the company's statement about the business as a going concern. Commenting on the company's position the report stated:

> This cash flow forecast includes several cash generating transactions over the next 12 months to provide further liquidity in addition to that arising from ordinary business trading. The Directors believe these transactions will provide sufficient liquidity for the Group's needs and to manage potential consequences of downside risks as noted above. The financing actions range from short-term actions that are currently at an advanced stage and relate to the sale or sale and leaseback of assets or disinvestment of non-core elements of the business, and further medium-term plans that are being prepared to be transacted during 2019.[27]

One of its longstanding investors, Aberford Holdings sold most of its shares in the company, reducing its holdings from 15% to 4%.[28] Shareholders approved the proposal in December 2018.

On 14 November 2018 the company told its shareholders that it was looking at a range of different strategies to address the company's situation including putting the business up for sale.[29]

Grounded by strong headwinds

In January 2019 the company accepted a 1p a share takeover offer from Connect Airways, a new company set up by a consortium of Virgin Atlantic, Stobart Aviation and Cyrus Capital.[30] Shareholders formally approved the offer in March 2019. The new consortium committed to invest £100m in the company, including taking over a net debt of £80m. In February the company received loans from the three new owners. The last of the company's remaining assets including buildings, equipment and intellectual property were pledged as security. The CEO stepped down in July 2019 and was replaced by a senior manager from Virgin Atlantic.

Business continued until January 2020 when Flybe sought state aid to resolve recurring cash flow problems, including potential deferment of APD. The government was initially sympathetic to providing aid, due in part to its commitment to providing support for regional development and Flybe service to many different parts of the UK. This was criticised by other airlines, citing European regulations that required any support to be commercially viable which would not be possible since Flybe had no remaining tangible assets to offer as security. As a final blow, the outbreak of coronavirus across the world in the first few months of 2020 spelt the end for Flybe. The company entered administration on 5 March 2020.

Table 8.1 in Chapter 8 uses the Flybe Group plc case study to illustrate how the generic benchmarking framework introduced in Chapter 1 can be applied. Readers are recommended to look at this table for a summary of the case and the issues that it raises.

Notes

1 Flybe Group Ltd, (2010), *Flybe announces its intention to list on the London Stock Exchange* [online]. 30 November. Available at: https://www.investegate.co.uk/flybe/rns/intention-to-float/201011300700140156X/ [Accessed: 10 December 2021].

2 Flybe Group plc, (2011) *UK Leadership-European Growth* Annual Report 2010/11.

3 Flybe Group plc, (2012) *Building Europe's Leading Regional Aviation Group* Annual Report 2011/12.

4 Flybe Group plc, (2013) *Delivery and Future Direction* [online]. 23 January. Available at: https://www.investegate.co.uk/flybe-Group-Plc–flyb-/rns/delivery-and-future-direction/201301230701031416W/ [Accessed 26 November 2021].

5 Flybe Group plc, (2013) *Fit to Compete* Annual Report 2012/13.

6 Flybe Group plc, (2013) *Directorate and Management* [online]. 05 August. Available at: https://www.investegate.co.uk/flybe-Group-Plc–flyb-/rns/directorate-and-management/201308050700229233K/ [Accessed 26 November 2021].

7 Flybe Group plc, (2013) *Update on Strategic Review* [online]. 16 September. Available at: https://www.investegate.co.uk/flybe-Group-Plc–flyb-/rns/update-on-strategic-review/201309160700080098O/ [Accessed 26 November 2021].

8 Wild, J. (2015) Flybe yet to hit a purple patch. *Financial Times* [online]. Jan 29. Available at https://www.ft.com/content/130adfec-a7a1-11e4-8e78-00144feab7de [Accessed 26 November 2021].

9 Flybe Group plc, (2013) *Notification of Sale of Shares by Rosedale* [online]. 13 November. Available at: https://www.investegate.co.uk/flybe-Group-Plc–flyb-/rns/notification-of-shares-sale/201311130700198660S/ [Accessed 26 November 2021].

10 Flybe Group plc, (2014) *Proposed Firm Placing and Placing and Open Offer* [online]. 20 February. Available at: https://www.investegate.co.uk/flybe-Group-Plc–flyb-/rns/proposed-firm-placing-and-placing-and-open-offer/201402200700195171A/ [Accessed 26 November 2021].

11 Flybe Group plc, (2014) *Transforming Flybe* Annual Report 2013–14.

12 Flybe Group plc, (2014) *Aircraft agreements* [online]. 17 September. Available at https://www.investegate.co.uk/flybe-Group-Plc–flyb-/rns/aircraft-agreements/201409170700298889R/ [Accessed 26 November 2021].

13 Flybe Group plc, (2015) *Continuing our Transformation* Annual Report 2014–15.

14 Finnair Plc, *Stock Exchange Release* 12 November 2014.

15 CAPA (2015) *Flybe Swot Analysis: strengths as an airline do not necessarily convert to sustainable profits* [online]. 6 February. Available at: https://centreforaviation.com/analysis/reports/flybe-swot-analysis-strengths-as-an-airline-do-not-necessarily-convert-to-sustainable-profits-208471 [Accessed 10 December 2021].

16 Flybe Group plc, (2015) *Continuing our transformation* Annual Report 2014–15.

17 Flybe Group plc, (2016) *Delivering our transformation* Annual Report 2015–16.

18 Flybe Group plc, *Shaping a sustainable future* Annual Report 2016–17.

19 CAPA, (2016) *Flybe: largest regional airline in Europe leads the airline capacity growth charge in winter 2016/17* [online]. November 7. Available at: https://centreforaviation.com/analysis/reports/flybe-largest-regional-airline-in-europe-leads-the-airline-capacity-growth-charge-in-winter-201617-311034 [accessed 10 December 2021].

20 Flybe Group plc, (2017) *Shaping a sustainable future* Annual report 2016/2017.

21 CAPA, (2017) *Flybe plans post peak fleet profit progress; new CEO introduces a business improvement plan*[online]. 20 June. Available at: https://centreforaviation.com/analysis/reports/flybe-plans-post-peak-fleet-profit-progress-new-ceo-introduces-a-business-improvement-plan-349670 [Accessed 10 December 2021.]

22 Flybe Group plc, (2018) *Statement regarding withdrawal of Stobart Group* [online], 22 March. Available at: https://www.investegate.co.uk/flybe-Group-Plc–flyb-/rns/statement-regarding-withdrawal-of-stobart-Group/201803220718085662I/ [Accessed 26 November 2021].

23 Flybe Group plc, (2018) *Close to You* Annual report *2017–18.*

24 Flybe Group plc, (2018) *Interim management report Adjusted profit up despite fuel and currency headwinds* [online]. 14 November. Available at https://www.investegate.co.uk/flybe-Group-Plc–flyb-/rns/2018-19-half-year-results/201811140700032614H/ [accessed 10 December 2021].

25 Spero, J. (2019) Flybe owners seek tens of millions in withheld payments' *Financial Times* [online]. May 5. Available at: https://www.ft.com/content/387ac81a-6ce0-11e9-80c7-60ee53e6681d [accessed 10 December 2021].

26 Flybe Group plc, (2018) *Interim management report Adjusted profit up despite fuel and currency headwinds* [online]. 14 November. Available at https://www.investegate.co.uk/flybe-Group-Plc–flyb-/rns/2018-19-half-year-results/201811140700032614H/ [accessed 10 December 2021].

27 Flybe Group plc, *Interim management report for the six months ended 30th September 2018*, 14 November 2018. Available at https://www.investegate.co.uk/flybe-Group-Plc–flyb-/rns/2018-19-half-year-results/201811140700032614H/ [accessed 10 December 2021].

28 Flybe Group plc, (2018) *Holdings in Company* [online]. 16 November. Available at: https://www.investegate.co.uk/flybe-Group-Plc–flyb-/rns/holding-s–in-company/201811161524236665H/ [Accessed 26 November 26 2021].

29 Flybe Group plc, (2018) *Formal Sale Process as Part of Strategic Review* [online]. 16 November. Available at: https://www.investegate.co.uk/flybe-group-Plc–flyb-/rns/formal-sale-process-as-part-of-strategic-review/201811140703012615H/ [Accessed 26 November 2021].

30 Flybe Group plc, (2019) *Recommendation of the Connect Airways Offer* [online]. 11 January. Available at: https://www.investegate.co.uk/flybe-Group-Plc–flyb-/rns/recommendation-of-the-connect-airways-offer/201901111131009002M/ [Accessed 26 November 2021].

3 Resilient planning

Director (n)
Corporate world "one of a number of persons having authority to manage the affairs of a company"
Theatrical world "the leader of a company of performers"
(Online Etymology Dictionary, 2021)

Directing the show

A board of directors has a range of responsibilities that include setting the overall vision and purpose of the company, agreeing the plans that are necessary to take the business forward and making sure that such plans are executed effectively. Borrowing an analogy from the theatrical world members of the board write the story line, secure financial backing for the production, recruit an artistic director (CEO) to manage the delivery of the performance and oversee delivery. Their role is also to make sure that the story line (the business plan) is developed by the artistic director in a compelling way that delights different audiences (customers) and professional critics (external auditors, investors, creditors and suppliers). They provide feedback where the interpretation of the performance is not consistent with the original script (business plan). In the theatrical world the biggest challenge is to come up with a storyline that is sufficiently compelling and unique to keep potential theatre goers interested. Whilst there are still considerable challenges in recruiting the right cast and directing the production, success is ultimately dependent on creating a performance that attracts new audiences and brings others back on a regular basis to repeat the experience.

Resilient planning in the commercial world reflects many of these different considerations, beginning with the creation of a business proposition that is sufficiently distinctive and enduring, followed by setting specific objectives and plans. Writing the plot for a new theatrical production cannot be done by formula. In the same way there are no established principles or routines to create a new business concept that will have value in the market place. In the theatre once the story line is agreed putting the show together and presenting performances is a more straightforward and programmable task, with key stages well rehearsed in advance and practiced in a wide range of different settings. Equally the implementation of business plans (as distinct from strategic thinking) can also be a logical process, once the business concept is clearly identified. Strategy creation (writing the plot) and strategy implementation (delivering the performance) are two separate and clearly distinct activities.

Whilst some theatrical plays are relatively enduring and will continue to draw in audiences for an extended period, eventually audience interest is likely to decline

https://doi.org/10.1515/9783110689495-004

and a new production is needed. Business models also have a finite lifespan and need to be renewed, either as a result of competitive activity or a reduction in overall demand for the product or service. Resilient businesses continuously challenge the assumptions that lie behind the existing model seeking to identify whether modifications are needed to existing plans or a new direction is indicated to take the business forward in a different direction.

Table 3.1 sets out the specific questions that we suggest are included in a review of business planning. As we indicated in the previous chapter, readers who are interested in benchmarking the performance of a specific business may want to make some notes under each of the main areas as we progress through the discussion. We have included another extended case study (Arcadia Group Ltd) at the end of

Table 3.1: BFQ 3 Resilient planning: How effective is the board in setting the overall direction of the business and monitoring how well plans are implemented?.

Benchmarking questions	Commentary (Evidence)	Score
Recognition that planning can make a difference BFQ 3.1 Do members of the board and business as a whole believe that the business plan and/or business planning adds value?	Regular review and updating of business plans A plan for planning with appropriate resources and external support where required Strategic items on regular agenda rather than as infrequent events A clear statement of business strategy that is set out simply and briefly All members of the board actually know what the company's business plan is and can explain it clearly in one sentence	
Knowledge, skills and experience BFQ 3.2 Does the business have the right range of knowledge skills and experience to put in place and implement a resilient planning process?	Regular review of management competences and develop and train approach rather than fire and replace Explicit budget and resources for skills development and benchmarking performance at all levels The mix of skills of non-executive directors is deliberately chosen to reflect the challenges that the business faces Well thought through partnerships with external parties including professional support (accountancy and legal) as well as commercial consultancy to add supplementary skills Non-executives in specific roles such as the audit and remuneration committees are given appropriate information to fulfil these roles	

Table 3.1 (continued)

The process of planning BFQ 3.3 Is there an explicit process where the major assumptions in the business plan are regularly revisited and modified to reflect changes to the market place and competitive behaviour?	Business planning is informed by the application of specific approaches including SWOT analysis, analysis of competition and core competences, value chain analysis, and portfolio analysis Each of these formal approaches is applied in an appropriate way that is relevant to the needs of the organisation and the competences of those running the business

this chapter. Again, readers may want to skip ahead and read this case first prior to beginning this chapter.

Recognition that planning can make a difference

BFQ 3.1 Do members of the board and business as a whole believe that the business plan and/or business planning adds value?

Business planning is frequently described as though it were a logical controllable process, beginning with analysis of the situation followed by the identification of appropriate objectives and then strategies to achieve those objectives. Alternative strategies are costed, revenues calculated and a series of targets emerge that are typically presented in terms of financial outcomes such as sales and profitability. This approach might be unfairly characterised as "think–then do–check the results–then think again–then do" [repeat as necessary typically as part of an annual process]. At the other extreme planning and implementation can be part of a more randomised set of actions that might be better represented by the expression, "do–check the results–do–think–reconsider–do" [repeat as necessary frequently in a random manner at different times potentially over the same year]. In the second situation planning and doing are intermingled with an emphasis on flexibility and change. Resilient approaches to planning lie somewhere between these two extremes.

Readers may recall the discussion of Nestlé's declared business purpose in the last chapter. If we add "who?" and "when?" to the three questions posed by Nestlé Chair Paul Bulcke ("how?", "what?" and "why?") then we get close to the essential questions that are typically covered in most business plans. Formal business plans are focused on what the company intends to do, why it proposes specific actions, who is responsible for making things happen and how and when such actions will be implemented. A sixth element, "how much will it cost to implement the plan?" and a seventh question "what do we expect to gain as a result of implementing the plan?" complete the picture.

Such plans are statements about the future. They are based on assumptions about cause and effect. In a rapidly changing environment it is reasonable to ask what is the value in producing a plan in the first place if the actions set out in the original plan rapidly become obsolete? Projections of financial results beyond a few months are rarely accurate. Whilst companies might be able to control costs in a predictable manner, they cannot control revenues in the same way. Those responsible for producing a plan are aware that there is little or no chance of every assumption in the plan being correct. In some companies planning is a process of continuous adjustment to circumstances with no formal explicit event at a particular moment in the year. In others planning may be a formal elaborate ritual linked to away days for the senior team and subsequent staff briefings. For other companies planning takes on a greater significance at key moments in the development of the business when those responsible are faced with a major change in circumstances such as the replacement of the CEO or potential threats to business continuity.

Continuous adjustment

In many small and medium-sized businesses, particularly business start-ups there is no perceived need to produce a formal business plan. The directors get on with running the business, making adjustments to new challenges or perceived opportunities as they arise. They have wide discretion as they are frequently not accountable to third parties, and it is their ambition rather than any formal plan which provides direction. Lenders are willing to provide support if they can see that business basics are in place, and more importantly that borrowing is secured by assets or personal guarantees. Very often in such circumstances business plans, if they are formalised at all, are expressed in financial terms with performance judged against specific indicators. External investors back their judgement and do not get involved, subject to the business meeting certain basic parameters such as growth targets.

The decisions that such a company may face when challenged to produce their first business plan are illustrated in "Sustainable Foods". Sustainable Foods is a fictional small business. The case is based on one of the writer's experiences in working with such businesses and draws on a range of different situations.

Planning needs to be a practical process

The owners of Sustainable Foods, a supplier of ready-made meals with an on-site café never saw the need to produce a formal business plan whilst sufficient cash was generated to pay staff and suppliers and cover overheads including income for its owners. The first time they were asked to produce a plan was when they sought external funding to support building an extension to their premises.

Describing a long-term vision, the first question that is typically asked by potential funders may not be a major problem. Owner-entrepreneurs including the directors of this particular business frequently have a clear idea of where they want to take the company and can describe this enthusiastically – this is what drives them to set up in the first place and keep the business going. The real problem begins when they are then asked to describe the way in which they run the business (their business model) and quantify their vision in terms of sales and cost estimates.

In the description that follows we review the areas that the owners of this small company might have considered as they began to formulate an explicit business plan. We have linked this discussion to the language of business planning that is often used to describe the process (*in italics*). The owners of this particular business are unlikely to have ever used this language.

Identification and description of purpose or vision
The stated purpose of the business owners is to use natural ingredients as far as possible in imaginative and constantly changing café menus and takeaway meals. The mix of different foods will reflect changing trends in food preparation and consumption and be designed to meet the needs of different customers with specific concerns about diet and health.

Analysis of business situation
No one else is operating a similar business in the same area and the immediate threat of direct competition is low. They believe that their focus on organic foods and innovative recipes will continue to give them a long term business advantage. Much of their success has been due to the efforts of one key member of staff - an experienced and innovative chef - who would be difficult to replace. She has indicated that she intends to retire within the next five years.

Description of business model
In this business the owners have decided to focus on two main groups, families with small children and mature customers, and develop menus that constantly change from season to season reflecting the availability of ingredients. They have attempted to create a distinctive business through their focus on sustainability. A range of different events and activities are organised throughout the year to attract different audiences. These include an exhibition area for local artists and a series of musical performances by local artists targetted at younger audiences.

Development of strategies
New options constantly appear on the menu designed to provide variety and new dining experiences for its target customers. The proposal to extend the premises that generated the need to produce a business plan is designed to create greater capacity to meet expanding demand for takeaway meals.

Action plans
Forward orders are placed with local produce suppliers, and staff working in the kitchen and serving customers are regularly briefed on new menu choices. The owners have recently updated their website which now gives more information about menus, special deals and new products, up-coming events and visitor feedback.

Implementation and control
The owners check every week how much money has come in and where it has been spent. Every month they produce a summary of cash flow and look ahead to forecast what the next month might look like. The owners have a regular meeting with an independent bookkeeper who provides advice on what information to collect and how well the company is trading. During the meeting they discuss any new ideas for business development and the costs that may be involved.

From the above description it looks like some of the different elements that might be needed to produce a formal plan are already in place. There is evidence of strategic thinking designed to create a unique position for the business in its immediate locality. There is some awareness of strengths and weaknesses as well as consideration of alternative strategies and an implementation plan. Finally there is a budgeting and planning process in place that focuses on cash flow and financial control.

Presenting each of these actions in the form of a written plan may appear to be a relatively straightforward process. However, asking such a business to consciously consider these questions and produce such a plan can still be seen as a difficult task, particularly if this is the first time that this has been asked for. There is a more fundamental question, namely will such a plan add real value? This is often more directly expressed in conversations with the typical owners of many such businesses as "what's the point of all of this?"

Some key questions that a potential lender might ask could include "How quickly can such a business change direction if circumstances change and the original assumptions behind the plan are no longer correct? What might happen if a key employee decides to leave or retire? How competent is their assessment of the situation?" Many directors in small companies when faced with this process for the first time conclude that it is too complicated a process and seek external help.

On a positive note a formal written plan once completed can be used to inform discussions with a range of different stakeholders including lenders, possible investors or ultimately potential buyers interested in acquiring the business. It also can generate specific guidelines for those involved in running such an enterprise, particularly where the owners are considering handing over some or all of the responsibility to new management and stepping back. More fundamentally perhaps, producing such a plan for the first time may force the owners to concede that problems are emerging and put in place plans to address potential threats.

Regular ritual

The assumption that directors in larger companies spend a significant proportion of their time on business planning could not be further from the truth. We
have rarely found a company where an extended debate about strategy takes
place during regular scheduled board meetings. Most of the discussion tends to
focus on ongoing business and day-to-day decision-making in the form of reports from the executive members of the board on each of their areas of responsibility. Perhaps more worryingly when boards do take time out to discuss
broader strategic issues there is often no shared consensus on the overall strategy or direction of the business. As a facilitator of such exercises the initial briefing given to one of the authors by the CEO/chair of the business prior to running
such a session has frequently not been consistent with the expectations and values of those involved in the discussion. Beyond personal anecdotes, research evidence shows that most executive directors only allocate a small proportion of
their time to strategic planning (Mintzberg, 1975). Most of their time is taken up
with the daily routine of keeping the business going. Many non-executive board
members also tend to be distanced from the day-to-day work of the board and
less involved in strategy development.

Discussions of strategy and planning in many organisations tend to be
reserved for specific designated sessions that take place less frequently (often
annually). In such settings planning may become a check on progress where executive directors review performance against targets, discuss variations with
non-executive directors, agree marginal changes and then get back to running
the business. Having observed a range of meetings in a variety of different commercial and public sector settings such events have often seemed like an annual
vehicle service, designed to check that the business is operating effectively
against previously agreed criteria and fix any minor problems that are seen to
be likely to interfere with its smooth running. Following the meeting the CEO or
chair then frequently issues an update on progress for investors and other
stakeholders which often presents an optimistic picture despite underlying
problems that may be emerging.

In many situations inertia may set in with a reluctance to step back and take a
more detailed look at emerging business problems. When a more fundamental review
is proposed, particularly by a new board member this proposal may be regarded with
suspicion or outright opposition, particularly if there are vested interests in maintaining the status quo. There may be no incentive for the rest of the board to dig more
deeply into some of the assumptions that have guided the business up to that point. In
such circumstances planning can appear to be a comprehensive exercise but may not
go beyond the boundaries of the existing business to explore alternative business scenarios. The challenge for a chair in such circumstances is to create an environment

where challenges to assumptions are encouraged and executive director decisions are regularly reviewed.

Strategic shift

A major review of the current business model may be linked to the arrival of a new CEO. We briefly discussed the role of a new CEO as an agent for change in the previous chapter. There are examples of this situation in each of the major case studies that are featured in this book. A challenge from an activist investor may also force the board to reconsider the existing assumptions that underpin the current strategy. A newly appointed non-executive director may also question the appropriateness of current business plans. More fundamentally, a major strategic review is more likely to be undertaken at key moments in the evolution of a business, when the board itself acknowledges that it needs to reset direction to avoid potential business failure.

Such a review may be repeated over several iterations with new senior teams involved on each occasion as a business tries to put a sustainable plan in place that reflects the challenges that it faces. Several of the case studies reported in this book describe how independent advisors were also used at various stages to address emerging business problems (for example the discussion of the role of Ernst & Young in the Carillion case study at the end of Chapter 4).

Aston Martin Lagonda Global Holdings plc

The recent history of Aston Martin Lagonda demonstrates how one company has faced a series of different challenges, each of which has required the board to adjust the business model, seek new sources of finance and attempt to relaunch the business. The enduring factor that has served to keep the business going over this period has been the intrinsic value of the brand, positioned as a luxury performance car for a specific market segment (buoyed up in no small measure by its association with one of the most iconic film franchises ever – the James Bond movies). Its recent history has been punctuated by changes of ownership, repeated calls for new investment and the introduction of new management teams (Burgess, 2019). Critics of the company point to claims of poor product quality and inadequate dealer support, combined with increasing competition from other niche manufacturers that have moved faster into more sustainable vehicle power trains. Covid-19 had a major impact on company sales with losses almost quadrupling in the first year of the pandemic (Jolly, 2021).

The company's risk and viability assessment produced as part of its annual report in 2019 ran to over 10 pages of detailed description of risks (Aston Martin Lagonda,

2019). Each of the risks had a clearly identified champion responsible for progressing mitigation actions. The risk assessment identified the inability to maintain a favourable competitive position in the high luxury segment of the car market as an increasing problem. It also identified the failure to incorporate automotive technological advances as a significant increasing issue (e.g. active safety, connected car, electrification and autonomous driving).

These risks, the annual report stated could be mitigated by a range of actions including changes in the company's portfolio driven by investment in strategic alliances that "would enable the company to develop and implement new technology quickly and cost effectively" and "talent recruitment to sustain the company's ability to analyse market trends". Aston Martin Lagonda also recognised the potential risk of relying on key suppliers and the need to ensure uninterrupted production by improving supplier performance through supplier engagement and development programmes led by "supplier champions".

Comments from the outgoing chair made in the same report illustrate the position that the company had reached following several years where it had attempted to raise fresh capital for the business (Aston Martin Lagonda, 2019).

> This has been a disappointing year for Aston Martin Lagonda. Revenues of £997m, (9% lower) and a significant fall in adjusted EBITDA to £134m (down 46%), have contributed to severe pressure on liquidity which has left the company with no alternative but to seek £500m of additional equity financing, without which, the balance sheet is not robust enough to support the operations of the group.

The report goes on to discuss the company's Second Century plan which they had committed to in 2015. The chair admitted the plan itself had proved to be too ambitious and could not stand the scale of investment needed including building new manufacturing facilities. It was also recognised as "[not able to] support the unexpectedly large downside risk and costs of underperformance that was being experienced by the business". The board admitted that it had needed to change some of its major decisions on capital structure and its business plan. This had led to the raising of an additional $190m in additional debt in April 2019 to maintain liquidity.

Throughout the 2019 financial year business trading continued to be weak putting further pressure on liquidity, meaning that the board needed to increase debt even further including raising another $150m in senior secured notes. Following a strategic review a decision was taken in January 2020 to accept a strategic investment bid from an external consortium to raise further proceeds of up to £500m to sustain the company. A new business plan was announced that included a reduction in the overall volume of production to match demand and reduce inventory, delay in investment in electric vehicles until no earlier than 2025, focus on the launch of a new sports utility vehicle (SUV) and critically a reduction in operating costs and capital expenditure to give priority to improving cash flow.

The report describes how external consultants were involved in improving business forecasting and short-term cashflow modelling as well as providing advice on director duties. It also announced that the CFO and the chair would be stepping down to be replaced by nominees of the new shareholder group.

During 2020 the new owners also replaced the CEO. A new transformational plan "Project Horizon" was announced.

In his report for 2020–2021 the new executive chair commented on progress against the plan (Aston Martin Lagonda Global Holdings plc 2021).

> 2020 has been a transformative year for Aston Martin. Since I became Executive Chairman in April, we have made significant progress to position the Company for success to capture the huge and exciting opportunity ahead of us. We have appointed a world-class executive leadership team with deep experience of this industry and earlier this month announced new non-executive appointments to the Board bringing a wealth of relevant luxury and automotive experience. I am extremely pleased with the progress to date despite operating in these most challenging of times. I both welcomed the strong support we received from existing investors and was delighted to attract new investors to Aston Martin through the successful refinancing actions taken during 2020. I, and my co-investors, are fully committed to delivering this plan and are confident in the future success of Aston Martin as we transform the Company to be one of the greatest luxury car brands in the world.

The case study illustrates the complexity of different decisions that a board can face as they attempt to turn a business around. The purpose statement "[transforming] the company to be one of the greatest luxury car brands in the world" set a serious challenge for those involved in working in the business.

Knowledge skills and experience

BFQ 3.2 Does the business have the right range of knowledge skills and experience to put in place and implement a resilient planning process?
Business plans can take a variety of different forms ranging from no apparent formal plan (the ideas inside the head of the original entrepreneur) to the elaborate statement of purpose, objectives, situation assessment, evaluation of strategic alternatives, business model and implementation strategies that might be produced in some of the largest companies. The value of any plan will be determined by the extent to which planning informs the thinking of those involved and enhances their appreciation of the best way to take the business forward. Planning's value can also be measured in terms of the extent to which the outcomes (a formally agreed set of actions) are communicated and implemented effectively across the business. Planning can develop new skills and knowledge about the business amongst those involved (strategic learning). It is also a resource management process linked to the allocation of specific resources to different activities across the business (implementation of strategies).

Planning as learning

Each of the different approaches to planning that we have described (continuous adjustment, regular ritual and strategic review) has different elements of learning. Those responsible for running a small or medium-sized business may have no explicit process for capturing their experience and reflecting on the quality of the decisions that they make, but direct involvement in decision-making and the impact of such decisions is an important learning experience in its own right. Working with such companies it is frequently possible to draw out examples of successful practice or re-examine assumptions about the nature of the business that may shape future decisions. Since decisions are typically made by relatively few controlling managers it is often easier to discuss cause and effect more directly and agree areas for review and improvement.

When planning becomes a ritual review, typically in larger organisations critical review and learning become more difficult. The awayday format which is often used for such events can often inhibit critical review of the position of the business and inhibit effective learning. We discuss alternative ways of addressing this problem in Chapter 8. A major strategic review that is triggered by the arrival of a new CEO, the appointment of new members of the board, or obvious challenges to the current business model is more likely to provide a productive focus for the review of assumptions about the direction of the business and the most appropriate way forward.

Knowledge, skills and experience

Table 3.2 sets out some of the key questions that might be asked as part of a broad initial review of business position. These questions reflect the general discussion that we set out in the Sustainable Foods example. The answers to these questions will typically inform the content of a formal business plan although the level of detail and the assumptions that are made will depend on a wide range of different circumstances including the scale of the business, the knowledge, skills and experience of those involved in the planning process, the importance that has been given to formal plans as an explicit activity and the use that is made of any plans that are produced.

Many businesses lack the broad range of commercial skills and experience that underpin effective planning and may find it difficult to answer the questions that are posed in Table 3.2. Back in the late 1980s one of the authors conducted a survey of chief executives and HR directors in 91 large UK companies (with turnovers greater than £20m). The research was designed to explore the extent to which executive development was a priority for boards (Parkinson, 1990). In the survey approximately two thirds (69%) of the companies had an explicit plan for development in place.

Table 3.2: Strategic learning: What do we need to know?

	Related questions
Description of purpose	Why are we in business? What principles guide the overall direction of the business and how is this informed by our broader responsibility to external stakeholders?
Analysis of business situation	What broad assumptions are the board making about the range of external environmental factors that are likely to affect the business over the next year, three years, five years or longer?
	How are these factors likely to affect the demand for different products and services supplied by our business? Which markets are likely to grow, stay the same or decline?
	How well is the business currently performing against plans for sales, profitability and cash generation? How does this pattern look for each of the key areas of the business?
	How will competition emerge in each of the major markets in which the business operates and to what extent will the business's current position relative to each of these major competitors in each market improve, stay the same or decline?
Description of business model	What are the main determinants of customer behaviour in each of the core markets and how competitive are we in each of these key areas of performance in each segment of the market?
	How does the business compare with other significant competitors across the whole of the value chain from procurement, through manufacturing and supply and customer service in terms of security, cost, flexibility and value added?
Development of strategies and action plans	What plans do we have to develop new areas of business/reduce activity in other areas/divest specific areas of business?
	What could our projected profit and cash plan look like given a range of different assumptions about changes to the market and to the current business model?
	What are the investment implications of business development in terms of capital, human resources and other support infrastructure?
	How do current investors, lenders and suppliers view the business? What are the main factors that are influencing their perceptions including profit margins, sales growth, dividend payments (where relevant) and level of indebtedness?
	What additional capacity/resources have we built into the plan to deal with unexpected events or outcomes?
Implementation and control	What are the financial implications of the strategies that we have chosen and what are the margins for error if there are unforeseen problems in delivery?
	Do we have the level of skills and knowledge across the organisation to address each of these questions and respond to the challenges identified in each of the above areas?

In half of these companies (approximately 34%) the plan had been in place for less than three years. Some of the largest Plcs represented in the sample had no explicit plan at all, preferring to recruit executive talent as and when required (a fire and re-place strategy). One of the biggest problems identified by HR directors was to get the board to put executive development on its formal agenda. Formal performance re-view and development programmes for executives were in place in approximately one third of the sample (35%). Companies with such schemes typically identified spe-cific development requirements and tailored personal development plans to meet in-dividual needs.

Thirty years ago it was obvious that the attention that was given to develop-ment varied considerably from company to company with some companies recog-nising this as a priority area whilst others preferred to replace underperforming managers rather than focusing on improving skills. Over the years this position does not appear to have radically changed. In 2013 a survey of over 15,000 organi-sations, again in the UK identified significant skills gaps amongst executives in a wide range of sectors, including financial services, agriculture, construction and public administration (Campbell, 2013). The top five skills most lacking were strate-gic management skills (46%) and planning and organisational skills (44%). Sixty-one percent of the businesses surveyed had provided some training for managers over the previous year. Reflecting the findings of the original survey conducted some 30 years earlier, 30% of those surveyed did not have a business plan, a train-ing plan or a training budget. The survey concluded that executive development was still a significant problem in 2012. It seems unlikely that this position has changed significantly between 2012 and 2022 when this book was being finalised. The conclusions of this recent review are particularly striking in terms of one of the broader findings that "around 166,000 managers are deemed to be not fully profi-cient in their job".

This skills gap remains one of the most critical problems that many businesses face. Potential remedies include the use of specialist advisors, particularly account-ants in the case of small business and a wide range of commercial consultants who may provide temporary support at specific times for many other businesses. Non-executive directors with appropriate experience can make an effective contribution. More generally a regular review of competences across the business and enhanced training for key individuals may make more sense in the long run rather than firing and replacing staff in key roles. We touched on this in our discussion of board skills in the previous chapter, but the problem can extend more broadly across the whole business. Resilient businesses are more likely to take this issue seriously and have an explicit budget for skills development across the whole organisation.

Strategic planning roles

In larger companies specialist planning roles with titles such as strategic planning director, strategic planner or financial analyst may provide more specialist inputs. The job descriptions for such roles in two companies that were for advertised in 2020 shed some insight into the contribution that such a role might make and the personal characteristics that are seen as desirable. We have highlighted (*in italics*) the specific aspects of the broader strategic planning tasks and the skills that were identified as necessary to fulfil the roles.

Company A

The Senior Director of Strategic Planning [. . .] will have frequent interactions with executive management as well as strategic business unit Presidents and functional leaders. S/he will work across functions such as finance and legal and will be expected to access and hone the strategic plans and actions of [. . .]. To strengthen the [. . .] business portfolio, the successful candidate will participate in *identifying potential business development opportunities*. [. . .]

You have the ability to mobilize the organization around the key "must wins".

Curious mindset, "out of the box" thinker willing *to test organizational boundaries and anticipate changes in priorities and technology. You are keenly attuned to the marketplace and continually push the status quo.*

You will solve problems and *see the world through the customer's eyes and aggressively focus on new opportunities.*

You understand what creates value for customers.

Most importantly you are able to make *strategic recommendations actionable* for the organization.

Make an impact *on long-term shareholder value.*

Shaping the portfolio for future growth.

Company B

The Director of Strategic Planning will be responsible for planning and directing [. . .] strategic and long-range goals, focusing on executing the bold vision that will lead to a sustainable competitive advantage. The Director will be a thought leader to [. . .] most senior leaders and will play an instrumental role in planning and implementing [. . .] next generation strategy. This leader will successfully navigate a complex organizational structure and continuously bring forward an outside-in view that challenges internal thinking and provides objective views of opportunities and risks. Specific responsibilities include:

Develop implementation plans and corresponding *go-to market plans* for the next gen [sic] growth strategy, with emphasis on *financial modeling and competitive analysis*, that drive transformational growth from inception through execution

Apply *strategic frameworks to develop the broader programs, projects, financial investment, and organizational strategies*

Provide *recommendations to senior management and business leaders based on emerging trends, expansion opportunities, competitive threats, viability of outside business partners, and internal business process improvement*

Leverage in-depth consumer and market data, *translating consumer-driven understandings into business observations and recommended actions that drive growth*

Identify and develop domain-specific management tools and methodologies to further define strategic priorities; provide weekly and monthly updates to senior executives

       Lead *cross-functional teams to develop detailed business plans*, including acquisition analyses, technology development assessment, roll-out communication strategy, and training

       Conduct *business reviews to identify strengths and weaknesses and to evaluate operational effectiveness*

       Ensure *strategic planning is consistently integrated* throughout the organization by partnering closely with Consumer counterparts, including Product teams, Marketing, and Finance

       Ability to lead through influence, build engagement and partner across a diverse set of stakeholders including development, network, finance, strategy, marketing, advertising, and sales teams

       Embodies *an incredible passion for consumer product and services subject matter, applications, and content; understands emerging technologies* and how [company] can leverage them to address customer needs.

       Stellar presentation skills and gravitas

       Ability to predict market trends and focus on high impact initiatives that capitalize on future opportunities; expertise in revenue planning and forecasting

Reading both of these job descriptions it is tempting to ask if these are the knowledge skills and behaviour levels that are required of someone who ultimately reports to the CEO, what is left for the CEO to do that goes beyond these roles? It is even more tempting to consider the reaction of the management team in businesses such as "Sustainable Foods", to the range of expectations and the personal characteristics required in such posts.

The contrast between planning in a small or medium-sized company and the description of the roles in these two large multi-national businesses is stark. It illustrates the challenges of discussing strategic planning as a one size fits all approach. The reality is that each company will approach this process in different ways that reflects its unique combination of circumstances, resources and capabilities.

The process of planning

BFQ 3.3 Is there an explicit process where the major assumptions in the business plan are regularly revisited and modified to reflect changes to the market place and competitive behaviour?

Despite the apparent diversity of approaches some basic principles have emerged that can provide some guidance for those involved in the development of strategy. Mintzberg and Lampel (1999) have produced a useful overview, making a distinction between planning by design and logical analysis and other more judgmental approaches that put greater emphasis on adaptability and leadership. Table 3.3 summarises some of the more formal analytical approaches that are widely applied. Each of the different activities in Table 3.3 can be linked back to the general questions that were asked in Table 3.2.

We discussed the importance of identifying and describing business purpose in the previous chapter. Assuming this process has created a sound foundation then

Table 3.3: Strategic implementation: What are we going to do?

Process	Actions
Identification and description of purpose	**Affirmation of purpose or vision** Clarity of purpose and follow-on objectives is realised through discussion and negotiation with key stakeholders including shareholders, customers, employees and other stakeholders and broader community.
Analysis of business situation	**SWOT analysis** Objectives are moderated by an assessment of opportunities and threats and the company's relative strengths and weaknesses. Market attractiveness and market share are key determining factors linked to a careful analysis of product and market life cycles. **Competitive analysis** Assessment is made of the potential impact of direct and indirect competition. **Value chain** Careful assessment of the company's value chain is used to inform analysis of specific areas of competitive strength and weakness seen from a customer perspective (value drivers).
Determining priorities for focus	**Portfolio analysis** Based on this analysis the company develops a business model that describes how the purpose will be realised. This model is based on a careful analysis of the opportunities that exist to serve different target markets including where to invest, where to hold position and where to divest.
Development of strategies	**Positioning** Strategies evolve from the business model to exploit opportunities and counter potential threats. Such strategies are designed to create a unique position in the minds of target customers. The selection of the optimum combination of strategies is likely to be based on consideration of the different surplus that each may generate separately and in combination.

Table 3.3 (continued)

Action plans	**Implementation**
	Strategies then require action plans and resources to implement
	Ultimately this generates a financial plan, setting out the anticipated resources required and the projected surplus of revenue over costs over a specific timescale.
Monitoring and control	**Financial planning and KPIs**
	Responsibility for production and monitoring of the final business plan is frequently delegated to a company's finance function. Financial and non-financial KPIs are developed to monitor business progress against agreed performance dimensions.
Getting buy-in and commitment: Allocation of responsibility	**Setting individual accountabilities**
	Targets are owned by specific functional areas/individuals who are held responsible for delivery. Balanced scorecard measures may be used to monitor performance.

in theory attention should focus on analysis, planning and control decisions. Practical experience in a range of different settings indicates that a debate about purpose may cause many businesses to revisit assumptions about their market place and competitive position. This in turn may lead to different perspectives of purpose with a degree of recycling of assumptions.

Studies of the impact of business planning on performance indicate that the two most important factors to consider in business planning are the choice of which markets to serve and the business's relative position in each market (Schoeffler, Buzzell and Heaney, 1974). These two basic questions drive the rest of the planning process. The quality of any formal business plan is driven by these basic fundamentals. Get the decisions right and a poor or incomplete plan for implementation may still bring some degree of success. Get the choice wrong and even the most well-thought-through and well-articulated plan is unlikely to bring substantial rewards. Turnaround strategies for established businesses that have run into difficulties are unlikely to succeed in markets where the company's competitive position is weak and the overall market is in decline.

Returning to the basic toolkit SWOT analysis is one of the most popular and widely applied techniques (analysis of Strengths Weaknesses, Opportunities and Threats). Most presentations of a business plan will typically contain such an analysis either implicitly or explicitly. The popularity of the approach and its widespread use reflects the apparent ease with which the exercise can be completed and the impression that it can create of a degree of objectivity and thoroughness in the interpretation of a business's position. The analysis of strengths and weaknesses is designed to identify core competences and areas for improvement. The review of opportunities and threats is designed to identify areas for development, areas for consolidation and areas where withdrawal may be the most appropriate decision.

Core competences need to be relevant and distinctive (Hamel and Prahalad, 1989). Any evaluation of relative strengths and weaknesses should be based on market feedback and competitive analysis. An effective review process will also take account of the views of different stakeholders including existing investors as well as investment analysts. The analysis of opportunities and threats is also ultimately a subjective process, with the potential for alternative conclusions being drawn from the same information.

Porter's five forces model (1979) is another influential framework that has stood the test of time. Porter's model is designed to explore the different elements of competition that a company may face. The model stresses the importance of analysing not only existing competitors but also new possible market entrants, the actions of buyers and suppliers and possible substitute products or services. This approach underpins much of our discussion of risk and scenario planning in Chapter 5. Porter (1985) is also responsible for the concept of the value chain, stressing the importance of examining all of the interlinked activities of a business from innovation through sourcing and manufacture or service supply to marketing and sales and service to determine how far each element creates competitive advantage or adds to cost.

In terms of setting priorities the growth-share matrix, commonly referred to as the Boston Box, is a portfolio planning model that uses market share and market growth rate to identify strategies for different areas of a company's business. Applying this approach, each product or service in a company's portfolio is classified into one of four categories. Areas of the business with a high share in high growth markets are areas for investment. Low-growth–high-share situations indicate areas where the company should seek to maximise cash flow, gradually diverting resources from such areas to other parts of the business. High-growth–low-share businesses pose a more fundamental problem. Should the company take a risk and try to expand its business knowing that competition may be intense or should it decide to get out of such markets? Finally low-growth–low-share situations might seem to offer the most obvious strategy. Get out of the market, drop the product or service and use the funding elsewhere. This approach has been refined to include more detailed analysis of the factors that determine industry attractiveness and competitive position that go beyond market growth and market share (for example the GE-McKinsey matrix that identifies different strategies for business areas in nine different situations) (Coyne, 2008).

The basic message of such approaches is invest where there are opportunities, hold on in markets where the business has competitive strengths but be prepared to get out when the market begins to decline or competition becomes too strong. Simple enough to describe in general terms but when applied to an analysis of a company's current position these basic strategies begin to break down as those with vested interests in the fortunes of specific business areas make their own case for continued support. The problem becomes even more acute when a business realises that all or most of its current activities lie in markets that are no longer attractive, its competitive position is weak and it is rapidly using up available funds to stay in business.

Strategies then require action plans and resources to implement, which in turn generates a financial plan. Key performance indicators are defined to monitor the overall performance of the business and set individual targets for review and appraisal. We discuss these two elements, financial planning and KPIs in Chapters 4 and 5.

Arcadia Group Ltd

In the following case study we trace the development of business planning decisions in Arcadia Group Ltd, better known in the UK for its major clothing brands including Topshop, Dorothy Perkins and Burton. This case study follows the evolution of the company from its origins as a menswear supplier in the North of England founded in 1916 to a major international business offering a wide fashion range under different brand names through a large and diverse retail estate. Ultimately the business was not able to compete with younger more agile market entrants and entered administration in November 2020. The story did not end there with most of the company's brands being sold-on as part of the administration process to find a new life in other online businesses.

Some of the areas that you might want to focus on in the case could include:

- The evolution of the Montague Burton brand over 100 years of history as it experienced different patterns of ownership and control
- The pattern of innovation, growth, maturity and ultimate decline of different shopping formats that formed the background for many of the decisions taken by successive boards as they attempted to take the company forward
- The problems of dealing with a legacy of acquisitions and mergers that created potential overlap in specific areas of the business with associated cost inefficiencies
- The difficulties created by supply chain problems and the impact of new distribution models on the business's competitive position
- The relative importance given by successive boards at different times in the company's evolution to business expansion, business rationalisation, cost efficiency and brand awareness.

Case study: Arcadia Group Ltd

Origins

Arcadia Group Ltd's origins can be traced back to its founder Meshe David Osinsky (1885–1952), an immigrant from Kovno (modern day Lithuania) who arrived in the UK in 1900.[1] The first "Burton & Burton" store was opened in Sheffield in 1909, selling ready made clothing to working men with the number of stores increasing to 14 stores primarily in the North of England and the Midlands. In 1916 a major contract to produce military uniforms provided the platform for a rapid growth in the company's business, leading to the establishment of a limited liability company, Montague Burton, The Tailor of Taste Ltd based in Leeds, UK. By 1929 when the company went public with a capital of £4m, it had already grown to almost 300 shops, offering a "made-to-measure" service for its customers. By the time that the company's founder died there were 616 branches.

In the 1960s "Burtons" began to diversify into women's ready-to-wear clothing, reflecting a boom in casual fashion. The company's businesses included the original Burton menswear outlets, the Peter Robinsons chain of department stores, and Jackson the Tailor. Top Shop, one of the company's longstanding brands was launched in the Peter Robinsons chain in 1964, targeted at the younger female fashion buyer. The two brands quickly separated with Top Shop becoming an independent brand and Peter Robinsons gradually disappearing. In 1978 the Group launched Top Man, targeted at the younger fashion-conscious male market. The original brand names were changed to Topshop and Topman as the brands grew in popularity. The Group bought the Dorothy Perkins chain in September 1979.

The Group Chair's report in December 1981 refers to major reductions in menswear manufacturing capacity and a move to outsourcing production to "increasingly competitive and flexible sources of supply" as well as the sale of peripheral businesses including Ryman. It also refers to the company's continuing strong asset base in its retail property portfolio, a factor which increased its vulnerability to future acquisition bids.[2] In 1985 the Group acquired Debenhams Ltd, a major UK department store chain.

By 1993 the company had grown to £1,893.1m turnover with a profit before exceptional costs and taxation of £38.1m. The company had added the Principles brand to its portfolio, aimed at A, B and C1 target markets, segments that were not as well served by its Burton and Dorothy Perkins brands. Its Topshop and Topman brands (womenswear and menswear, respectively) were primarily focused on young consumers.[3] In 1996 the Group announced the introduction of a home shopping division, following the acquisition of Innovations, a mail order catalogue business. The CEO described the strategy as follows.[4]

https://doi.org/10.1515/9783110689495-005

Building a brand is about creating and then meeting expectations- even exceeding expectations- in the mind of the customer. We are making long-term investments in the quality of our brands, which are all achieving measurable gains in their efforts to build customer confidence–the most important factor for improving the profits.

Each division focuses on a clearly defined and different target market. We build our brands by listening to our customers and delivering what they want, by offering distinctive and desirable products in the right store environment. [. . .]

We believe home shopping is an exciting area of the retail market. Innovations brings considerable skills and expertise in database management systems and marketing in specialist Mail order and a database of approximately 5 million names to add to the Burton Group's expanding list of store card customers which already exceeds 5 million. [. . .]

The skills of Innovations combined with the financial and brand strength of the Burton Group, offer considerable marketing potential to generate additional sales both within the new home shopping division and at the Group's traditional stores. Catalogues give the customer the choice of either shopping from home or visiting our stores. They can help to make small stores larger with order fulfilment either to the store or delivered direct to the home.

The CEO described how the company had implemented a strategy to rationalise and update high street outlets (reduced from over 1600 in 1992 to 1500 in 1996). The strategy was described as "designed to improve relationships with key suppliers and build product quality, supply flexibility, stock availability and accuracy into the entire supply chain". Commenting on the strategy he said: "The drive is to build a powerful supply chain that is fast and flexible from end to end–from the conception of the product to its arrival in the store."

In July 1997 the CEO of subsidiary companies Burton Menswear, Dorothy Perkins, Evans and Principles left the company to join Argos Plc as their CEO.

In 1998 the retail chain Debenhams demerged from the Group, although Debenham stores continued to stock the Group's major womenswear and childrenswear brands. The Group was renamed Arcadia Group PLC. The company's annual report described its first moves into home shopping and the potential benefits that it could bring in positive terms.[5]

Since the trial began in September 1997, customers have been able to visit the websites for each of the Group's brands, browse for clothes, place an order and then have the goods delivered to their chosen location. Along with the paper based home shopping catalogues internet stores provide the customer with 24 h shopping.

But one of the most important things about the sites is the knowledge they bring the Group. As pages are accessed these hits are recorded so that customers can be tracked as they browse or shop the sites. By this method the Group has learned that customers like to shop outside the traditional trading hours. The biggest peak of shopping activity is a Sunday evening while the most browsing of the pages takes place at lunch times and in the evenings.

Online marketing had arrived for Arcadia by 1998 – the question was how fast would the company's capabilities in this area develop and could they keep up with competition?

Arcadia Group's trading profit in the year to 28 August 1999 reduced to £52m (before exceptional items) compared with £172m in 1998.[6] The purchase of Sears

Womenswear for £155m combined with generally poor conditions in the UK High Street contributed to an increase in net debt to £227m at the year end (up from £57m at the previous year end). The Group issued a profit warning on 18 November 1999, citing "difficult conditions in the clothing sector of the high street, including increased promotional activity combined with selling price reductions..[this] resulted in our taking a more aggressive stance [. . .] consequently our gross profit margin has reduced".[7]

A preliminary results announcement for the 52 weeks ending 26 August 2000 on 19 October 2000 confirmed that Group performance was continuing to deteriorate.[8] Net debt had increased to £257m, gearing to 64% and loss before tax and exceptional items was £8.5m. The Group described its progress on project Brand-MAX, designed to review its existing portfolio of stores across all its brands in towns across the UK and create a rationalised structure with fewer, more profitable outlets. The initial conclusion of the review was that 332 towns had been identified for action, and a total of 55 sites had been identified for disposal. Many of these sites were a legacy of periods of brand acquisition over previous years. The company expected to realise a cumulative total of £180m savings as these disposals took effect. The board announced that it would not be recommending a dividend for the year. On 13 November the company announced the appointment of a new CEO.[9]

Following his appointment the CEO initiated a review of options for the Group. His update on progress on 5 April 2001 identified five main areas on which the planned recovery would be based: disposal of brands that were not seen as part of the core business going forward, focus on the remaining brands for growth, improving efficiency primarily by reducing central costs and the efficiency of the process from product design to manufacture and delivery, reducing debt and finally "adding excitement".[10]

On 10 October 2001 Arcadia announced that it had reached agreement to dispose of the Warehouse, Principles, Racing Green and Hawkshead brands to Rubican Retail Ltd, a management buyout vehicle.[11] In the year to 26 August 2000 the brands had cumulatively incurred an operating loss, before allocation of Arcadia Group central costs of £0.6m on sales of £265m. Publication of final results for 2001 on 25 October 2001 indicated an improvement in profit to £53m (compared with a loss of £8.5m in the previous year), dividend payments were resumed, like-for-like sales on core brands were up 6.6%, total costs had been reduced 5.6% year-on-year and net debt had been reduced by £117m and stood at £140m.[12] The CEO's report detailed substantial progress on each of the five planned recovery objectives. The Group had also been able to make substantial reductions in borrowings, leaving a long-term loan of £126m secured on its signature premises in Oxford Street London and a revolving credit facility of £185m.

Later on the same day 25 October 2001 Arcadia confirmed that it had received a takeover approach from Baugur hf., stating that "discussions are at a preliminary stage and there can be no certainty that any offer will result".[13] On 1 February the company confirmed that discussions with Baugar had been discontinued, with the board stating that "Arcadia is well placed to create further shareholder value as an independent company".[14]

A trading statement issued following the critical trading period immediately before and after Christmas 2001 announced a further improvement in like-for-like sales for its core brands, which were reported to be up 8% trading from 3.5% less space.[15] The CEO commented "The Group's performance over the 1st 19 weeks of the year, and especially over the Christmas trading period, reflects the improvements that have been made in the business over the last year. We have made significant progress in developing our product offer and brand marketing, improving the efficiency of our supply chain and reducing Group debt."

The continuing improvement in the Group's position was confirmed in an announcement of interim results on 23 February 2002.[16] Profits from core brands (Dorothy Perkins, Burton, Evans, Wallis, Topshop/Topman and Miss Selfridge) had increased by 60% to £57.9m (2001: £36.3m) and net debt had reduced to £11m (February 2001: £195m). The CEO commented:

> Arcadia is a changed business. We operate 6 brands from significantly fewer stores, trading less space. We have reduced our rent bill. Our debt is £11m, significantly lowering our interest costs. We have tightened all aspects of working capital and reduced operational gearing.
>
> We are working on our supply chain and can already see the benefits. We have less stock in the business and we have built greater flexibility into our buying operations [. . .]
>
> We have significantly reduced forward commitments so that we remain flexible to changes in market and fashion demand. This gives us the ability to take advantage of good times and to be more resilient in difficult ones.
>
> We have commenced a review of our back-of-house operations with the initial objective of increasing time available for staff to serve our customers. We have already increased the proportion of deliveries made during non trading hours from around 35% to 45% and eliminated one million pieces of paper from the business saving 20,000 work hours.
>
> Our primary focus is now on driving our brands, by offering better fashion and outstanding value in an exciting retail environment, reinforced through powerful visual imagery, strong advertising and wide PR activity.

On 18 August 2002 the board of Arcadia confirmed that it had received a proposal from Taveta Investments Limited, in relation to a possible offer for the company at 365 pence per share.[17] The board stated that "it had concluded that this undervalued the company and therefore did not form an acceptable basis for further discussions." Taveta increased the value of its offer to 408 pence per share on 29 August. On 6 September 2002 the board concluded that the proposal could be recommended to shareholders, subject to Taveta concluding its financing arrangements.[18] On 15 October 2002 the recommended cash offer by Taveta Investments for Arcadia Group PLC was declared unconditional. All of Arcadia's non-executive directors resigned from the board. The CEO resigned on 31 December 2002. The company was delisted from the London Stock Exchange on 9 December and re-registered as a private limited company on 10 December 2002.

From its foundations in 1916 to its ultimate sale in 2002, Arcadia had grown massively, driven initially by the adoption of a business model in the early 1920s and 1930s which integrated sales and customer service with its own production and supply capability, to the owner and innovator of leading market brands. By 2002 much of the business had been simplified and was focused on the company's core markets. It had substantial cash reserves (cash at bank and in hand £302m) and an apparently strong trading position (turnover in 2002 had reached £2,019m, operating profit was £124m). The average number of employees in the Group was 22,826 (including 15,589 part-time employees). The net book amount shown for tangible fixed assets (land and buildings) was £349m with a further £149m in fixtures and fittings.[19] By most standards it appeared to be well positioned for the next stage in its development.

Under new ownership

Taveta Investments Ltd's accounts for the period ended 30 August 2003 reported a turnover of £1,619m, total operating profit of £207m and retained profit of £103m.[20] The company was inactive prior to acquiring Arcadia. Details on the acquisition of Arcadia show a purchase price of £866m, net assets acquired (book value) of £475m and goodwill of £319m. Tangible fixed assets were revalued to £603m (an increase of £109m on their book value at acquisition).

Cash at bank and in hand was £175m. The consolidated cash flow statement for the period ended 30 August 2003 showed an issue of £918m bank borrowings and a repayment of bank borrowings of £409m (a net increase in bank borrowings of £509m). Net cash inflow from financing including the issue of discounted subordinated bonds amounted to £552m. Details of bank loans show £392m of financing secured by way of a fixed charge over certain Group properties and a legal charge over other assets.

By August 2005 Taveta's total turnover for the financial year had grown to £1,772m, total operating profit was significantly higher at £310m, but due to the payment of £1,299m dividends retained loss for the year was £1,114m.[21] The consolidated cash flow statement (for the year) showed an issue of bank borrowings of £1,675m and a repayment of bank borrowings of £689m. Between financial year 2004 and 2005 bank loans and property mortgages increased from £332m to £1,314m. The scale of the dividend payment was criticized some 16 years later as the company's finances ultimately deteriorated and the company entered administration.[22]

Taveta Investments Ltd was a complex structure of individual companies. Whilst Taveta Investments Ltd was the ultimate holding company the company's activities were managed through Taveta Investments (no 2) Ltd. The Arcadia Group Ltd was in turn a services company through which the main actions of the Taveta Group were managed. When Arcadia Group Ltd was placed into administration in 2020 the administrator's report identified 28 Group companies within the overall Taveta Investment Ltd portfolio.[23] This structure reflected Arcadia's history with eight major fashion brands, Topshop, Topman, Miss Selfridge, Dorothy Perkins, Burton, Evans, Wallis and Outfit Retail. Each of these brands had their own distinctive position in their respective markets.

The business model, primarily driven by extensive physical presence in a large number of outlets and unique brand identities sustained the company through the first years of its new existence, although by the beginning of the new decade in 2010 there were already signs that the fashion market had begun to change and move away from the approach that had underpinned Arcadia Group's development. Arcadia's business had a legacy of too many outlets (fascia's) in too many of the same locations, complex sourcing and distribution systems, and increasing pressures from landlords seeking rent increases. Its annual reports between 2010 and 2019 reflect continuing growing pressure on the company to deal with these major issues (problems that other traditional retailers in the same position were also attempting to address with greater or less success).

In the annual report for the year ended 29 August 2009 the directors wrote:

> The Group now trades from 3,114 outlets representing 12.4 million square feet of space. Enhancing the productivity of the portfolio, which now includes the recent acquisition of Bhs, through effective space management, the expansion of internet shopping and the Group's presence abroad, together with continuous profit improvement and realising 'back of house' synergies, will all contribute to the Group's objective of growing profitability. Ongoing supply chain improvements, including tight stock and commitment management, remain particularly important to ensure gross margins are optimised.[24]

By 2013 it is clear from the directors' comments in the annual report that trading was becoming increasingly difficult.[25] The report echoes many of the issues raised 4 years earlier:

> The Group now trades from 3,034 [. . .] outlets representing 11.6 million [. . .] square feet of space. The current retail environment remains challenging and the Group continues to focus on enhancing the productivity of its business through effective space management, whilst expanding its internet offering and overseas presence. The directors expect that further product improvement and ongoing supply chain improvements will contribute to the Group's objective of maximising profitability significantly.

The directors considered the company to be a going concern "due to the continued profitability of the underlying Group".

In the 2016 annual report retail the directors identified a series of new challenges that the company needed to address:

> The retail industry continues to experience a period of major change as customers become ev-ermore selective and value conscious and advances in technology open up more diverse, fast changing and complex sales channels. Clothing has also become a less important part of the household budget. Our customers are continuing to adopt different shopping habits as a result of these fast changing sales channels. This is set against an economic environment of a contin-ued slow recovery from a deep recession and the uncertainty caused by Brexit. As a result the Group's financial performance is below prior year levels including a significant additional charge on its trading results through the deterioration in currency exchange rates.[26]

The 2016 report set out five key values to take the company forward, namely customer focus, commercial flair, strategic focus, energy and drive, and people. The company was trading from a reduced number of outlets (2,766 representing 6.4 million square feet). During the year it closed 307 concessions within Bhs stores. It reported that it was now trading on 39 different brand specific web sites and 28 mobile sites and was focused on growing its social media presence.

By 2017–2018 the retail environment had become increasingly challenging and the Group explicitly recognised that it faced significant challenges.[27] The company announced a loss for the financial year after tax of £169m (2017: profit of £49m) and net liabilities at 1 September 2018 of £73.7m. Its strategic report for the year ending 1 September 2018 stated:

> The business operates in a challenging environment with UK and overseas consumer habits changing, and underlying consumer confidence low. In addition, the digital arena continues to see significant competition, particularly in the younger fashion market, from new entrants who do not have the high fixed cost base associated with retail stores. The Group has looked to respond to the changes in shopping habits and reduction in high street footfall through de-veloping a multi-channel offering that will allow customers to interact through the stores and websites of the individual brands in a seamless way. We believe that high quality stores in the right location can enhance the customer experience and the brands' relationships with their customers.[. . .] the Group continued with its ongoing investment in the digital web platform, developing an agile capability which will enable a programme of continuous investment once the project is delivered.

A report by the Retail Gazette indicated that the company's Topshop brand, its leading brand for young fashion conscious female markets had seen a steep drop in sales over the Christmas period 2016–2017 making it one of the worst performers in the sector.[28] The company announced plans to rationalise brand manager roles in stores which housed both Topshop and Topman with one manager looking after both as part of a restructuring of retail management roles across the Group.[29] Retail sales were badly hit by an overall decline in the number of shoppers visiting high streets, and a reduc-tion in consumer confidence, coupled with heavy discounting as retailers competed for customers. The national town centre vacancy rate increased to 9.2% in April result-ing in almost 1 in 10 retail outlets vacant.[30]

By 2019 the company's financial problems had significantly worsened, and Ar-cadia Group appointed two restructuring specialists to board roles indicating the extent to which business restructuring had become a major strategic imperative.[31]

As financial pressures built, on 22 May 2019 the Group launched seven company voluntary arrangement (CVA) proposals designed to improve the company's cash outgoings by seeking rent reductions from its landlords.

Arcadia was not alone in seeking such reductions. Other major retailers under the same pressures as Arcadia were also using CVAs to reduce lease costs. The CVAs related to 48 planned store closures in the UK and Ireland, and rent reductions in 194 other stores, 11 Topshop closures in the US and more than 500 job cuts. The company's flagship store, Miss Selfridge's on Oxford Street was identified as a candidate for closure. The CVA proposals included a change in focus for Topshop and Topman towards more competitively priced stock and a plan to increase the brands' presence on third-party websites such as ASOS. The plan also included proposals to restructure the company's pension scheme. The company's ultimate shareholder committed to make cash payments amounting to £100m into the pension schemes to support the restructuring.[32]

In early 2020 the arrival of the Covid-19 pandemic put Arcadia's business under extreme pressure, reducing consumer confidence, particularly in fast fashion segments of the market, and leading to very significant declines in customer footfall in stores. Whilst the company made significant attempts to mitigate the effect, the report of the joint administrators ultimately appointed to manage the company indicates that the impact could not be fully absorbed by the Group, noting that the Group's financial position had materially deteriorated by October 2020.[33] Topshop and Topman between them had gross liabilities of over £550m at the time of entry into administration. The directors concluded that continuation of trading was not viable, given a potential cash shortfall forecast for early 2021, and concerns about the ability to turn around the Group's trading profitability. They also acknowledged the potential long-term impact of competition from better funded retailers in online sales. A board meeting held on the 27 November 2020 concluded that the Group did not have a reasonable prospect of avoiding insolvency and resolved to place the company into administration. The company and its associated brands had reached another key moment in its 100 years history.

With the benefit of hindsight critics of the company's strategies point to the failure of the company to respond quickly enough to digital challenges and the arrival of new aggressive challengers on the high street such as Primark, H&M and Zara. They also cite the extent to which the company's ultimate owners took cash out of the company, leaving it with limited reserves to sustain periods of poor trading.[34] Writing in December 2020 after Arcadia had been placed into administration, a leading retail analyst Mary Portas took an alternative view. She blamed the ultimate failure of Topshop on a long-term failure to sustain brand values, which she argued was far more important than other broader issues such as the death of physical retail, the rise of digital and how much money was drained out of the business.[35] Her description evokes a broader concept of the essence of interaction between the brand and its (previously) loyal customer base that had been gradually eroded. She said:

In its heyday, Topshop wasn't just a 'shop'. It was a destination where you could tap into the zeitgeist. Its finger was not just on the pulse–it generated that pulse. The key to that was the creative vision of brand director Jane Shepherdson and her team. [. . .] She understood how we live is also how we buy, which is how to sell. When she left the numbers and systems people got over-involved, and the creative voices were stifled and sidelined. Topshop became a cookie cutter volume store, sticking to the formula that once made it great but didn't evolve to meet the changing demands of younger shoppers. [. . .] The retailers who are winning today have vision. They create brands that people feel a part of – buying into, rather than mindlessly buying from.

Stores without frontiers

On 1 February 2021 ASOS plc, a major online retailer with no physical outlets announced that it had acquired the Topshop, Topman Miss Selfridge and HIIT brands out of administration for £265m.[36] The CEO described how the newly acquired brands fitted into the company's multi-brand strategy:

> This acquisition represents a compelling strategic opportunity in support of our mission to become the number one destination for fashion loving 20-somethings worldwide. These are strong brands that resonate well with our core customer base. Brand equity is strongest in the UK and they have an established presence in both the US and Germany, two of our key strategic markets.

Further insights into ASOS's business model indicated what ASOS proposed to do with the brands. The CEO continued:

> The brands we have acquired are strong consumer facing brands that have continued to grow through key channels and we see a significant opportunity to drive further growth for these brands globally. We will do so through applying our industry leading design talent and online retail experience. They will also benefit from investment into customer engagement and brand positioning in line with our existing model.
>
> Beyond this, we will work to maximise the opportunity for the brands' global distribution. Our international warehouse infrastructure and localised online experiences will support continued growth through our own platform. In addition to this there is significant scope for selective development of strategic retail partnerships.
>
> [. . .] We will work to integrate these brands into our business quickly. Our capacity to do so is supported by our ability to use our existing warehouse and technology infrastructure. [. . .] As part of the integration process we will undertake a thorough review of the supply chain to ensure it complies with all our Fashion with Integrity principles [. . .] Our familiarity with these brands and our experience developing and running in house brands, together with our well developed technology and warehouse infrastructure, gives us confidence in our ability to execute the transition with as little disruption as possible.

On 25 January boohoo plc another major online retailer announced its acquisition of the intellectual property but none of the physical outlets of Debenhams, one of the UK's oldest retailers and another casualty of the changing UK retail market place, that had gone into administration in April 2020. boohoo stated that the acquisition would allow the company to own Debenham's retail website, one of the top 10 retail websites in the UK, with 300 m visits and £400m of sales in the year to August 2020.

On 8 February the boohoo Group consolidated its position announcing that it had bought the other three major Arcadia brands Dorothy Perkins, Wallis and Burton out of administration, paying £25.2m in cash.[37] boohoo's CEO John Lyttle commented on his ambitions for the acquisition.

> We are delighted to announce the acquisition of the assets associated with the online businesses of the three established brands Burton, Dorothy Perkins and Wallace. Acquiring these well known brands in British fashion out of administration shows their heritage is sustained, while our investment aims to transform them into brands that are fit for the current market environment. We have a successful track record of integrating British heritage fashion brands onto our proven multi-brand platform, and we're looking forward to bringing these brands on board.

With the sales to ASOS and boohoo complete, Arcadia and ultimately Burton the original foundation brand moved off the high street and began their new future as stores without frontiers.

Notes

1 Building our past, (2017) *The Story of Montague Burton–the Tailor of Taste, 28 January.* [online] Available at: https://buildingourpast.com/2017/01/28/the-story-of-montague-burton-the-tailor-of-taste/ [Accessed 12 February 2021].
2 The Burton Group Limited, (1981) *Report and Accounts.* p4, 15 December.
3 The Burton Group plc, (1993) *Report and Accounts*: 10 November. 8.
4 The Burton Group plc, (1996) *Report and Accounts* (ND). 6–7.
5 The Burton Group plc, (1998) *Report and Accounts* 21 October. 7.
6 Arcadia Group PLC, (1999) *Report and Accounts*, (ND) October. 34.
7 Arcadia Group PLC, (1999) *Trading Update–Total Retail Sales Up 35%* [online]. 18 November. Available at: https://www.investegate.co.uk/arcadia-Group-Plc–ag–/rns/trading-update—total-retail-sales-up-35-/199911180701390388B/ [Accessed 13 February 2021].
8 Arcadia Group PLC, (2000) *Preliminary results 52 weeks ended 26 August 2000* [online]. 19 October, Available at: https://www.investegate.co.uk/arcadia-Group-Plc–ag–/rns/preliminary-results/200010190700397386S/ [Accessed 13 February 2021].
9 Arcadia Group PLC, (2000) *Arcadia Group Board Changes* [online]. 13 November, Available at: https://www.investegate.co.uk/arcadia-Group-Plc–ag–/rns/board-changes/200011130700369826T/ [Accessed 13 February 2021].
10 Arcadia Group PLC, (2001) *Interim Results, 26 Weeks ended 24th February 2001* [online]. 5 April. Available at: https://www.investegate.co.uk/arcadia-Group-Plc–ag–/rns/interim-results/200104050700196622B/ [Accessed 13 February 2021].
11 Arcadia Group PLC, (2001) *Disposal* [online]. 10 October. Available at: https://www.investegate.co.uk/arcadia-Group-Plc–ag–/rns/disposal/200110101024413938L/ [Accessed 13 February 2021].
12 Arcadia Group PLC, (2001) *Final Results* [online]. 25 October. Available at: https://www.investegate.co.uk/arcadia-Group-Plc–ag–/rns/final-results/200110250700471164M/ [Accessed 13 February 2021].

13   Arcadia Group PLC, (2001) *Statement re Possible Offer* [online]. 25 October. Available at: https://www.investegate.co.uk/arcadia-Group-Plc–ag–/rns/statement-re-possible-offer/200110251109541322M/ [Accessed 13 February 2021].

14   Arcadia Group PLC, (2002) *Offer Talks Terminated* [online]. 1 February. Available at: https://www.investegate.co.uk/arcadia-Group-Plc–ag–/rns/offer-talks-terminated/200202011511168748Q/ [Accessed 13 February 2021].

15   Arcadia Group PLC, (2002) *Trading Statement and update on discussions* [online]. 9 January. Available at: https://www.investegate.co.uk/arcadia-Group-Plc–ag–/rns/trading-statement/200201090700196843P/ [Accessed 13 February 2021].

16   Arcadia Group PLC, (2002) *Interim Results* [online]. 18 April. Available at: https://www.investegate.co.uk/arcadia-Group-Plc–ag–/rns/interim-results/200204180700297095U/ [Accessed 13 February 2021].

17   Arcadia Group PLC, (2002) *Response to Press Comment* [online]. 18 August. Available at: https://www.investegate.co.uk/arcadia-Group-Plc–ag–/rns/response-to-press-comment/200208190700191060A/ [Accessed 13 February 2021].

18   Arcadia Group PLC, (2002) *Response to Taveta* [online]. 6 September. Available at: https://www.investegate.co.uk/arcadia-Group-Plc–ag–/rns/response-to-taveta/200209060937048449A/ [Accessed 13 February 2021].

19   Arcadia Group Ltd, (formerly Arcadia Group Plc) (2002) *Annual report for the year ended 31 August 2002*. 11 December.

20   Taveta Investments Ltd, (formerly Ibis (780) Ltd) (2003) *Report for the Period ended 30 August 2003*, October 2003.

21   Taveta Investments Ltd, (2005) *Annual Report for the year ended 27 August 2005*. 19 October.

22   Jahshan, E. (2020) Arcadia Group "legally robbed by the Greens", says peer. *Retail Gazette*, December 9 https://www.retailgazette.co.uk/blog/2020/12/arcadia-Group-legally-robbed-by-the-greens-says-peer/ [Accessed 15 February 2021].

23   Deloitte (2020) *Arcadia Group Limited (in administration)*. 25 January.

24   Taveta Investments Ltd, (2009) *Annual Report for the year ended 29 August 2009*. 21 October.

25   Taveta Investments Ltd, (2013) *Annual Report for the year ended 31 August 2013*, 13 November.

26   Taveta Investments Ltd, (2017) *Annual Report for the year ended 27 August 2016*, (ND).

27   Taveta Investments Ltd, (2019) *Annual Report and consolidated financial statements for the 53 weeks ended 1 September 2018*, 30 August.

28   Stevens, B. (2017) Topdrop: Sir Philip Green's fashion brand struggles over Christmas. *Retail Gazette*, 6 February. https://www.retailgazette.co.uk/blog/2017/02/topdrop-sir-philip-greens-fashion-brand-struggles-over-christmas/ [Accessed 16 February 2021].

29   Stevens, B. (2018) Jobs at hundreds of Topshop/Topman stores to be cut. *Retail Gazette* [online] 29 January. Available at https://www.retailgazette.co.uk/blog/2018/01/jobs-hundreds-topshop-topman-stores-cut/ [Accessed 16 February 2021].

30   Wood, Z (2018) ' Shoppers desert UK high streets, putting more jobs at risk', *The Guardian*, [online] 14 May Available at: https://www.theguardian.com/business/2018/may/14/shoppers-desert-uk-high-streets-to-put-more-jobs-at-risk [Accessed 16 February 2021].

31   Jashan, E. (2019) Sir Philip Green appoints restructuring experts to Arcadia board. *Retail Gazette*,[online] 11 April. Available at: https://www.retailgazette.co.uk/blog/2019/04/sir-philip-green-appoints-restructuring-experts-to-arcadia-board/ [Accessed 16 February 2021].

32   Deloitte (2020) *Arcadia Group Limited (in administration)*. 25 January Arcadia Group Ltd.

33   See ref. 32.

34   Eley, J. (2020) The Rise and Fall of Philip Green's Arcadia retail empire. *Financial Times* [Online]. 30 November, Available at: https://www.ft.com/content/cd2e9b8a-c9b6-4a2f-8810-cb749ea37421 [Accessed 16 February 2021].

35 Portas, M. (2020) Covid-19 didn't kill Topshop: a lack of creativity did. *Financial Times*, 8 December Available at: https://www.ft.com/content/f8bd6c9e-7b91-4fe3-af3a-d35d7fc617b5 [Accessed 16 February 2021].

36 ASOS plc, (2021) *Acceleration of ASOS Brands Strategy* [online]. Available at: https://www.investegate.co.uk/asos-Plc–asc-/rns/acceleration-of-asos-brands-strategy/202102010700095062N/ [Accessed 15 February 2021].

37 boohoo Group plc, (2021) *Acquisition of Dorothy Perkins, Wallis and Burton* [online]. 8 February Available at: https://www.investegate.co.uk/boohoo-Group-Plc–boo-/rns/acquisition-of-dorothy-perkins–wallis—burton/202102080700008236909O/ [Accessed 16 February 2021].

4 Financial stewardship

If you are the kind of person who is waiting for the "right" thing to happen, you might wait for a long time. It's like waiting for all the traffic lights to be green for five miles before starting the trip. (Robert Kiyosaki, 2011)

Resilient companies are better than their competition at identifying opportunities and problems and reacting fast to deal with evolving situations. They are fleet of foot and proactive in terms of closing down areas of business that are no longer attractive, and capable of diverting resources into new opportunities. They have identified the essence of their company's purpose and business direction and create unique ways of adding value that are difficult to copy. Such businesses have also built sustainable relationships with investors, lenders and suppliers, and their broader base of stakeholders. They have put in place effective governance systems with good audit procedures that provide timely feedback on strategic choices. Critically, they have an appetite for risk which enables them to contemplate changes to established strategies and implement as appropriate.

They are also quicker than other businesses to see when the traffic lights are at red, "stop what we are doing and reconsider whether we should keep going in the same direction", amber "let's get on with it cautiously or reconsider whether or not to stay in this area of business" or green "go for it". Checking whether the lights are red, orange or green is a critical area of judgement for the board. In most companies the traffic signals are monitored most closely by the accountancy and finance function.

Several studies have commented on the low level of financial literacy of many company directors (see, for example, Berman and Knight, 2009). Professional finance expertise is frequently limited to one or two members of the typical board. In such circumstances, the board will rely on such members and/or professional advisors to interpret financial results, interrogate the CFO on business performance and identify where problems may be emerging.

Small businesses are frequently challenged by accountancy basics, relying on external advisors (usually accountants) to provide help with tasks that they may not have sufficient time or skills to complete. As companies grow in size these functions are typically taken over by dedicated staff, broadening the range of responsibilities beyond basic record keeping and reporting functions to include financial planning and control and participation in the broader strategic planning and development of the company. Rather than being restricted to reporting how well the company is doing such roles also focus on providing insights into the future direction of the business. In the largest companies, this can involve strategic choices about sources of funding and long-term business viability. In time of business distress it is typically the accountancy and finance area of the business that provides an early "heads up" that problems are emerging and takes the lead in addressing

https://doi.org/10.1515/9783110689495-006

the problem. Effective performance in this area makes an essential contribution to creating and sustaining a resilient business.

Table 4.1 sets out the specific questions that we suggest are included in a review of financial stewardship. As we will continue to remind readers, we have included a table at the beginning of each chapter that contains a series of questions that a board might consider when evaluating its performance on the areas that the chapter discusses. Again readers who are interested in benchmarking the performance of a specific business may want to make some notes under each of the main sections as we progress through the discussion. We have included another extended case study (Carillion plc) at the end of the chapter. Readers may want to skip ahead and read this case first before beginning the chapter.

Table 4.1: BFQ 4 Financial stewardship: To what extent do directors give careful long-term consideration to the financial and broader commercial resilience of the company?

Benchmarking questions	Commentary (Evidence)	Score
Accountancy's core contribution **BFQ 4.1** **Is there a conscious and strategic recognition of accountancy and finance roles, and the impact of effective performance on business outcomes?**	An explicit financial plan as an integral part of the overall business plan	
	Accountancy and financial planning expertise appropriate to the size and type of business	
	Appropriate and regular review of performance of external advisors	
	Job description and accountabilities of key finance and accounting personnel and nature of performance review	
	Extent of involvement of accountancy and finance personnel in strategic decision-making	
Accountancy and financial management functions **BFQ 4.2** **Has the company consciously recognized the contribution that this area can make to business resilience and put in place effective systems to establish standards and monitor performance?**	Check of accountancy and finance competences across the business against basic procedures	
	Distributed responsibility to specific individuals for costs and expenditure	
	Evidence of evaluation and use of automated processes (small business)	
	Appropriate use of AI and cloud-based resources (larger companies)	
	Regular analysis and briefings across the business of key financial KPIs (see broader discussion in the next chapter)	

Table 4.1 (continued)

Going concern **BFQ 4.3** **How does the board reach its conclusions about the going concern status of the business, beyond considering the immediate reporting requirements required to comply with legislation?**	Awareness and compliance with ACCA and ISA 570 recommendations Consideration of broader resilience in business planning and implementation linked to strategic assessment of market and industry fundamentals. An effective internal audit process including the role of an audit committee (where in place)
Managing funds effectively **BFQ 4.4** **Is there an explicit plan for long-term management of funds that establishes alternative strategies to deal with potential future periods of business distress?**	Use of stress testing to evaluate financial resilience and make a balanced choice about future development Effective use and monitoring of supply chain finance and invoice factoring An explicit strategy for financial emergencies that maps future funds and determines the best way to release such funds in the optimal way Separate accountability for treasury functions alongside financial performance in larger organisations Regular briefings and discussion with major shareholders and other external stakeholders on optimal pattern of funds flow into and out of the business, including payment of dividends, pension contributions and director remuneration

Accountancy's core contribution

BFQ 4.1 Is there a conscious and strategic recognition of accountancy and finance roles, and the impact of effective performance on business outcomes?

In 2020, the Department for Business, Energy & Industrial Strategy estimated that there were 5.98m private sector businesses in the UK. About 99.9% of these were small businesses (with 0 to 49 employees), 76% did not employ anyone apart from the owner(s) and many of these (59%) were sole proprietor businesses. Similar statistics can be found for most other economies. Whilst many of these small companies do monitor cash flow, keep effective records and have effective systems for budgeting and costing, a significant number do not. Accounting basics are frequently missing, leading to potentially serious business problems.

In a typical small company the existing senior team is likely to be keenly aware of emerging problems because they are close to the day-to-day running of the business. These problems can be created by events such as cancelled orders, customer default on payments, unexpected demands for tax and VAT payments, suppliers' refusal to provide credit or the end of current banking arrangements. Each of these on their own may not be sufficient to force the management team to step back and look at the broader picture, but when the impact is cumulative or one element creates a major problem then they may be forced to take stock of the situation and accept that urgent action is needed. There is a limit on the extent to which such companies may be able to resolve immediate financial concerns without seeking professional advice.

This problem is reflected in professional journals, and government and academic reviews. Common themes that emerge are the need for improved record keeping, accurate tracking of costs and income, careful management of tax and VAT payments, close monitoring of cash flow and the importance of specialist advice either by employing an experienced finance professional or an independent advisor.

A range of basic accountancy tasks that are generally recognised as critical were included in a job advertisement posted in November 2020 for a bookkeeper for a small family business (Company A). Duties included:

- Posting purchase invoices and maintaining the purchase ledger
- Processing and managing payroll
- Statutory payment processing
- Assisting with VAT returns
- Reconciling invoices and bank accounts
- Producing monthly reports
- Assisting external auditors with month and year-end processes.
- Weekly payments to suppliers
- Reconciling supplier statements and chasing missing invoices

Dealing with such fundamentals may put considerable pressure on the time and attention of many small owner-manager businesses, particularly where most of their time is taken up with building new business and satisfying current customers. Making the decision to recruit someone to do this is frequently one of the most difficult choices for a small business that may have been used to buying in specific services as and when required. Typical doubts might be "Will the person who is appointed add sufficient value to justify the extra costs that will be involved? How do I know that the person that we appoint will do a good job?"

Low-cost automation

In many small and medium-sized companies one of the biggest changes in bookkeeping and accountancy practice has been the increased availability and use of software packages that have been designed to support many basic tasks. The development of online packages such as QuickBooks[1] and Sage[2] with built-in standardised processes that automate many relatively straightforward tasks such as invoicing, payment records and payroll offers the potential to simplify, standardise and reduce costs, whilst improving the overall accuracy and timeliness of such information. The time spent in periodic analysis and sorting of piles of paperwork can potentially be freed up for other purposes by a set of consistently prepared analyses instantly available to anyone with approved access.

Spotting the opportunity many professional accountants have integrated such packages into their services, offering support to their clients in implementation and use. Where this includes online access by such accountants to client financial systems this has the potential to considerably enhance the client-accountant relationship, speeding up advice based on real-time information. Continuous updating of transactional information such as invoices, payments, payroll and tax payments that is fed into financial models and reproduced as a set of specific performance indicators has changed the nature of many small business operations and enhanced response times, whilst freeing up time for other business generation or revenue earning activities.

Choosing the right advisor

Making the right choice of professional advisor is a critical decision. The importance of this relationship was emphasised in 2014 in an ICAEW (Institute of Chartered Accountants in England and Wales) survey of 500 small and medium-sized businesses, exploring the perceptions of the relationship between such businesses and their accountants. The primary services used by respondents were accounts preparation with a report (65%), tax services (62%), bookkeeping and/or preparing management accounts (32%), financial audit (28%) and business advice (25%). According to the survey the popularity of such services diminishes as companies grow in size, due to the growth of in-house capability and experience, with a greater emphasis on the importance of business advice in larger companies. In a memorable phrase the ICAEW described the relationship as follows: "Accountants are the most trusted and consulted advisors for businesses from sole traders up to medium-sized enterprises. They can be seen as the garage mechanics that keep the engine running with a range of crucial services."

This advisory role should be distinguished from the role that such accountants may have in auditing a company's financial statements as part of any statutory process. We look at this in greater detail later on in this chapter.

Accountancy and financial management functions

BFQ 4.2 Has the company consciously recognised the contribution that this area can make to business resilience and put in place effective systems to establish standards and monitor performance?
As companies grow in size and complexity the nature of financial management is likely to change with two separate functions emerging, financial management and in some companies a separate and identifiable role of funds management (treasury). These skills may be combined in one role CFO or split into two distinctive positions (CFO and treasury).

In November 2020, a UK-based operator of a chain of convenience stores and a restaurant advertised for a finance director (Company B). Its formal accounts for its financial year ending 30 April 2019 were prepared and delivered under the provisions applicable to the small-companies regime indicating a relatively small company. The company described the new role as follows:

> We are looking for a detail orientated individual who can deliver accurate results and also identify where things can potentially go wrong. We have had our fair share of things going missing through poor stock accounting, void/refund control etc. and paid the price so we are very keen to work with someone diligent who can identify any potential stock losses or theft.
>
> Previous experience in food retailing and restaurants would be great but not a prerequisite – we'd prefer you to be good at maths;)
>
> We require a qualified accountant with a strong process driven, commercial management accounting track record and the ability to work closely and interface effectively with owners, part time finance director and non-finance stakeholders to continue and become an integral part of the company's expansion.
>
> You must be prepared to be confident in your own decisions and take charge of financial processes & systems and lead this change with the managers throughout the company.
>
> We are looking for a 'common sense' accountant who understands the big picture and our industry as a whole.
>
> We are looking for up to date reporting as fast as possible and you will have the support of 3–4 others to help you achieve the weekly KPI deadlines and require a good leader who can make sure he/she and their team can meet deadlines for checking off all necessary tasks.

Whilst the advertisement focused on the core functions of the accountancy role, it is clear that there is a strong expectation that the appointee will make a significant contribution to the overall health of the company.

Another advertisement appeared at around the same time, this time placed on behalf of a start-up company (Company C). At the time of its most recently filed financial statement, this UK-based company confirmed that it qualified as a small company. Its accounts indicated the start-up nature of the business. In the description of accounting policies the directors stated:

> The financial statements are being prepared on the going concern basis. The company has incurred losses during the year. The directors were successful in raising additional share capital during the period and further capital post year end, together with issuing convertible loan

notes and therefore have a reasonable expectation that the company should have sufficient cash resources to meet its future obligations, if and when they become due. The directors are therefore of the opinion that they should adopt the going concern basis of accounting in preparing the financial statements.

The job description described the role as follows.

We're looking for a CFO (Chief Financial Officer) to help support the company through our next stage of growth. As CFO, you will work closely with the CEO (Chief Executive Officer), COO (Chief Operating Officer) and the rest of the Senior Leadership team. Your mission will be to lead and grow our Finance function. As the first hire in the finance function you'll shape the team and how Finance collaborates with other departments from the beginning.

In this role you will be working closely with the operations side of the business. You will also be working with people from a variety of backgrounds, who truly care about how what we're building can help others.

Detailed responsibilities were set out across four key areas, financial management, funding and investor relations, strategy and commercial development and team development. These included:

The appropriate use of financial systems. Maintain a tight focus on cash management and liquidity. Prepare and maintain regular financial planning reports. Analyse and expand upon the company's capabilities to track performance and adapt strategic decisions. Develop financial business plans and forecasts, develop and monitor budgets, and lead financial and tax strategies. Build and maintain relationships with the VC (Venture Capital) community with the view to securing further rounds of funding. Engage the Board around issues, trends, and changes in the operating model and operational delivery.

These considerations reflect the nature of the role, with an emphasis on investor and venture capital relationships as one of four main areas of responsibility alongside core accountancy functions.

Finally, also around the same time a large and diversified business operating across a number of international markets was seeking to recruit a director of strategy and finance – (Company D). The advertisement stated: "The Director of Strategy & Finance is responsible and accountable for the analysis of strategic initiatives and financials for reporting and planning."

Responsibilities included:

Maintain up-to-date forecast for revenues and expenses partnering with operating teams to provide updated information and clear understanding of deviations. Provide timely feedback to management about risks and opportunities to the company objectives and financial targets, including recommended actions to mitigate potential risks and capture opportunities. Deliver required inputs to corporate finance and accounting group responsible for consolidated financial reports, including uploading information into corporate systems and completing other standard documents. Lead budget and long-range plans, integrating company strategy with information about economic environment and industry trends. Develop innovative analyses that measure financial and operational performance in ways not captured in basic financial statements. Produce financial projections, business plans and detailed operating models associated with new initiatives, highlighting the P & L impact to the company, returns/sensitivity analyses and cash flow models. Review business case projections developed by operating groups and business development team to ensure consistent frameworks and criteria for analysis and evaluation of initiatives.

This was a pan-company role that was clearly designed to make a major contribution to the development and implementation of business plans across a large multinational business.

Whilst the roles explored above reflect a wide range of different circumstances and challenges there are some fundamental similarities in the contributions that the roles are expected to make. In essence all of these roles enhance resilience. Poor performance in any of these areas is likely to have a significant negative impact. When we were looking at specific cases for inclusion in this book we found several examples where CFOs had departed following the disclosure of apparent weaknesses in financial systems. Typically these departures occurred several months ahead of formal acknowledgment that a company was in business distress.

A survey of senior managers in finance and treasury roles in large multinational companies around the world by the Association of Corporate Treasurers (ACT) in 2021 confirmed the strategic role of cash management and liquidity. These two areas were cited as key concerns occupying most of the respondents' time, not just during the Covid-19 pandemic of 2020–2021 but as a major part of their ongoing long-term responsibilities. There was also evidence of the central role of the CFO in risk management and performance measurement. According to the respondents, these were the givens on which successful financial performance was built. Treasurers also indicated that they were becoming increasingly involved in discussions about financial dimensions of business strategy ahead of board briefings on treasury operations and controls, technology and pensions management.

Going concern

BFQ 4.3 How does the board reach its conclusions about the going concern status of the business, beyond considering the immediate reporting requirements required to comply with legislation?

Going concern has a specific interpretation when applied to the preparation and reporting of financial accounts. Financial reporting standards oblige directors to state on a periodic basis that a company is able to continue to operate as a solvent entity capable of meeting its debts and other obligations (Financial Accounting Standards Board, 2014). When directors believe that this position may no longer be tenable, then they are required to warn shareholders that the going concern based of accounting no longer applies, issue appropriate warnings about potential problems and ultimately prepare for the liquidation of the company. Where accounts are subject to external audit, then the auditor is required to comment on the realism of the statement and its underlying assumptions.

Statements in company annual reports about going concern are explicit statements about business resilience. Directors have a legally defined responsibility to ensure that a company can continue to trade as a going concern. Failure to do so is a breach of directors' duty and can lead to personal repercussions. The quality of this ongoing assessment depends on the underlying skills and motivation of directors, the scale of the company and its financial reporting resources, the support directors may receive from professional accountants and ultimately external review by independent auditors.

Whilst financial reporting in annual or interim company reports must follow specific accounting conventions, the commentary about going concern can range from a comprehensive discussion of the company's strategic position to limited even cursory compliance. Inspection of a range of annual reports on file at Companies House (UK) or with the SEC (US) reveals a wide variety of different standards and approaches to reporting, reflecting the circumstances of individual companies. Readers who are not familiar with the format of such reports are invited to search for a specific company using the UK Companies House website or the US Stock Exchange Commission (SEC) website and access the most recent filing for that company.

It is useful to cross check the reports that are filed with other company announcements that have been filed with different regulatory bodies. In the UK Companies House filings, readers will find details of director appointments, reporting dates and filings of accounts and any charges (secured borrowings). The SEC database has a range of similar information, with the most useful source being form 10-K, the company's annual filing, equivalent to the UK-based annual report and accounts filing.

In many small companies, realistic assessment of the company's ongoing viability is typically down to the knowledge, experience and motivation of individual directors. Directors' confidence in many small companies that the company still remains a going concern is frequently linked to the conviction that they will be able to secure continuing funding either from personal resources or lender support (backed by personal guarantee). The case of NMU Realisations Ltd illustrates how one small business approached this area in the year immediately prior to its entry into administration in January 2020.

NMU Realisations Ltd

NMUL Realisations Ltd (previously Norton Motorcycles (UK) Ltd. was a small company (annual turnover of £6.7m in 2017–2018, with two directors and total employment of 85). Norton was one of the most widely known and celebrated motorcycle brands in the world with a history going back to its foundation by James Lansdown Norton in Birmingham UK in 1898. The company's annual report for the year ended

31 March 2018, and reports from the administrators involved in dealing with the case give some insight into the factors behind the company's ultimate demise.

In the last filing of an annual report (on 26 April 2019), the directors provided a brief description of performance as follows:

> The company has performed strongly over the last few years with revenues and EBITDA continuing to grow, creating a stronger balance sheet. Intangibles have grown significantly over the past three years as the business has invested money into the research and development of new engine platforms and model ranges.

Risk management was described in a few short phrases. "Risk management is a high priority. Processes are designed to identify, mitigate and manage risk. The board of directors are ultimately responsible for the risk management." Strategy formulation was described as follows. "Strict processes are followed to evaluate various level of opportunities, whether this be new funding opportunities, investment in new motorcycle models, entering new markets and geographical locations of the selection of new suppliers."

At one level based on the directors' comments, all might seem well with the company. However, the report of independent auditors included as part of the commentary in this last formal filing, indicated that they (auditors) were unable to express an opinion on the financial statements that accompanied the final report, and had not been able to obtain sufficient appropriate audit evidence to provide a basis for an audit opinion. The report goes on to say that the information they had been able to access had led them to conclude that there was a material uncertainty that the company would be able to continue as a going concern. They also reported that they were unable to determine whether adequate accounting records had been kept.

On 29 January 2020, an application was made for the company to be placed into administration by Metro Bank PLC, the company's largest lender. The administrator's proposals confirmed the existence of outstanding sums due to a range of creditors including Metro Bank PLC (£4.04m) and HM Revenue and Customs (£695k). A further £3.4m was owed to customers who had placed orders to purchase motorcycles. Readers can track the process of administration from this report and a further progress report on 17 September 2020. Both of these are available from UK Companies House.

The administrators' reports provide some insight into the growing problems that the company was facing, including a series of different attempts by directors to resolve the company's financial problems up to the point that the company was put into administration. On 17 April 2020 TVS Motor Company, an India-based manufacturer of two and three-wheeler motorcycles announced that it had paid £16m for some of the assets of Norton Motorcycles (UK), including its brand name and knowhow. Commenting on the acquisition, the joint managing director of TVS, indicated why the Norton name had such value.

> This is a momentous time for us at TVS Motor Company. Norton is an iconic British brand celebrated across the world, and presents us with an immense opportunity to scale globally. This

transaction is in line with our effort to cater to the aspirations of discerning motorcycle customers. We will extend our full support for Norton to regain its full glory in the international motorcycle landscape. [. . .] Norton will continue to retain its distinctive identity with dedicated and specific business plans. TVS Motor will work closely with customers and employees in building the success and pre-eminence of the Norton Motorcycles brand and we look forward to growing together globally in the years to come.

Directors may lack the necessary level of time or expertise to keep track of business fundamentals such as payments to suppliers, payment of taxes and records of cash receipts from customers. We have commented earlier on in this chapter on the positive impact that online accountancy packages has made to this process. An effective monitoring system should provide an early warning of potential problems. On the other hand a sudden unforeseen shock, such as the financial liquidation of a key customer or a major external threat (for example, enforced closure due to lockdown during the Covid pandemic) may put the long-term survival of such a business into question and raise immediate questions about the company's going concern standing.

In 2009 the FRC (Financial Reporting Council), the UK regulatory body responsible for financial reporting and standards, produced detailed advice for large companies on the production of going concern statements. Readers who want to explore this in more detail could usefully consider the key questions set for boards that are a central element of the report. These questions include the quality of preparation of cash flow forecasts and budgets, together with the assumptions that underpin the budgets, and the extent of appropriate sensitivity testing of assumptions. They also include the extent of compliance with lending covenants, potential cash flow deficits that mean that covenants may not be met, and the existence of alternative plans where necessary to deal with any problems where financial commitments may not be met including potential asset disposal or sale and lease back provision.

Significantly perhaps, this advice, written in 2009 is almost entirely focused on financial issues with the exception of one section which addresses market and supply chain factors. The emphasis on financial liquidity reflects the time when the report was produced and the target audience in the period immediately following the financial crisis of 2008.

Three years later in 2012, the ACCA, one of the UK's major accounting bodies addressed the same topic, providing simplified advice on the assessment of going concern, potentially more directly relevant to small and medium-sized companies. The recommendations were summarised as follows:

The assessment required to be performed by directors should consider all the facts and circumstances of an individual company known at the date of approval of the accounts. The level of detail of the assessment and extent of procedures required would vary in accordance with the size and complexity of the entity. It is recommended that it should involve, as a minimum, the preparation of a budget, trading estimates and cash flow forecasts and an analysis of the company's borrowing requirements and facilities, albeit smaller entities may not prepare such a detailed analysis. Larger companies or those with more complex business models may need substantially more procedures as part of the going concern assessment, such as annual reviews of medium and long-term plans, analysis of the major aspects of the economic environment in which they operate (market size, market share, competitors etc.) and financial and operational risk management.

In 2012, the Sharman inquiry recognised the priority that many companies were giving to short-term plans when preparing going concern statements and recommended a broader long-term perspective that took account of future business prospects (estimates of risk and business viability over an extended future periods modelled against alternative assumptions) (Financial Reporting Council, 2012).

Going concern: Auditor responsibilities

In the UK auditor responsibilities are determined by International Standard on Auditing UK 570, Going Concern (Financial Reporting Council, 2019-a). Section 10–1 of ISA 570 focuses on risk assessment procedures including an evaluation of the company's business model, its operations and investments/divestments and the measurement and review of financial performance, including forecasts, future cash flows and budgeting processes. The advice given covers a range of different areas. These are reproduced below.

Events or conditions that may cast significant doubt on the entity's ability to continue as a going concern (Ref: Para. 10-1) A3.
The following are examples of events or conditions that, individually or collectively, may cast significant doubt on the entity's ability to continue as a going concern. This listing is not all-inclusive nor does the existence of one or more of the items always signify that a material uncertainty related to going concern exists.

Financial
Net liability or net current liability position. Fixed-term borrowings approaching maturity without realistic prospects of renewal or repayment; or excessive reliance on short-term borrowings to finance long-term assets. Indications of withdrawal of financial support by creditors. Negative operating cash flows indicated by historical or prospective financial statements. Adverse key financial ratios. Substantial operating losses or significant deterioration in the value of assets used to generate cash flows. Arrears or discontinuance of dividends. Inability to pay creditors on due dates. Inability to comply with the terms of loan agreements. Change from credit to cash-on-delivery transactions with suppliers. Inability to obtain financing for essential new product development or other essential investments.

Operating
Management intentions to liquidate the entity or to cease operations. Loss of key management without replacement. Loss of a major market, key customer(s), franchise, license, or principal supplier(s). Labour difficulties. Shortages of important supplies. Emergence of a highly successful competitor.

Other
Non-compliance with capital or other statutory or regulatory requirements, such as solvency or liquidity requirements for financial institutions. Pending legal or regulatory proceedings against the
entity that may, if successful, result in claims that the entity is unlikely to be able to satisfy.
Changes in law or regulation or government policy expected to adversely affect the entity. Unin-
sured or underinsured catastrophes when they occur. Substantial decrease in share price.

Whilst these areas are flagged by ISA 570 as potentially negative indicators, con-
versely if these areas are all well managed this may make a strong contribution to
business continuity (subject to any unexplained or unexpected events). A positive
performance across the range of different areas identified is likely to indicate significant business resilience.

Even if all of these areas are monitored and performance regularly reviewed
there is still no guarantee that the company will not run into difficulties. The best
that can be said is that the main bases have been covered and basic assumptions
have either been validated or at least tested. The auditors' main role in this process
is to check the quality of analysis that has been undertaken internally and report
on the extent to which the materials presented for audit contain no material incon-
sistencies and have been prepared to appropriate external standards.

There is considerable controversy and debate about the value of going concern
statements, particularly given the number of significant cases where companies
with several consecutive positive external audits suddenly fail. Auditors may de-
fend this anomaly, pointing out that whilst they can determine that specific processes are in place, they are not in a position to influence the quality of director
decision-making, especially given the independent role that they are required to
have in the audit process.

Managing funds effectively

**BFQ 4.4 Is there an explicit plan for long-term management of funds that establishes
alternative strategies to deal with potential future periods of business distress?**

Over 50 years ago, in a seminal work, Donaldson (1969) set out a strategy for financial emergencies focused on flexibility and long-term planning. Donaldson summarised the overall strategy as follows:

> Considered in these terms, the task of financial management involves anticipating the pattern
> of release of funds from, and commitment of funds to, various specialized uses, identifying
> points where a surplus or deficiency of liquid funds may be expected, and taking action to
> employ the surplus or cover the deficit. This process involves mapping out future funds re-
> quirements both in the immediate future and longer term and determining the best way to
> meet such commitments or use surpluses effectively.

Back in 1969, when Donaldson wrote this article computer based simulation models were emerging that enabled such mapping to be undertaken quickly taking a wide range of different elements into account. Donaldson commented: "In this connection I am impressed with the potential of a computer model of the company's funds flow system designed so that it can generate cash or funds flow statements, income statements, balance sheets and related analyses for any desired time horizon and for any set of assumptions."

Whilst the recent pandemic has drawn specific attention to the importance of cash management, effective management of funds flow has always been a major factor in the evaluation of companies of all sizes. Investors have a specific interest in how well directors are using the cash that a company has generated, particularly in terms of the balance between reinvesting in new business opportunities, payment of dividends or share buy-backs. Lenders monitor cash flow to determine decisions on renewal or extension of borrowing facilities. Private equity firms use estimates of cash holdings (or near cash that can rapidly be turned into liquid funds) as part of the calculation to determine whether a company may be a potential candidate for a hostile takeover. Investment analysts use cash measures to determine whether company shares are under or overvalued.

In 2019 the FRC undertook an investigation into what investors wanted to know about funds management (Financial Reporting Council, 2019-b). Investors indicated that they wanted to know more about how much cash would be generated from the operations of the business both in the current period and in the future, and whether or not generated cash was sufficient to meet the company's strategic objectives. They wanted to know where cash flows were inadequate, where the required cash would come from, what was the company planning to do with the cash it generated and was the company being efficient in its use of cash.

In their discussions with investors, the FRC identified a series of key metrics that were seen as important. These included free cash flow, cash conversion and operating cash flow, new debt/net cash and cash remitted to group, and metrics that focused on the use of cash such as cash returned and cash expenditure. From the investors' perspective, such metrics should be aligned to strategy, be transparent in terms of what they relate to, and put into context in terms of the business where they are applied. They should also be reliable from one period to the next and applied consistently. Investors also expressed a desire to see how companies proposed to use the cash that was generated and the priorities that would determine its use, particularly in terms of reinvestment in the business, maintenance of strategic cash reserves and return to shareholders as dividends. The report reviewed best practice across a series of different sectors using a range of specific examples from companies including J Sainsbury, Rio Tinto, Burberry and Anglo-American.

Funds management is a key element in all four of the job descriptions in companies A to D discussed earlier on this chapter. In company A it is an implicit task linked to a general range of bookkeeping responsibilities. In company B funds management is linked directly to the role of improving stock accounting and reducing theft. In company C the tasks of the incoming manager include maintaining a tight focus on cash management and liquidity and building and maintaining relationships with the VC (venture capital) community with the view to securing further rounds of funding. Company D's requirement is for someone who will produce financial projections, business plans and detailed operating models associated with new initiatives, highlighting the profit and loss impact to the company, returns/sensitivity analyses and cash flow models.

Donaldson advocated creating an inventory of the resources available to management to cover any unexpected problems in funds flows, something he called "an estimate of the purchasing power available for commitment in the future" or "checklist of resources for covering a funds flow deficit". He split this list into three categories. The first was uncommitted reserves such as surplus cash, unused credit lines, additional bank loans, additional long-term debt and issue of new equity. The second was reduction in planned outflows including changes in production scheduling, reduction of expenditure on marketing, R&D, administration, capital expenditure and dividends. The third category included business shutdown or sale of business unit.

Some of these resources such as surplus cash could be used immediately, potentially to buy time until other resources could be made available through negotiation with lenders or new equity issue. Other areas such as reduction in planned outflows, or the sale of business units can only be achieved over longer time frames and are less flexible. Donaldson argued that management should consider all of these potential resources in a systematic manner and create an explicit plan to maximise flexibility ahead of times of financial emergency.

Donaldson's original arguments generated widespread discussion of the importance of strategic funds management reflected in a range of different academic and practitioner contributions. Some 50 years later, Birshan, Gerken, Kemmer, Petrov and Polyakov (2020) were still exploring the same agenda discussing the potential to release the cash sitting in a company's balance sheet. They identified five key areas where CFO's can create value, including funding and capital structure, management of strategic liquidity, risk-adjusted capital allocation, foreign exchange and interest rate management and commodity price and risk management. The following case, Next Plc illustrates this in action.

Next Plc: Testing for financial stress

In its strategic report for 2018–2019, Next Plc described how it applied stress testing to model the effect of alternative business systems on its business over a 15 year period. The analysis was based on the company's existing business model and reviewed outcomes when changes were made to assumptions about sales mix, rental costs, rates and staffing costs. The report described the process as follow:

> We have asked ourselves what the combination of Online opportunities and negative Retail like-for-likes might mean for the long-term financial performance of the Group. Last year we issued a fifteen-year stress test modelling the cash flows from our Retail business in an environment of −10% compound like-for-like retail sales. We have updated this model in the following ways:
>
> > Maintaining the minus 10% decline in like-for-like sales
> >
> > Accounting for the improving outlook for retail rent, rates and staffing costs
> >
> > Layering on the potential cash flows from the compound annual growth of + 7.5% in Online business (including overseas)
> >
> > The model implies sales growth over the period of +3% and cash generation of around £12bn over the next 15 years, in addition to growing our online nextpay debtor book by another £900m.
> >
> > [. . .] It is important to emphasise that the 15- year stress test is not a plan or a forecast. No one can predict the future and the numbers are very likely to turn out exactly as modelled. They depend on too many unknowns, not least the quality of our execution and continued innovation (which, by definition, cannot be foreseen).
> >
> > [. . .] Nonetheless the model is important because it demonstrates that, using a reasonable set of sales and cost assumptions, Next's economic structure allows its profitable transition into the online world. It shows what is *possible* within the constraints of our balance sheet, current lease structures, warehousing and distribution capacities, infrastructure costs and likely changes to our revenue cost base *if* we continue to see a migration online similar to that which we are currently experiencing.
> >
> > It is not necessarily the path we will follow but it is a way through the woods: a realistic scenario under which we might deliver a growing profitable and potentially world-class online clothing and homeware business. And at the same time generate around £12 bn of pre-tax cash flow over fifteen years.

Most companies are unlikely to contemplate the level of analysis illustrated in the Next Plc example. In Next's case, the company has used its existing business model as a baseline. It has then applied a range of assumptions to the baseline data to explore what effect future changes in its operating environment might have on revenue and costs.

Carillion plc

In the case study which follows we examine the collapse of Carillion plc, a major UK-based construction and services company that entered insolvency in 2018. The collapse of Carillion plc was one of the UK's most significant business failures of recent years. Many of Carillion's business partners and sub-contractors felt an immediate impact as they became responsible for the completion of Carillion contracts. UK government provided short-term funding to protect the incomes of employees pending transfer of contracts to joint venture partners. A substantial number of Carillion's employees continued to work on existing contracts that were taken over by other companies. The Group's pension scheme was transferred to the Pension Protection Fund, affecting an estimated 27,500 members who faced a reduction in pension benefits. When the company collapsed the construction trade body, Build UK estimated that it had over 30,000 direct and indirect suppliers many of whom would not receive payment following the declaration of insolvency.

As we suggested in the previous chapter you may want to look back at the questions that we ask in Table 4.1 as you review the case.

Some of the areas that you might want to focus on in the case could include:

- The impact of a business strategy based on the acquisition of rivals on long-term debt and cash flow
- The problems of managing costs and profitability in a traditionally low-margin industry subject to a wide range of possible impacts on performance including government policy, difficulties in planning and delivering complex contracts and coordinating a wide range of different subcontractors
- Fluctuations in cash flow associated with project cancellation and delays
- Difficulties in creating and maintaining an accurate and up-to-date picture of costs, revenue and cash flow in over 400 subsidiary companies
- The difficulties of maintaining investor and creditor confidence in an industry characterised by traditionally low margins, complex projects and a high degree of uncertainty about project completion, revenue and costs.

Case study: Carillion plc

Background

Carillion plc was created in July 1999 through a demerger from Tarmac plc. Businesses which were previously part of Tarmac plc were reorganised into five main divisions: private finance initiative (PFI) construction, infrastructure management, services, capital projects and building. At the time the business had a significant dependence on the UK government as a major client. The then chairman described the new business as "more focused and better able to pursue its strategy for growing shareholder value – a strategy that is changing both what we do and how we do it. Despite the considerable effort demanded by the demerger, all our businesses remained clearly focused on their customers. Their success is evident in the Group's improved results, which reflect an increasingly prudent approach to profit recognition."[1]

In the same report, the company's financial director referred to a review of cash management where he stated that the intention was to smooth over the large year-end cash peaks which had historically been part of the business. Much of Carillion's work in the UK was for public sector agencies where demand was driven by government procurement policy (36% of Carillion's revenue in 1999, its first full year of trading was from the UK government). PFI contracts, forming a significant part of Carillion's work, were widely used to secure private sector investment to deliver public infrastructure (schools, road and rail, hospitals) and then operate and maintain the infrastructure. The chairman's report underlined the perceived importance of this sector to the company, commenting that "Significantly our order book in these segments has increased tenfold to £1.4 billion [over the past five years] and now represents some 64% of our total order book, which has nearly trebled to £2.2 billion. In addition, we will benefit from more than £1 billion of turnover over the next 25 years from our equity investments to date in PFI concessions."

Business focus

Carillion's business was focused on two areas of activity: new build and service projects. Typical construction projects have a long gestation period from original agreement to proceeding with the contract and then to completion and it is important for businesses in this sector to be able to maintain a pipeline of new projects to replace those that are nearing completion. In its early years, Carillion chose to grow its business through the acquisition of other construction companies, each of which had their own portfolio of activities. In 2006, the company bought Mowlem, one of the largest UK construction and civil engineering companies for £350m. In 2008,

https://doi.org/10.1515/9783110689495-007

the company bought Alfred McAlpine, another major competitor for £565m. These acquisitions were financed through increased borrowings and were reflected in an increase in goodwill shown in the company's balance sheet following each acquisition. Valuation of this goodwill became a critical issue in the last few months of 2017 immediately prior to the company's failure.

Dramatic reductions in public spending following the election of a new coalition government in the UK in 2010 caused major problems for the whole of the UK construction industry. Government policy shifted away from PFI projects to favour more direct public control. Following a policy review in 2012 changes to the organisation of such projects increased the amount of scrutiny of these schemes, making them more onerous undertakings for contractors. Profit margins became increasingly slimmer as companies bid for the limited amount of work that was available and had to comply with the increasingly demanding conditions placed on the award and delivery of such contracts. Simultaneously, major cutbacks in economic activity following the financial crash in 2008 continued to have an effect on new construction projects, not just in the UK but also in the Middle East and Canada, markets that Carillion had identified as areas of potential growth.

In this climate, in March 2011 Carillion chose to pay £298m to buy Eaga Plc, a contractor specialising in major government service contracts including the promotion and administration of green energy initiatives. This initiative was designed to increase the company's presence in low-carbon energy services. The company added a further £329m to goodwill in its balance sheet, with a commensurate increase in debt. The anticipated growth in demand for such services never materialised, due to major government cutbacks in green energy programmes.[2]

Strategic review 2009

A board strategy session held in Dubai in November 2009 identified the potential risks and opportunities of Carillion's four major business segments.[3] UK construction was seen as a risky sector which would be very difficult going forward, particularly since the business was over three quarters public funded. A presentation during the meeting commented on the company's situation as follows:

> The challenge will be for us to manage the business so that we retain a quality UK construction business – whatever the consequent size–whilst ensuring that the cash flow implications are properly managed. [. . .] Recession is clearly hurting our core FM (Facilities Management) business as the requirement for our 'value added' offering is less critical in the eyes of our customers who are now seeking a low cost solution. The clear risk is that we will lose business to in-house and to cheaper competition. On the other hand the government must reduce costs drastically so we expect that this will create renewed outsourcing opportunities for us.

Some potential was identified for the Middle East and Canada, subject to the caution that overseas markets had become increasingly volatile and unpredictable. The report commented: "Project delays and cancellations are widespread as customers 're-prioritise' their development plans and seek liquidity to move projects forward. As a result of the dramatic slowdown, the market has become fiercely competitive with contractors expected to accept more risk at less margin. Contract terms are being renegotiated and payments unreasonably withheld."

The incoming CEO who would take the company forward in this new stage of development was first appointed to the board as an executive director one month after the completion of the strategic planning exercise in December 2009. He was subsequently promoted to CEO in January 2012 and remained in this role until 9 July 2017, overseeing a business strategy that reflected the conclusions of the strategic review. He described the options facing the company when he became the CEO:

> We did not have any money to buy competitors, as we had done in the past. We had to win our work organically. We had to bid and we had to win because future cash flows are in my mind more important than the (pension) deficit contribution [. . .] Those are the future cash flows that the pension is absolutely dependent on.[4]

General pressures on the industry

Carillion was not alone in recognising the changes that were impacting on the construction and service infrastructure markets. The new CEO of Balfour Beatty, Carillion's major UK competitor, also appointed in 2012, identified similar market trends and announced comparable measures to take the company forward, including growing the business in new segments, delivering greater value to clients, improving operating efficiencies and cost-effectiveness through better utilisation of resources. In July 2014, Carillion approached Balfour Beatty about a possible merger. The bid was ultimately turned down by Balfour Beatty with the board dismissing the proposed combined business plan saying that it had "very significant delivery and financial risks".[5]

On 3 May 2014, Balfour Beatty's board announced that the current CEO would step down and they would seek to appoint "an experienced, top-flight Chief Executive from outside the Group with strong turnaround credentials". An independent review by KPMG, conducted for the Group, identified three critical issues in the company's UK construction business. The chair's discussion in the annual report for 2014 summarised the major problems as follows:[6]

> Firstly tendering for certain lump sum fixed price projects at very low margins at the bottom of the market, assuming optimistic buying gains which didn't materialise as costs escalated during the course of the project, leading to losses. Secondly inadequate commercial and contract management processes and a lack of management supervision, leading to poor control over projects and failures to recover genuine contract entitlements. Thirdly poor cost and programme forecasting leading to insufficient visibility on project deterioration. In this part of the

Group we saw failures in risk management and the control environment particularly commercial and operational controls was not effective.

Following KPMG's analysis, the board made further provisions of £118m write-down for delays in project completion for 2014 year end. A business transformation programme "Built to last" was announced in February 2015, setting out priorities for development of the Group, including streamlining activities to remove duplication and reduce layers and costs not related to frontline activity, strengthening financial controls and investment in training and talent. This was linked to a cash generation drive throughout the Group. Two years later, a review of Carillion by Ernst & Young (EY) as part of the attempt to transform the company following the departure of its CEO identified many of the same issues and suggested very similar remedies (see below).

Early investor concerns

Returning to Carillion plc by December 2015, doubts were beginning to emerge about the company's financial position. Standard Life Investments, one of Carillion's significant investors with over 10% of Carillion shares, began to reduce its shareholding. In a letter to the chairs of the joint committee set up to investigate the circumstances of Carillion's ultimate collapse Standard Life representatives wrote: "There were a number of interconnected reasons for this divestment. In summary, there were growing concerns from late 2015 on a number of fronts, including the company's strategy, its vulnerability to worsening market conditions and financial management, including the strength of its balance sheet. As a consequence our investment position on Carillion moved from a 'hold' to a 'sell' from December 2015 onwards." Specific concerns cited included:

> High levels of on and off balance sheet debt for a cyclical, low margin business with limited possibility of this debt burden being reduced in the near term due to acquisitions and a high dividend payout.
> Widening pension deficit (from £317m to £663m in 2016).
> Downward pressure on earnings in spite of revenue growth due to narrowing margins on new business, particularly in support services, UK construction and projects in the Middle East.
> Weak cash generation due to working capital outflows, restructuring costs, pension contributions and capital expenditure needs.
> Our engagement on corporate governance matters left us with concerns about the willingness of the board to alter the strategic direction of the company to address our concerns.
> These issues were raised with the management through our ongoing engagement. However, it was felt the management was not giving sufficient weight to the probability that trading may deteriorate further or to the downside risk from this scenario given the high level of debt. The board showed no inclination to drive the management to change.[7]

Summarising Carillion's business model in 2020, Sasse, Britchfield and Davies commented:[8]

Carillion exemplified bad business practices. It was renowned for bidding aggressively (and unsustainably) low to win work, undercutting other companies. Even as its debts piled up, it continued to take huge risks, acquiring companies for more than their value and bidding for work in uncertain markets, particularly in the construction sector. It paid its suppliers extremely late, offering standard payment terms of four months and demanding a price cut for earlier payment–an arrangement it used to shore up its balance sheet without care for its suppliers. It failed to make adequate contributions to pension schemes and disguised all of its problems with aggressive accounting practices. Rather than challenging such behaviour, Carillion's board continued to award generous bonuses even as performance declined.

An accounting issue

On 1 March 2017, the company published its report and accounts for 2016.[9] The report summarised performance as follows: "High-Quality order book [. . .] and strong pipeline of contract opportunities." It proposed a full-year dividend increase of 1% to 18.45 pence (2015: 18.25). Reasons given to invest in Carillion included "leadership positions in good markets", "broad capability and trusted partner", "a track record of performance" and "integrated and sustainable business". The chair's report was an up-beat message that described "strong revenue growth" with a "slight overall increase in profit from operations" and "substantial liquidity", noting that "The vast majority of the Group's £1.5 billion of funding matures in November 2020 and beyond."

On 9 May 2017, a board meeting was called to discuss an accounting issue which had been raised by a colleague returning from an overseas assignment to take up the role of finance director of construction services. The issue related to "some issues with which she was not comfortable".[10] At the meeting the board discussed the progress of specific projects and the provision that had been made for delays or variations in the performance of contracts. The CEO briefed the board on current major projects where adjustments to projected outcomes had been considered and the assumptions about performance that had been applied. The company's finance director, who had been in post since the beginning of January 2017 commented that the Group's position had always been to discourage negative accruals, "save where cost escalation had been the consequence of supplier incompetence". The board agreed to implement a broader review of the overall position, to be led by KPMG.

In June, the company begun to explore the possibility of raising capital through an issue of equity, but were ultimately unsuccessful. Advice from brokers indicated that the scale of the contract provision would likely damage any prospect of successful fund-raising.[11]

A first half trading update, published on 10 July 2017, contrasted markedly with the optimistic tone of the Annual Report and Accounts published some 4 months earlier.[12] It revealed that the company had reviewed all of its contracts, with the support of KPMG and had made a contract provision of £845m as at 30 June 2017. As a result, revenue estimates for the full year had been downgraded to between £4.8bn and £5bn, and net borrowings were expected to increase to £695m (full year: 2016 £586m). The update also identified deterioration in cash flows across a significant number of contracts. The board announced a series of actions designed to reduce borrowings including disposal of companies within the Group to focus on core markets, further annual cost savings as part of a strategic and operational review, maximising the recovery of receivables (monies owed by customers) and the suspension of 2017 dividends. This would be the first time that dividends had not been paid since the formation of the company in 1999.

The company's non-executive chairman said:

> Despite making progress against the strategic priorities we set out in our 2016 results announcement in March, average net borrowing has increased above the level we expected, which means that we will no longer be able to meet our target of reducing leverage for the full year. We have therefore concluded that we must take immediate action to accelerate the reduction in average net borrowing and are announcing a comprehensive programme of measures to address that, aimed at generating significant cashflow in the short-term. In addition, we are also announcing that we are undertaking a thorough review of the business and the capital structure, and the options available to optimise value for the benefit of shareholders. We will update the market on the progress of the review at our interim results in September.

The company also announced that the CEO had stepped down and that the search for a successor would begin. In the meantime, the company would be led by the board's senior non-executive director.

Business review

EY were appointed on 14 July to support the business review. The company initiated weekly cash flow forecasts.[13] The initial findings of the EY review were discussed at a board meeting on 22 August 2017.[14] Key problems identified included:

> A number of non-profitable contracts, under investment in systems and platforms, outsourced solutions not optimised for delivery, lack of accountability, proliferation of reporting, inability of senior managers to make fast decisions based on evidence, too many managerial layers, limited standards on ways of working, lack of professionalisation and expertise, an inward looking culture, with limited adoption of market best practice, and a culture of noncompliance. The key themes emerging from the review were the need to ruthlessly rationalise the company's portfolio of different activities to focus on where it made money, simplify and delayer the organisation, and upgrade the organisation through the right systems, processes and skills to enable quality delivery.[15]

These findings and recommendations echo those of the report KPMG produced for Balfour Beatty some 2 years earlier (see above), suggesting that both of these companies had failed at different times to address weaknesses in their business models that had been exposed by an increasingly difficult and demanding market place.

Both companies had grown through acquisition, both delivered projects through a complex structure of contractors and subcontractors with a large number of individual financial transactions. Both had experienced delays and potential setbacks in project completion dates as clients changed specifications or attempted to vary payment terms. Both had to coordinate their work with a significant number of joint-venture partners, and monitor and consolidate their financial results for a large number of subsidiaries (in 2016 Carillion listed over 400 subsidiary companies in its report and accounts). On construction projects both had experienced significant delays and setbacks in project completion due to unforeseen site-specific problems or the failure of a subcontractor to execute their part of the project effectively.

Critical success factors

Major construction projects can carry large risks, depending on assumptions about the nature of the project and its delivery. Contracts typically contain clauses that cover delays or unexpected events that make it difficult to control the exact progress of a specific project or deliver it on time. The company's finance director described the problems that this created for financial planning in his evidence to the UK Joint Committee enquiry that investigated Carillion's failure.[16]

> . . . if your supply chain does not perform, and you are signed up to deliver your contract at a particular point in time, you have to supplement that and fund the costs until you can get some sort of recovery off them. That recovery, again, is subject to lengthy debate, discussion and negotiation with the supply chain. If your customer makes changes as you go through the contract, again, you are obliged to act on those changes, because if you do not you are going to be late delivering the contract, but again, the compensation for that takes time. You have all of these dynamics. You are boxed in, where you have to deliver but in terms of your ability to make a sensible return or keeping hold of the cash, you are dependent on people doing the right thing.

Worsening financial position

Publication of the financial results for the 6 months ended 30 June 2017 on 29 September updated the market on the company's position.[17] A further £200m for support services contracts was added to the previously announced construction contract provision of £845m, and a goodwill impairment charge of £134m was recognised in respect of the UK and Canadian construction businesses. At the end of 2016 the level of net debt had already been recognised as a significant problem and in oral evidence to the subsequent enquiry into Carillion's collapse members of the board indicated that they had asked management to develop a plan to address the issue.[18] Nevertheless, net borrowing on 30 June 2017 had increased to £571m from £291m at the same time in the previous year.

The announcement also updated investors on the business review that it had begun with EY, citing actions underway to improve cash flow and strengthen the balance sheet, and expected proceeds from disposals of non-core businesses of £300m including discussions related to the sale of Carillion's businesses in Canada and the UK Healthcare business. It also announced a further committed credit facility of £140m with a number of the Group's core lenders.

The company's interim CEO described the company's situation as follows:

> This is a disappointing set of results which reflects the issues we flagged in July and the additional £200m provision for our Support Services business that we have announced today. We now expect results for the full year to be lower than current market expectations.

> The strategic review that we launched in July has enabled us to get a firm handle on the Group's problems and we have implemented a clear plan to address them. Our objective is to be a lower risk, lower cost, higher quality business generating sustainable cash backed earnings. In the immediate short term our focus is to complete the disposal programme, accelerate action to take cost out of the business and get our balance sheet back to a place where it can support Carillion going forward.

On 11 September 2017, the company announced that its finance director had left the company with immediate effect and a chief transformation officer had been appointed on secondment from EY. The company also announced a series of other departures from the senior team that would occur on 30 September, including the previous the CEO, the chief operating officer, the managing director of Carillion construction services and the managing director of Carillion services. It also announced that its group strategy director would be leaving the company by the end of the year.[19]

Investor perceptions

A letter to the joint enquiry held in 2018 to investigate the collapse of the company from Kiltearn Partners LLP, an investment management company with clients with over 10% of Carillion's outstanding shares on 10 July 2017, describes two meetings with the interim CEO on 17 July and 13 October.[20] According to the account of the first meeting, the issues discussed were (i) the £845m provision, (ii) Carillion's balance sheet and (iii) Carillion's future outlook. Kiltearn stated to the enquiry that it had decided to steadily exit the investment in Carillion on behalf of its clients as it believed that it was in their best interests to do so. It cited material reservations about Carillion's capital base and its cash flows, and the reliability of its published information, including its historic annual reports. The account of the 13 October meeting reports comments made to Kiltearn by the interim CEO who stated that there would be little point in trying to raise significant debt or issue equity until (i) cost reductions and disposals had been delivered, (ii) Carillion had shifted its focus to its core business, namely UK support services, and (iii) a permanent CEO had been recruited. The letter describes how Kiltearn continued to liquidate its clients' holdings in Carillion, finally selling out completely on 4 January 2018.

Managing the crisis

Between September 2017 and November 2017, the management team began the process of attempting to turn the business around, following the principles set out in the EY report. This involved disposal of marginal interests, cost reduction and cash collection. On 24 October 2017, the Group announced that it had signed an agreement with Serco Group Plc for the disposal of most of its UK healthcare business for an agreed price of £50.1m, with the aim of receiving the bulk of the proceeds during the first half of 2018.[21]

In a move to reassure investors, creditors and employees, the Group announced the appointment of a new CEO, who would take up his office with effect from 2 April 2018. On 2 November 2017, it was announced that a new non-executive director would be joining the board. He was described as having specific turnaround experience: "[His] extensive executive career has included several chief executive roles. [. . .] These roles included working with companies at times of financial stress and in turnaround."[22] A significant new contract was announced on November 15 in Oman for a Carillion joint venture worth an estimated £250m. A further non-executive director was appointed with effect from 1 December 2017. His expertise was described as follows: "He has substantial operational experience across the finance function of significant and international businesses, having served as a Group Finance Director for over eight years and a proven track record of driving business growth."[23]

Despite these efforts, the Group was forced to issue a profit warning on 17 November 2017 for the final quarter to the end of December 2017 citing delays in the disposal of a number of public private partnerships, a slippage in the start date of a significant project in the Middle East and lower than expected margin improvements on a number of UK support service contracts.[24] As a result, the Group warned that it expected a breach of its borrowing covenants as on 31 December 2017. The announcement described discussions with its principal lenders related to securing their support for amendment to the agreements to defer the test date from 31 December 2017 to 30 April 2018. The Group stated that "Carillion had now commenced a process to seek the consents that would be necessary to make this amendment".

Creditor engagement

On 10 January 2018, the Group presented a plan to take the company forward to a coordinating committee of creditors. The programme reflected the strategic decisions set out in the company's announcement of half year results, including exit from high-risk businesses, cost reduction, disposal of non-core assets and selective growth. An independent review of the plans by FTI Consulting estimated that the Group's strategy implied an additional funding commitment of up to £360m of which the majority would be required by May 2018. The review also identified a further requirement for bonding and letters of credit of up to £309m.[25] The conclusions of the review were negative, citing doubt about the true historic trading position and cash generation of the business. It commented: "Rather than addressing the underlying challenges facing the Group in respect of problem contracts and the strength of the balance sheet, transactions were entered into, and accounting treatments and assumptions made, to enhance the reported profitability and net debt position of the Group."

Management was harshly criticised with the report stating:

> Whilst circumstances outside of the Group's control are a factor in the operational challenges faced on certain projects.. [we found].. a lack of management attention to (and accountability for) addressing key issues, governance failures over the amount of risk being taken on, and a focus on short term financial benefits (net debt and cash) at the expense of long-term profitability and viability.

The Group's pension liabilities were seen as a major risk factor in any further extension of borrowings, since in the event of insolvency the schemes' relative claims would take priority. The report acknowledged that "management believe our sensitivities overstate the risks and are too harsh".

Appeal to government

On 13 January 2018, Carillion plc's chairman wrote to the Permanent Secretary for the Cabinet Office, setting out two options, namely "the provision of short-term funding from HM Government and certain key banks to enable Carillion to bridge through to a restructuring; or an insolvency".[26] The email emphasised that any loan would carry a commercial rate of interest and be for a short period. It also stressed that the key beneficiaries of a restructuring would be employees, the supply chain and customers who would continue to receive uninterrupted support. Insolvency according to the email would lead to a series of very damaging consequences. The email set these out in stark terms.

> If HM Government determines in the near term not to support Carillion, that will lead very rapidly into what is likely be a very disorderly and value destructive insolvency process, with no real ability to manage the widespread loss of employment, operational continuity, the impact on our customers and suppliers, or (in the extreme) the physical safety of Carillion employees and the members of the public they serve. Any attempt to manage this process will come with enormous cost to HM Government, far exceeding the costs of continued funding for the business.

On 15 January 2018, an announcement from Carillion plc confirmed that this last min-ute appeal had not succeeded:[27]

> Further to the announcement made on 12 January 2018, Carillion continued to engage with its key financial and other stakeholders, including Her Majesty's Government ('HMG'), over the course of the weekend regarding options to reduce debt and strengthen the Group's balance sheet. As part of this engagement, Carillion also asked those stakeholders for limited short term financial support, to enable it to continue to trade whilst longer term engagement continued.
>
> Despite considerable efforts, those discussions have not been successful, and the board of Carillion has therefore concluded that it had no choice but to take steps to enter into com-pulsory liquidation with immediate effect. An application was made to the High Court for a compulsory liquidation of Carillion before opening of business today and an order has been granted to appoint the Official Receiver as the liquidator of Carillion."

Carillion's chairman said:

> This is a very sad day for Carillion, for our colleagues, suppliers and customers that we have been proud to serve over many years. Over recent months huge efforts have been made to re-structure Carillion to deliver its sustainable future and the Board is very grateful for the huge efforts made by (interim CEO), our executive team and many others who have worked tire-lessly over this period. In recent days however we have been unable to secure the funding to support our business plan and it is therefore with the deepest regret that we have arrived at this decision. We understand that HM Government will be providing the necessary funding required by the Official Receiver to maintain the public services carried on by Carillion staff, subcontractors and suppliers.

Footnote

The collapse of Carillion plc was one of the largest business failures in the UK in recent years. It had a significant impact both on direct employees and a large num-ber of subcontractors who worked with the business. A parliamentary subcommit-tee set up to investigate the collapse criticised the behaviour of many of those involved. The collapse raised a series of questions about the responsibilities of an independent auditor in the preparation and approval of financial statements and led to calls to overhaul the process by which such auditors were appointed. It also added to an increasing number of demands to increase the scrutiny of the behav-iour of directors at a time when other significant business failures in the UK such as Bhs were also under review.

In January 2018, the Financial Reporting Council (FRC), announced the opening of an investigation of KPMG's audit of the financial statements of Carillion plc for 2014, 2015, 2016, and additional audit work carried out during 2017.[28] KPMG subse-quently self-reported the results of its own investigation into its audit of Carillion plc. On 21 November 2021, *The Times* reported that the official receiver had lodged a High Court legal claim against KPMG in respect of its conduct of Carillion audits.[29]

On 19 March 2018, the FRC announced that it had also commenced an investigation into the conduct of two former Group finance directors in relation to the preparation and approval of the financial statements of Carillion plc for the years ended 31 December 2014, 2015 and 2016, and the 6 months ended 30 June 2017, and the preparation and reporting of other financial information during the period 2014–2017.[30]

On 12 January 2021, disqualification proceedings were issued on behalf of the Secretary of State for Business Energy and Industrial Strategy with respect to eight directors and former Carillion directors following a report about the conduct of each director submitted by the official receiver.[31] The grounds given were that "their conduct, whilst acting as a director of Carillion, makes them unfit to be concerned in the management of a company".

The series of events that we describe in this case reflect the situation as this book goes to press. As with the other case studies in this book we cannot anticipate what may happen with respect to outstanding or future investigations into the conduct of any of the individuals or organisations identified in this case study.

Notes

1 Carillion plc, (1999) *The results of what we do: Annual Report 1999*. 22 April.

2 Vaughan, A. and Macalister, T. (2015) The nine green policies killed off by the Tory government. *Guardian* [online]. Available at: https://www.theguardian.com/environment/2015/jul/24/the-9-green-policies-killed-off-by-tory-government [Accessed 8 February 2021].

3 Carillion plc, (2009) *November Board Meeting: Board Strategy Session-Dubai* [online]. 4 November. Available at: http://www.parliament.uk/documents/commons-committees/work-and-pensions/Carillion%20report/Board-Strategy-session-November-2009.pdf [Accessed 9 April 2020].

4 Howson, R. (2017) *Business, Energy and Industrial Strategy and Work and Pensions Committees, Oral Evidence: Carillion, HC 769 Response to q. 606 Oral Evidence* [online] 6 February. Available at: http://data.parliament.uk/writtenevidence/committeeevidence.svc/evidencedocument/work-and-pensions-committee/carillion/oral/78103.pdf [Accessed 8 February 2021].

5 Balfour Beatty plc, (2015) *Annual Report and Accounts 2014 Build to last*, 26 May.

6 Balfour Beatty plc, (2015) *Annual Report and Accounts 2014 Build to last*, 26 May.

7 Standard Life Aberdeen, (2018) *Letter from Standard Life to the Chairs of the Joint Committee* [online]. 2 February Available at: https://www.parliament.uk/globalassets/documents/commons-committees/work-and-pensions/Carillion/Letter-from-Standard-Life-to-the-Chairs-regarding-Carillion-2-February-2018.pdf [Accessed 10 December 2021].

8 Sasse, T., Britchfield, C. and Davies N. (2020) *Carillion: Two years on, Institute for Government, IfG Insight*, March. Available at: https://www.instituteforgovernment.org.uk/sites/default/files/publications/carillion-two-years-on.pdf [Accessed 6 October 2020].

9 Carillion plc, (2017) *Making tomorrow a better place* Annual Report and Accounts 2016. 22 April.

10 Carillion plc, (2017) *Minutes of a meeting of the Board of Directors, 9 May 2017* [online]. 9 May. Available at: https://www.parliament.uk/globalassets/documents/commons-committees/work-and-pensions/Carillion/Carillion-Board-minutes-9-May-2017.pdf [Accessed 7 February 2021].

11 Q238–239, Q337, (2017) *Business, Energy and Industrial Strategy and Work and Pensions Committees, Oral Evidence: Carillion, HC 769 Response to q. 606 Oral Evidence* [online]. 6 February. Available at: http://data.parliament.uk/writtenevidence/committeeevidence.svc/evidencedocument/work-and-pensions-committee/carillion/oral/78103.pdf [Accessed 9 February 2021].

12 Carilllion plc, (2017) *2017 First-half trading update Strategic review and management changes* [online]. 10 July Available at: https://www.investegate.co.uk/News/carillion-strategic-review-as-h1-operating-profits-fall-short/745203/ [Accessed February 7, 2021].

13 Q333, (2017) *Business, Energy and Industrial Strategy and Work and Pensions Committees, Oral Evidence: Carillion, HC 769 Response to q. 606 Oral Evidence* [online]. 6 February. Available at: https://data.parliament.uk/writtenevidence/committeeevidence.svc/evidencedocument/work-and-pensions-committee/carillion/oral/78103.pdf [Accessed 14 December 2021].

14 Carillion plc, (2017) *Carillion Board Minutes, 22 August 2017* [online]: Available at https://www.parliament.uk/globalassets/documents/commons-committees/work-and-pensions/Carillion/Carillion-board-minutes-22-August-2017.pdf [Accessed 7 February 2021].

15 (2017) *Extract from EY presentation to Carillion Board, 22 August 2017 Business, Energy and Industrial Strategy and Work and Pensions Committees, Oral Evidence: Carillion, HC 769 Response to q. 606 Oral Evidence* [online]. 6 February. Available at: https://www.parliament.uk/globalassets/documents/commons-committees/work-and-pensions/Carillion/Extract-from-EY-presentation-to-Carillion-Board-22-August-2017.pdf [Accessed 8 February 2021].

16 Q306, (2017) *Business, Energy and Industrial Strategy and Work and Pensions Committees, Oral Evidence: Carillion, HC 769 Response to q. 606 Oral Evidence* [online]. 6 February. Available at: http://data.parliament.uk/writtenevidence/committeeevidence.svc/evidencedocument/work-and-pensions-committee/carillion/oral/78103.pdf [Accessed 8 February 2021].

17 Carillion plc, (2017) *Financial Results for the Six Months ended 30th June 2017* [online] 29 September. Available at: https://www.investegate.co.uk/carillion-Plc–clln-/rns/half-year-report/201709290700092047S/ [Accessed 8 February 2021].

18 Q251, Q331, (2017) *Business, Energy and Industrial Strategy and Work and Pensions Committees, Oral Evidence: Carillion, HC 769 Response to q. 606 Oral Evidence* [online]. 6 February. Available at: http://data.parliament.uk/writtenevidence/committeeevidence.svc/evidencedocument/work-and-pensions-committee/carillion/oral/78103.pdf [Accessed 9 February 2021].

19 Carillion plc, (2017*) Directorate Change* [online]. 11 September. Available at: https://www.investegate.co.uk/carillion-Plc/rns/directorate-change/201709110700063018Q/ [Accessed 9 February 2021].

20 Kiltearn Partners LLP, (2018) *Re: Carillion* [online]. 2 February. Available at: https://www.parliament.uk/globalassets/documents/commons-committees/work-and-pensions/Carillion/Letter-from-Kiltearn-Partners-LLP-to-the-Chairs-regarding-Carillion-2-February-2018.pdf [Accessed 7 February 2021].

21 Carillion plc, (2017) *Update on financing, disposals and work winning* [online]. 24 October Available at: https://www.investegate.co.uk/carillion-Plc/rns/update-on-financing–disposals-and-work-winning/201710240700044245U/ [Accessed 9 February 2021].

22 Carillion plc, (2017) *Board appointment* [online]. 2 November. Available at: https://www.investegate.co.uk/carillion-Plc/rns/directorate-change/201711020700063340V/ [Accessed 9 February 2021].

23 Carillion plc, (2017) *Board Appointment* [online]. 01 December. Available at: https://www.investegate.co.uk/carillion-Plc/rns/directorate-change/201712010700080711Y/ [Accessed 9 February 2021].

24 Carillion plc, (2017) *Update on discussions with stakeholders, trading and financial covenants deferral* [online]. 17 November https://www.investegate.co.uk/carillion-Plc/rns/update/201711170702318037W/ [Accessed 9 February 2021].

25 FTI Consulting, (2018) *Project Ray: Independent Business Review* [online] Available at: https://www.parliament.uk/globalassets/documents/commons-committees/work-and-pensions/Carillion/Project-Ray-FTI-consulting-15-January-2018.pdf [Accessed 9 February 2021].

26 Carillion plc, (2018) *Letter from Carillion Plc to Permanent Secretary for the Cabinet Office*, [online] 13 January. Available at: https://www.parliament.uk/globalassets/documents/commons-committees/work-and-pensions/Correspondence/Letter-from-Carillion-to-Permanent-Secretary-for-the-Cabinet-Office-regarding-Carillion-13-January-2018.pdf [Accessed 9 February 2021].

27 Carillion plc, (2018) *Compulsory liquidation of Carillion* [online]. 15 January. Available at: https://www.investegate.co.uk/carillion-Plc/rns/compulsory-liquidation-of-carillion/201801150700028399B/ [Accessed 9 February 2021].

28 Financial Reporting Council, (2018) *Investigation into the audit of the financial statements of Carillion plc* [online]. 29 January. Available at: https://www.frc.org.uk/news/january-2018-(1)/investigation-into-the-audit-of-the-financial-stat [Accessed 10 December 2021].

29 Meddings, S. and Treanor J. (2021) Carillion liquidators hit KPMG with £250m claim. *Sunday Times* [online]. November 21. Available at: https://www.thetimes.co.uk/article/carillion-liquidators-hit-kpmg-with-250m-claim-jsnvr377f [Accessed 10 December 2021].

30 Financial Reporting Council, (2018) *Investigation into the preparation and approval of the financial statements of Carillion plc* [online]. 19 March, Available at: https://www.frc.org.uk/news/march-2018/investigation-into-the-preparation-and-approval-of [Accessed 10 December 2021].

31 The Insolvency Service, (2021) *Carillion–directors' disqualification proceedings* [online] Available at: https://www.gov.uk/government/news/carillion-directors-disqualification-proceedings [Accessed 10 December 2021].

5 Risk management and KPIs

Everything that can be counted does not necessarily count; everything that counts cannot necessarily be counted. (Widely attributed to Albert Einstein although the exact provenance is uncertain)

This chapter is focused on executive judgement. It looks at the extent to which directors attempt to identify future risks that may affect a business and put in place mitigating plans to deal with unforeseen developments. The second part of this chapter considers the role of information in decision-making, specifically the extent to which key performance indicators are used to inform judgements about progress and identify priorities for action.

Risk management

Table 5.1 sets out the key questions that we ask boards to consider when reviewing their approach to risk management. As with each of the other chapters in this book, readers who are reviewing a specific business may want to consider the applicability of these questions to that business as they progress through the first part of this chapter. Other readers may prefer to skip forward to the case study at the end of the chapter that describes the unexpected collapse of a major UAE healthcare business, NMC Health Plc (NMC), before beginning this chapter.

Table 5.1: BFQ 5 Risk management: how well does the board assess and manage potential risks to the business?

Benchmarking questions	Commentary (Evidence)	Score
Risk assessment **BFQ 5.1** **Is risk assessment recognised as an explicit responsibility for members of the board?**	Clear identifiable procedures are in place for risk assessment and review by board	
	Systematic briefing and updating for board on progress against key risk performance measures	
	Explicit ownership of key risks established at board level and delegated appropriately	
	Board regularly challenges executive members on the risks that the business faces and supports a culture of 'informed risk-taking'	

https://doi.org/10.1515/9783110689495-008

Table 5.1 (continued)

Practical approaches to risk management BFQ 5.2 To what extent are business risks regularly identified, prioritised and monitored and mitigating actions specified?	Risk assessment occurs on a continuous basis not just as part of a mandated external reporting process such as 10-K submission or preparation of formal strategic report
	Alternative business scenarios are openly discussed and explored systematically in terms of potential impact on the business position as a pro-active rather than defensive process
	Risk assessment includes surveys of customer experience, cyber-security, and supply chain performance
	Risk assessment includes future ESG related issues
	External investor opinions of risk are taken into account in decision-making
	Going concern statements are supplemented by detailed assessment of business viability that extend beyond one year and model alternative commercial scenarios including competitive action
	Long-term business risks are evaluated regularly through a process of stress testing funds flow and cash balances against alternative assumptions about future performance

Risk assessment

BFQ 5.1 Is risk assessment recognised as an explicit responsibility for members of the board?

In 2021, Allianz, a leading international insurance company, asked clients, brokers and industry trade organisations to identify the three main risks to their business. 2,769 respondents from 92 countries replied. The top three business risks for 2021 in order of priority were business interruption (including supply chain), pandemic outbreak and cyber-incidents. Market risks linked to intensified competition, new market entrants and market stagnation or decline were ranked fourth. Other broader risks included changes to legislation and regulation, natural catastrophes, fire or explosion, macroeconomic developments, climate change and political risks and violence.

A similar survey of business leaders and insurance buyers across 10 sectors in the UK and the USA found a similar pattern (Beazley Group, 2021). About 85% of those replying to this survey felt that they were operating in a moderate to high-risk environment. Technology (systems failure) and cybercrime were seen as the most important immediate problems, followed closely by supply chain problems. Respondents were less concerned with political, economic and environmental risks. Priorities are likely to change again significantly following the outbreak of war in Ukraine in 2022. At the time of writing, it is already becoming apparent that major shifts in economic conditions and political relationships are occurring across global markets following this event that are likely to have a long-term impact on patterns of trade between nations, price inflation, and the security of supply chains.

Risk reporting

In the USA and the UK, companies over a certain size are required to publish a review of risks that is updated annually. In September 2014, the FRC provided guidance on risk management for companies that are subject to the UK Corporate Governance Code (all companies with a premium listing of equity shares on the London Stock Exchange). Risk management is viewed as a board responsibility and part of the broader corporate governance process. In this interpretation, the board should drive the process of risk assessment, both directly in main board meetings and also potentially in subcommittees, primarily the audit committee. Effective boards should challenge those with executive responsibility to clarify the assumptions that are being made about different risks, their potential impact and the steps planned to resolve potential problems.

In the USA, directors' legal responsibility to provide full guidance on the position of the business may be one reason for the long and detailed analysis of risks that typically appear in many annual 10-K reports. Virgin Galactic's 10-K statement illustrates how one US company described its situation in its 2019 filing.

Virgin Galactic Holdings Inc – on the edge of space

Virgin Galactic Holdings Inc describes itself as a "vertically-integrated aerospace company pioneering human spaceflight for private individuals and researchers, as well as a manufacturer of advanced air and space vehicles. [. . .] Our goal is to offer our Future Astronauts an unmatched, safe and affordable journey to space without the need for any special prior experience or significant prior training and preparation."

Early sections of the filing describe the company's business model, linked to five main drivers: differentiated technology and capabilities, significant pent-up customer demand, an "iconic brand", limited competition with natural barriers to entry and highly specialised and vertically integrated design and manufacturing facilities. The commercialisation of space had begun and Virgin wanted to be one of the early pioneers.

Understandably perhaps, given the nature of the business, the 10-K filing cited a large number of potential risks including significant financial losses, the uncertainties of pioneering in a market that had yet to be established, future delays to flight testing that could significantly delay commercial launch and safety performance (including accident or catastrophe). An analysis of the company's financial position concluded that there was a risk that the company might not be able to secure additional funding at the right time and under terms that would be acceptable to the company. The filing also pointed to possible problems of securing adequate supplies of the raw materials and components that were needed to meet anticipated manufacturing needs and the increasing international competition that was emerging in the area. Other sections detailed potential risks associated with government regulation and competition for highly skilled personnel, natural disasters and unusual weather conditions.

Consolidated financial statements, reported as part of the same 10-K filing, indicated that whilst revenue had increased from $1.8m in the year ended 31 December 2017 to $3.8m in the year ended 31 December 2019 (largely through customer deposits), net losses had increased from $138m to $211m over the same period. Predictably perhaps, research and development expenditure ($133m) and selling, general and administrative expenses ($82m) were the largest areas of cost in 2019. Cash and cash equivalents increased from $74m as at 31 December 2018 to $480m in December 2019, following the company's transition to listed status and share issue. The report outlined the major demands that were likely to be made on this cash reserve including operational costs and further research and development activity as the company scaled up its activities.

In terms of internal processes, the company acknowledged in the report that it did not have sufficient skilled personnel to handle the process of closing books for the year and reporting results. It also recognised that it did not have adequate levels of information technology to support its financial reporting systems. Both of these areas were identified as areas for improvement and performance indicators were being developed to monitor progress. Virgin Galactic admitted that many uncertainties lay ahead and that it was still in the process of identifying and building a long-run strategy. It also acknowledged that some of its systems were not yet sufficiently well developed to provide information on an ongoing basis on some of the performance indicators that would be needed to guide operations.

Readers might want to compare the analysis of risk in the 2019 10-K report with Virgin Galactic's reports for future years which will have been filed since this book was published. It will be interesting to see how the company's risk assessment changes and why.

In the UK companies are required to produce an analysis of risk as part of their annual strategic report, although the level of detail is typically far less detailed than the risk analyses that appear in 10-K reports. Careful reading of such reports reveals the extent to which risk management is taken seriously. Some companies regularly update their review on a year-to-year basis. They describe risk management structures and the role of the board in reviewing different elements of risk as well as the actions taken to mitigate risks. In other companies, risk reporting is essentially a cut and paste activity with the same lists and the same strategies to handle risk appearing for several years in a row.

Different types of risk

Organisations face a range of different types of risk. Kaplan and Mikes (2012) distinguish between internal risks, strategic risks and unforeseeable risks. Internal risks are best controlled by rules and procedures designed to minimise the chances of business disruption. Most organisations have evolved standard procedures to deal with such risks and can be covered by insurance against many eventualities. Business decisions by contrast have a degree of uncertainty linked to the potential problems of implementing a specific strategy, the reaction of the market and competitive behaviour (strategic risks). Unforeseeable risks or "Black swan" events (Kaplan, Leonard and Mikes, 2020) can disrupt business in a range of different and unexpected ways. Covid-19 has been a classic example of such a black swan event for many companies that were not prepared for its severe and long lasting impact. We have already mentioned the war in Ukraine in 2022. This has been another such event that drew many different countries into a local conflict that had been ongoing for several years and led to massive disruption for many companies in terms of escalating energy costs and interruptions to the supply chain for many strategic components.

In Chapter 2 we discussed how Impossible Foods Inc had decided to take a bet on the growing importance of the plant-based meat market. In the words of its CEO and founder, this would be achieved through "an audacious yet realistic strategy to turn back the clock on climate change and stop the global collapse of biodiversity". At the time of the statement (2020) this may have seemed like an optimistic view. The main challenge to Impossible Foods in the USA since then has not been consumer acceptance. The demand for plant-based meat has grown rapidly and its products are now widely available in mainstream supermarket outlets and on the menus of Burger King and Starbucks. A more substantial challenge has come from other competitors which have entered the market since Impossible Foods original launch (such as Beyond Meat) that have developed their own competitive products (Tepper, 2022).

More generally with the benefit of hindsight many decisions may subsequently seem to have been reckless as new circumstances emerge that seriously challenge the original business model. Members of the board may claim that they were not fully informed about the potential consequences of decisions or more likely that they were aware but felt that potential benefits outweighed any possible negative impacts. An experienced member of the board will challenge the level of risk that may be involved in strategic decisions and any contingency plans that have been put in place to allow for unexpected developments. An informed board may then often decide to move forward with a specific venture, despite potential difficulties with implementation and make subsequent adjustments to plans along the way as new factors emerge. We look at the legal issues associated with the exercise of such executive judgement in Chapter 7.

Practical approaches to risk management

BFQ 5.2 To what extent are business risks regularly identified, prioritised and monitored and mitigating actions specified?

In many small companies the closest that some directors may get to an explicit consideration of risk may be the annual requirement to produce a going concern statement. In such companies risk management is not a formalised process and only one aspect of the owner-manager's role. It is typically a sporadic activity linked to a significant change in business direction such as a move to new premises or a decision to hire new staff. The primary challenge in such businesses may be to get directors to even consider the potential risks that their company faces and think about how they would deal with problems that might arise.

In larger companies the quality of risk assessment is linked to the nature of interaction between members of the board and other executives who may have done the background analysis before presenting their conclusions. We commented more generally on the impact of board effectiveness on decision-making in Chapter 2. Failure to brief the board on the implications of specific decisions may lead to a lack of critical review of specific initiatives. Hall and Davis (2017) observe that if members of the board are not involved in the initial review of business risks, this can lead to members feeling that they do not own the conclusions. In an alternative scenario where directors are involved but are not given sufficient information they may favour a more conservative approach. In either situation, decisions may not benefit from the experience and advice of all members.

One relatively straightforward approach to explore risk is to invite different people in the company to identify a list of potential future events that might have an impact on the business. In small businesses, everyone might be invited to contribute. In larger businesses, different areas might be involved to generate a greater range of opinions. The process could be led by members of the board or facilitated by an external advisor. This is an area where an independent board member who is likely to be more distant from day-to-day decision-making can make a significant contribution provided that they are involved at an early stage in the process. Once an initial list of potential risks is established, participants are then asked to evaluate each risk in terms of potential impact on the business and likelihood of occurrence. The final stage is then to discuss different scenarios for dealing with priority areas and allocate responsibilities to individuals or areas of the business to develop strategies to miti-gate such risks if they arise.

This process can also involve the use of expert opinion. Back in the 1980s, one of the writers spent some time on future planning for companies involved in the offshore oil industry which was developing rapidly at the time off the northern coastline of Scotland. As part of this process, he and a colleague conducted a Del-phi study of expert opinion of likely technological change in the sector (Parkinson and Saren, 1981). Leading experts in universities and businesses around the world in areas related to offshore construction, inspection and maintenance were recruited as participants. These experts were asked to produce a list of major technical devel-opments likely to disrupt the market, the likelihood of such events happening, their impact on existing operations and the date when this might happen. The findings were used by a range of companies in the sector to evaluate their current competen-ces and prioritise areas for development.

A third approach involves creating a dynamic model of key financial parameters to evaluate the impact of different potential situations on financial performance. In its simplest form, this could amount to asking what would happen to cash flow if one or more key customers decided to move their business away from the company or entered formal administration procedures. In its more sophisticated form this can involve build-ing a financial model that could be used to explore a range of different future assump-tions about the business. We looked at an example of this approach in Next Plc in the last chapter.

Finally, a cautionary note: risk management is not always seen in a positive light. In 2011, the ICAEW compared the approach to risk reporting taken by compa-nies in the USA, Canada, Germany, Italy and the UK. The report was published in the immediate aftermath of the financial crisis of 2008 against a background of growing concern about the quality of risk reporting of many public companies, par-ticularly in the banking sector.

The analysis described how different regulatory bodies had attempted to improve the process from the 1980s onwards. The authors found that increased reporting re-quirements did not seem to have improved the quality of risk management. The au-thors commented "the effectiveness of a firm's risk management depends on the quality of its managers, and this is something that position statements and disclosure of internal structures and procedures are unlikely to reveal". This reflects a more gen-eral scepticism of the value of risk management or enterprise risk management as an exercise that adds little or no value to a business (Kay, 2011 and Power, 2009).

Risk management can be enhanced in several ways. These include integrating risk assessment into ongoing business operations rather than treating it as a one-off activity that is done to meet external statutory obligations. It is also important to make sure that there is an open and frank discussion about alternative scenarios that could affect the business. This discussion could be extended to include external investor perceptions. Risks can only be effectively monitored when there are key indicators to provide an early warning of emerging problems.

Rolls-Royce Holdings plc – linking risk management to business operations

Rolls-Royce Holdings plc described its risk management system in its strategic report to shareholders in 2019. The approach reflected the size and complexity of a major international company with a reported revenue of £16.6bn in 2018–2019, manufacturing activities spread across four major divisions (civil aerospace, power systems, defence and aero-engine design, manufacture and maintenance) and operating in 50 countries with over 51,000 employees.

Plans announced to offset potential risks included sustaining investment in adequate capacity, modern equipment and facilities, developing dual sources of supply and researching alternative materials as well as promoting and developing resilience in external supply partners. They also included providing finance in partnership with banks to enable suppliers to benefit from the company's own credit rating. This was designed to enable suppliers to access funds at low interest rates. Other mitigating measures included "building a resilient culture through flexible and collaborative working" and "developing, maintaining and regular focusing on business continuity in crisis management plans to prepare our people to respond quickly and confidently to any business disruption". The business also recognised the importance of "sharing lessons learned or identified through exercises or incidents" as well as "scanning the horizon to provide awareness of emerging risks and potential incidents".

Detailed plans to deal with risk may not be sufficient when a combination of circumstances arise that put a business into an extreme position. The company moved from private ownership into state ownership in 1971 due to major problems with one of its most important products at the time, the RB211 jet engine. In 1987, it returned to the private sector. Its business has always been subject to fluctuations in demand linked to changing patterns of international travel, economic downturn and recovery as well as the impact of international conflicts on the demand for military aviation products and technology. Technological problems have continued to affect confidence in the company and its products over its history. In November 2019, the board indicated that incidents of turbine blade cracking in its Trent 1000 engine would ultimately cost the business around £2.4bn between 2017 and 2023. Prior to the arrival of Covid-19 the company had already begun a programme of restructuring over a three-year period, involving the closure of major manufacturing facilities, workforce reductions and product and service elimination.

The collapse of the air transportation business in 2020 caused by the Coronavirus pandemic had a major negative effect on revenues and the assumptions in the previous year's plan since the company's revenues were linked to the number of hours flown by aircraft fitted with its engines. In May 2020, the company announced a further major restructuring involving 9,000 job losses and was forced to abandon targets for profit, cash and aircraft deliveries.

Effective risk management systems can make a major contribution to business continuity. However, they are unlikely to completely shelter any business from future uncertainties, even one that is as apparently as well organised as Rolls-Royce Holdings plc.

Key performance indicators (KPIs)

Table 5.2: BFQ 6 Performance indicators: how effectively does the board monitor key performance dimensions?

Benchmarking Questions	Commentary (Evidence)	Score
Resilience indicators **BFQ 6.1** **Is there an effective internal system that provides up-to-date information for the board on performance against financial and strategic objectives?**	Accounting basics are in place, including cash flow measurement and sales and cost analyses that are up-to-date and regularly reviewed in a systematic way There is a competence at board level in the specification and interpretation of financial performance measures including key ratios that indicate financial resilience such as current ratio, acid test ratio or operating cash ratio Willingness to look beyond financial indicators to analyse broader strategic problems and systematic use of KPIs that provide an early warning of potential problems – *see the more detailed discussion in table 5.3* Regular review and updates to the board on progress on areas of concern – honesty in situation review	
Performance reporting **BFQ 6.2** **Do published KPIs meet external expectations?**	How far has the business used feedback from external parties to determine what to include in its reported KPIs? Do reported KPIs include performance drivers as well as performance outcomes? How far do reported actions address concerns raised by adverse trends in KPIs? Is there a more comprehensive set of KPIs which the business uses internally to manage its activities that goes beyond those declared in reports for external use? How seriously does the board take the whole process of KPI reporting and seek to compare itself with best practice?	

Resilience indicators

BFQ 6.1 Is there an effective system that provides up-to-date information for the board on performance against financial and strategic objectives?

Financial indicators

As we have already noted, managers in many small and medium-sized companies may not put in place even the most basic controls to monitor financial performance. The importance of such measures is described graphically in the following comments made by a major supplier of accounting software for small businesses (Trimm, 2013):

> Get the accounting basics right from the start, [. . .] Cash flow is king . . . Set yourself targets and then stick to them. Setting realistic and measurable goals to aim for is an essential aspect of setting up a successful business. Without measurable goals, a business can end up sitting still or worse, spiraling out of control. Understand your KPIs–that's key performance indicators–and how you can measure them. Set yourself targets and budgets and then track them to identify improvements or declines over time. Always make sure you work within your limits and only set targets that you can realistically achieve [. . .] Understand your (profitable) customers [. . .] Get organised & KEEP organized–If these areas are left unattended, they can leave your business exposed to risks.

Whilst it may be easy to understand why small businesses may have problems in monitoring performance against financial targets, this problem may also exist in even the largest of businesses due to a range of factors including the application of different accounting procedures, the complexity of such businesses or in some cases the existence of business fraud where such information has been deliberately concealed or disguised.

In Chapter 4, we discussed the preparation of going concern statements as part of the annual reporting process. Readers may recall the advice given to auditors on the potential signs of emerging financial problems. Whilst this advice was originally written for external auditors, this is also a useful checklist for members of the board. Whilst they individually may not have a detailed understanding of specific areas, they might reasonably assume that someone in the business (starting with the CFO) should be able to address any questions they have on each of these areas.

Financial KPIs are the first reference point in any assessment of resilience. Specific indicators include the current ratio (current assets/current liabilities), the cash ratio (cash and cash equivalents/current liabilities) and the operating cash ratio (operating cash flow/current liabilities). Other useful indicators related to indebtedness include the debt ratio (total debt/total assets), the debt to equity ratio (total debt/equity) and interest coverage ratio (EBIT/financing costs). Adverse trends in any of these key ratios over time can provide a tangible indication of emerging business problems, particularly when such ratios are compared with industry norms. Each of these ratios can be readily calculated by external observers from statutory reports that are published on a regular basis, albeit frequently considerably after the period to which they relate. It might be assumed that the board is regularly updated on these and other financial performance indicators and understands the implications of adverse trends. In reality, this may not be the case. We have already commented on the lack of financial skills of many directors at various points in this book.

Performance drivers

The extent to which board members play a continuing role in the development and evaluation of business plans is a key governance issue. We discussed this in detail in Chapter 3. Members of a board without appropriate knowledge or experience in a related sector may not identify emerging problems that threaten long-term viability. Despite potential reservations about the way forward, they may also be reluctant to challenge the executive team on broader strategic issues if the business's underlying performance on key financial indicators continues to look positive. Having experienced this situation in a range of different circumstances, it has often seemed to one of the authors that financial measures (typically termed lag indicators) are given more credibility as measure of business resilience than evidence from other non-financial indicators (performance drivers).

Such performance drivers can be split into three broad categories: indicators that measure the quality of relationships with customers (marketing competences); indicators of operational capability, including supply chain management and overall administrative efficiency; and indicators related to the quality of strategic decision-making itself.

Marketing competence is a fundamental business driver. The relationships that are developed with customers through effective management of the marketing mix (product and service strategies, pricing, promotional strategies and distribution) reinforce the company's overall position and build future resilience. Marketing effectiveness can be measured in a wide range of different ways from quantitative information on sales volumes and profitability analysed by market segment, to measures of brand awareness and preferences. Some of the companies included in this book used net promoter scores to measure customer experience. Others used product return rates. Enhancements in artificial intelligence (AI) can now also be used to create a wide range of different measures of customer activity and preferences and monitor consumer behaviour on a continuous basis, combining information about a specific customer's online search, and the use of social media and buying habits.

Many board members may lack the necessary experience or competence to analyse the range of information that is now potentially available and might need help to interpret such information effectively. This was one of the primary criticisms aimed at Arcadia with many observers blaming the ultimate decline of the business on its failure to come to terms with online marketing and losing touch with its (predominantly younger) customers.

Measures of operational capability include supply chain costs and on-time availability and security, average levels of inventory and customer service times. Historically, businesses have sought to make each of these areas as efficient as possible, leading to integrated systems with low flexibility. Business may go through successive waves of rationalisation and business restructuring in attempts to enhance such efficiencies and restore resilience as all of our case studies demonstrate. Increasingly however, uncertain environments are now putting many businesses under pressure to move in the opposite direction and build in redundant capacity and flexibility to avoid business disruption.

The quality of strategic decision-making is much more difficult to assess. Some of the most useful indicators are more general questions. For example: What assumptions are we making about market size and growth rate? How much of our business comes from new products/services that we did not sell last year/three years ago/before then? How profitable are specific market segments? Do some products or services make more money in specific markets than others? How many products/services have we eliminated in the last year/three years/over a longer time frame? Most importantly perhaps, do we have systems in place to monitor how effective our decisions have been and make the best choices about the future direction of the business?

Identifying and scoring KPIs

Table 5.3 sets out all four areas (financial, marketing, operational and strategic), with suggested performance indicators and a brief commentary that describes some of the key problems that might be emerging in each area.

Readers who are reviewing a specific business may want to use the commentary column in Table 5.3 to record their own observations about each indicator.

Key questions to consider might include:

Is this specific indicator used to measure performance?

Who is responsible in the company for performance against the indicator?

How do we collect the information that is needed to measure performance?

How frequently do we do this? Who is responsible for follow-up actions?

Most importantly, is our performance in each area improving, staying roughly the same or deteriorating and are there significant emerging problems that need our attention?

Strategic shift

Improvements in one or more of the areas identified in Table 5.3 may indicate that adjustments to current plans have addressed a specific problem. When some or all of these indicators begin to show a significant and apparently irreversible deterioration, more direct action is needed (a strategic shift). We pick up this discussion in the next chapter.

BFQ 6.2 Do published KPIs meet external expectations?

The publication of KPIs is a mandatory part of the strategic report that must be produced by companies over a certain size in the UK (Companies Act 2006). Similar reporting requirements exist in a number of other countries with variations in the level of detail that is mandated by different legislations. This is an externally oriented process. Reports are unlikely to reflect the level of detail in the information that is used by those running the business. Nevertheless, it may well be the only information that is available to an external observer who is seeking to understand the potential viability of a business. Compliance with the requirement is variable. Inspection of the published report and accounts of many companies reveals considerable variety in the level and depth of KPI reporting. Some published reports contain detailed descriptions of KPIs used to run the business. Others contain a limited amount of information that is frequently not updated from year to year to reflect changing circumstances.

In 2014, KPMG conducted a survey of business reporting in companies in the UK, Australia, Canada, Denmark, France, Japan, Norway, South Africa, Sweden and the USA (90 companies in total) over a five-year period. The survey was based on annual reports (or the 10-K filing in the USA). One of the critical areas highlighted by the survey was the failure of many companies to present performance measures for the key drivers of shareholder value (lead indicators). Whilst operational efficiency (66% of companies), customer focus (56%), supply chain (42%) and brand and reputation (42%) were identified as key performance drivers, the percentage of companies providing a related operating measurement for each area was much smaller (21%, 7%, 8% and 2%, respectively). Companies had identified key performance drivers but were unwilling or unable to declare how well they were performing in each area. A second criticism was that too many companies relied on financial statements and outcome measures (lag indicators) at the expense of broader operating measures that might provide a better indication of the drivers of business value such as customer acquisition rates or product quality measures. The report was also critical of risk

Table 5.3: Resilience scorecard.

Area of concern	Indicators	Commentary
Financial standing	EBITDA Earnings per share ROCE Current ratio Cash ratio Operating cash ratio Debt ratio Interest coverage ratio Receivables/use of supply chain finance	Emerging financial problems are likely to be indicated by a deterioration on one or more of the key financial indicators Other more general indicators can include – The departure of key members of the finance team – Delays in the scheduled submission of accounts – Problems signing off going concern statements
Marketing competence	Sales volume and profitability analysed by market segment Product return rates Pricing surveys Brand awareness and preferences Number and type of service complaints Customer satisfaction surveys including net promoter score	Problems with marketing can be indicated by a range of different factors including: – Poor product/service quality and lack of continuous product/service improvement initiatives – Lack of price competitiveness in product/service markets that are increasingly commodities – Lack of sustained effective promotional support for brands (corporate and product/service related) – Poor levels of customer service and after sales support – Poor distribution cover and availability in emerging important distribution channels
Operational capability	Trends in supply chain costs and on-time availability and security Average inventory value Average customer service times. Unit supply costs Average production cycle times Indirect overheads Measures of employee engagement	Specific areas where poor operational capability can ultimately lead to higher costs and reduced effectiveness include: – Inflexible and inefficient production and supply systems that are less competitive than those of other major suppliers – Inefficient supply chain models based on assumptions about business continuity leading to higher costs/decreasing predictability and insecurity of supply – Changes to organisational structures that duplicate rather than reduce different organisational functions and lead to confusion about responsibilities and focus

Table 5.3 (continued)

Strategic choices	Total market size and growth rate/decline	Indicators of poor strategic planning can include:
	% of total sales from new products or services	– Lack of clarity in objectives – Costing models that do not measure the specific costs of staying in markets that are no longer large enough to sustain a profitable business
	Comparative margins for different product market combinations	– Emotional commitment to the 'status quo' of existing product/market combinations and lack of new product/service development
	Volume/value of new product development or market development activity	– Absence of any explicit attempts to eliminate specific products/services or divest marginal areas of the business
	Volume/value of product/service elimination	

reporting, describing the approach of many companies as focused on statements of "high-level mitigating actions" that could apply to any business.

Companies approach KPI reporting in a range of different ways. This is reflected in the performance indicators reported by the companies that are featured in this book. These included:

Flybe Group plc – Annual Report and Accounts 2017/18
Revenue per seat, cost per seat (including fuel), cost per seat (excluding fuel), on-time performance.

Taveta Investments Ltd (Arcadia Group Ltd) – Strategic Report September 2018
Best and least performing stores/product lines, margins, mark downs, profitability of different channels, EBITDA (earnings before interest, taxes, depreciation and amortization), cash flow, return on capital invested in store openings/refits, and like for like sales. EBITDA was identified as the Group's main KPI.

Carillion plc – Annual Report and Accounts 2016
Total revenue growth, underlying operating margin, underlying earnings per share, cash conversion, work won and secured and probable orders, book to bill ratio (work won as % of work executed and booked as revenue), net debt to EBITDA, net promoter score (measure of customer satisfaction), employee engagement score, lost time incident frequency rate, gender balance, contribution to profit from sustainability, percentage of employees volunteering, reduction in carbon footprint.

NMC Health Plc – Annual Report and Accounts 2018
Group Revenue, EBITDA, EBITDA margin (%), net profit, ROCE (return on capital employed). Patient numbers, licensed beds, operational beds, number of doctors.

Thomas Cook Group plc – Report and Accounts 2018
Underlying EBITDA and operating profit and margin, unlevered free cash flow, basic earning per share and underlying earnings per share and net debt. Employee satisfaction and commitment, customer satisfaction, how customers booked their holidays (online or through a retail outlet).

Analysis of investor requirements published in 2018 by the Financial Reporting Council (the Lab) indicated that investors welcomed the use of such KPIs in reporting and used these metrics for a range of purposes, including "analysis and valuation [...], assessing management's credibility, assessing long-term value and stewardship, and forecasting trends to build a picture about management and the company's performance, position and prospects" (Financial Reporting Council, 2018-c). In a subsequent report, the Lab commented:

Investors not only want to understand how a company monitors, manages and views its own performance, but may also use the metrics for a range of other purposes, including to: assess a company's use of capital or its capacity to add value; value a company; gain a greater understanding of a company's business model, strategy and risks; understand whether (and how) management are incentivised to drive the strategy of the company; make a forecast or assessment of future performance; understand a company's position within a market more fully; or make an assessment of management credibility. (Financial Reporting Council, 2018-d)

Published information may also provide the first indication to the external observer that problems are emerging. When a company announces the renegotiation or extension of loans, asset sale or attempts to issue new equity, these decisions may be interpreted as defensive processes designed to address funding problems. Borrowing agreements may become more expensive to renew without new security over assets. New funding may become difficult to secure from current shareholders or the bond market as investor confidence falls and the cost of issuing new fixed-term securities rises. The use of supply chain finance where companies offer early repayment of invoices to suppliers has been a long-standing business practice, which if used effectively can benefit both suppliers and their customers. The extent to which it is used as a form of off-balance sheet financing can create significant problems where the extent of liabilities is disguised and potentially increasing. Changes in each of these areas over time in a company's history may indicate emerging problems.

NMC Health Plc
Typically, companies do not suddenly collapse from a position of apparent strength to imminent closure. Usually the signs of any potential decline are clear well in advance and are flagged up as areas of concern long before there is a significant and immediate threat to business continuity. NMC is a significant exception. In less than five months between November 2019 and April 2020, NMC went from being one of the largest and apparently most successful LSE quoted Emirati companies to entry into administration. This case study tracks NMC's collapse and the attempts to revive a company that was a crucial part of the UAE healthcare system at a time when the Covid-19 pandemic was placing major strains on healthcare provision around the world.

As we suggested in previous chapters, you may want to look back at the questions that we ask in Tables 5.1 and 5.2 as you review the case.

Some of the areas that you might want to focus on in the case could include:

- The use of financial performance indicators by the external investment analyst who first identified potential problems with NMC's performance
- The actions of the board as it attempted to come to terms with the problems that the business faced
- The role of independent directors in monitoring and assessing performance
- The role of administrators following the entry of the company into administration.

Case study: NMC Health Plc

Overview

NMC Health Plc (NMC) was founded in 1975 and was amongst the first companies in the UAE to provide private healthcare services when the UAE government made healthcare services available to all residents.[1] The business began as a pharmacy, later extending to a clinic and in 1981 began operating a distribution business. The company grew quickly buoyed by a growth in the demand for healthcare services at a time of rapid economic development in the UAE. In April 2012 the company successfully completed an IPO on the London Stock Exchange, raising £117m from its flotation and was shortlisted for the Financial Times New Company of the Year Award in February 2013.

By 2018 NMC had grown to become one of the primary healthcare providers in the UAE and throughout other gulf states.[2] It had also expanded its overseas activities to include Europe and the USA. Its healthcare division operated 189 different facilities across 19 countries with 2,186 beds providing a wide range of different outpatient and inpatient services. Over 80% of its patients were covered by mandatory insurance in the UAE which had provided a key source of revenue that was forecast to grow strongly. A new joint venture agreement in Saudi Arabia was regarded as a key initiative to grow NMC's position in an important growing market. The product distribution and wholesale division offered clients more than 115,000 products across two segments Pharma and non-Pharma, providing clients with a wide range of services including sales, marketing, distribution and supply chain management. NMC also held stocks on behalf of customers as part of the distribution chain. This created a significant requirement for funding for working capital, a problem that was formally recognised by the business.

The annual report for 2018 presented a confident outlook. Revenue for financial year 2018 was $2057.3m, up 28% on financial year 2017, EBITDA was $487m, up 37.9% on financial year 2017 and earnings per share had increased by 28.5%. The company's financial report described a "healthy cash flow including improvement in the Group's working capital position through strong collections to reduce days' sales outstanding to 96", and an outlook for 2019 of "+22–24% year on year revenue growth and +18–20% year on year EBITDA growth". An interim report presented on 30 November also set out a confident position.[3] Profits for the first half of 2019 were shown as $358m and the directors indicated that the outlook was positive saying: "the Group has considerable financial resources including bank facilities. As a consequence, the directors believe that the Group is well placed to manage its business risks successfully. The directors expect that the Group has adequate resources to continue in operational existence for the foreseeable future. Thus they continue to adopt the going concern basis in preparing the financial statements."

https://doi.org/10.1515/9783110689495-009

On 17 December NMC's confident presentation was challenged by an external analyst's report that ultimately contributed to the company entering administration four months later on 9 April 2020. Subsequent accusations of fraud at a senior level and allegations of financial irregularities including unauthorised off-balance sheet financing raised severe doubts about governance mechanisms and identified an apparent failure of external auditors to recognise and address critical performance indicators.

This case study looks at the events that followed the publication of the initial critical report, and during the following months leading to the ultimate appointment of an administrator. It also looks at the process of restructuring that was still ongoing at the time when this book went to publication.

Who made the call?

On 17 December 2019 Muddy Waters LLC, an investment analyst, produced a report on NMC that was highly critical of the company's position.[4] The report cited "serious doubts about the company's financial statements, including its asset values, cash balance, reported profits and reported debt levels". These doubts included investment in assets "at costs we find too high to be plausible" and margins that appeared to be "too good to be true relative to UAE-focused publicly traded comps[sic]". The report accused the company of balance sheet manipulation to understate its debt, including reverse factoring used to convert NMC payables into debt. The report was also very critical of governance arrangements stating "each of these problems would be less likely to exist if NMC had sufficient governance. In our view, it falls well short. We do not see the independent board members as being truly independent. The company's relationship with its auditor, Ernst & Young raises flags. Executive compensation has nearly tripled in two years to $18.7m a year and insiders have monetised material amounts of stock. We are unsure how deep the rot at NMC goes, but we do not believe that its insiders or financials can be trusted."

NMC issued a detailed rebuttal on 19 December 2019 in which it described the report's conclusions as false and misleading and set out what it described as "factual inaccuracies".[5] The rebuttal cited regular rotation of its audit partner and disclosure of all share transactions made by board members, key shareholders and other key personnel. It referred to a future intention "to have a Committee providing independent oversight of related party transactions across the Group".

Supply-chain management, specifically the use of supply chain financing was identified as a particular issue in the report. To this point, in the rebuttal NMC stated:

> The Group has never given an impression to investors or other stakeholders that our suppliers have not used, or are not using, supply chain financing. These facilities remain commercial

matters for these suppliers and only have recourse to them. NMC has been publicly clear on that position for several years and the Group accounts for its obligations to such suppliers as trade payables [. . .].

Under these types of supply chain finance programs suppliers accept discounted payments for their invoices in return for receiving immediate payment from the financer, who then collects the full amount of the invoice from the purchaser (NMC in this case) at the original invoice payment date. Clearly for the purchaser (NMC) these payments relate to trade payables, with no actual borrowing by NMC from the financer to pay suppliers early or providing direct credit support for the suppliers.

On 20 December 2019 the Financial Times published a commentary on the report stating that it had had an immediate impact on the company's share price, taking an estimated £2.3bn off its market value.[6] NMC reacted to this report on the same day describing the Financial Times article as part of a "long running bear attack on NMC Health". In its statement NMC said:

> The company confirms that this article is based on false information and finds speculation regarding a transaction that didn't occur to be completely unproductive. [. . .] NMC considers this to be the latest in a long line of malicious attempts by certain parties to influence commentary around the Company in a negative fashion to damage its credibility and negatively impact its share price via methods which are at times nefarious, unethical and illegal.[7]

Three days later it appeared that NMC had recognised the need for a more detailed investigation that would satisfy critics when the company announced that it would conduct an independent review to be overseen by a committee consisting of a majority of the independent non-executive directors of the company.[8] This review was extended on 17 January 2020 when NMC announced that it had appointed a former FBI director to compile a report regarding allegations raised in the Muddy Waters report.[9]

On 10 February 2020 NMC announced that the company had been informed by its joint non-executive chairman that he and his advisers were carrying out "a legal review in order to verify the total interests of [the non-executive chair], his associated family members and his associated family holding companies in the Ordinary Shares of the Company and that this review also had implications for the holdings and interests of [two other major shareholders]".[10] The company stated that this announcement suggested that "the holdings and interests of [these three] have been incorrectly reported historically to the Company and the market". The announcement noted the board's concern about the extent to which shares owned by each major shareholder had been pledged or otherwise used a security "in any form of financial instrument or are subject to other arrangements under which third parties (eg banks, financial institutions etc.) have the ability to sell those shares without prior approval from the respective shareholder".

Four days later on 14 February 2020, the executive vice chairman retired from his role with immediate effect.[11] Three more directors resigned on 16 February 2020.

An announcement by NMC confirmed that one director would continue as the sole non-executive chairman of the Company.[12]

On 26 February 2020, the company provided an update on the independent review of allegations made by Muddy Waters.[13] The announcement detailed supply chain financing arrangements that had been entered into by the company stating:

> [These . . .] are understood to have been used by entities controlled by [the Related Parties]. Under these arrangements, supplies to companies owned by the Related Parties were paid by certain credit facility providers and, while those companies are responsible for settling the amounts payable to the credit facility providers, the contractual obligation rests with NMC, which has also provided a guarantee in event of non payment or default.

The announcement also described how these arrangements had been in place since early-2018, and stated that the current draw-down as of 31 December was estimated to be approximately $335m. These arrangements, the announcement stated were not disclosed to, or approved by the Board, and were not disclosed in related party transactions in accordance with Listing Rules. They were also not reflected on the company's balance sheet, nor reported in the company's financial statements for financial year ended 31 December 2018. The facilities would no longer be made available for further supplier financing. The report also identified "potential discrepancies and inconsistencies in the Company's bank statements and ledger entries". Following this initial review, the board announced that one member of the treasury team had been suspended, and the CEO had been removed from his position. The company's chief finance officer was granted extended sick leave.

On the following day, a report in the Financial Times described how public filings in the UAE showed that NMC had pledged future credit card payments from customers (receivables) to secure bank funding, a potential signal that the company had reached the limit of more conventional credit lines.[14] The company informed investors that the FCA had agreed to its request for a temporary suspension of its shares "to ensure the smooth operation of the market".[15]

Four days later on 2 March NMC announced that it had begun to address what it described as a process of "immediate stabilization".[16] It stated: "Moelis & Company ('Moelis'), PwC and Allen & Overy have been appointed as independent financial adviser, operational adviser and legal adviser respectively with immediate effect. Moelis will support and advise on NMC's discussions with its lenders, while PwC will assist on liquidity management and operational measures."

NMC described the appointments as necessary as part of a process of

> . . .safeguarding operational liquidity to continue funding existing operations throughout its various subsidiaries. In this context, NMC is asking for continued support and an informal standstill in relation to existing facilities from its lenders to achieve an immediate stabilisation of the group's financing. The informal standstill includes a request to lenders not to exercise any rights and remedies that may arise from any current or future defaults under the group's finance documentation.

Establishing the scale of the crisis

By 10 March 2020, the company's advisors had produced an update on the company's debt position which was estimated at around $5bn compared with the $2.1bn that had been reported on 30 June. $2.7bn in facilities had previously not been disclosed to or approved by the board. The company reported that it was continuing to work with its advisers to understand the exact nature and quantum of the undisclosed facilities and that some proceeds may have been utilised for non-Group purposes.[17] On 12 March the independent advisors confirmed that they had found evidence of suspected fraudulent behaviour in relation to some of NMC's previous financial activities.[18]

On 24 March 2020 NMC announced that the board had received another update advising that the Group's debt position was estimated to be around $6.6bn, including a $360m convertible bond and $400m sukuk. The Group's bilateral and syndicated debt obligations comprised over 75 debt facilities from over 80 financial institutions. Work on verifying the outstanding debt obligations was continuing. It was also announced that the board had been informed of the presence of cheques (written by Group companies), which may have been used as security for financing arrangements for the benefit of third parties. A preliminary view was that the amount of these cheques totalled approximately $50m. The existence of these cheques had only recently been brought to the attention of the board, and urgent investigation was ongoing.

The interim CEO also announced the appointment of a chief restructuring officer with effect from 22 March 2020 and the resignation of the CFO with immediate effect.[19] The effect of the growing crisis was reflected in the attrition rate of the senior team. This resignation meant that since the crisis began five main board directors had left the original board. None of the executive directors named in the annual report and accounts filed on 9 July 2019 remained on the board from March 2020 onwards. On 26 March the company announced that the non-executive chairman who had been in position since prior to the company's IPO in 2012 had left the board and ceased to be a director of the company with immediate effect, citing a period of ill health that had prevented him from participating in board activities.[20] A new executive chairman based in the UAE was announced with immediate effect. His comment on being confirmed in the post set out his perception of the challenges that lay ahead. He said:

> I recognise the challenges faced by NMC at the moment, but also see the underlying value of a business with its place at the heart of the infrastructure of the GCC. NMC has some outstanding assets and people working to provide the highest standards of care. My role will be to work with them and to focus on the governance of the business to enable it to deliver value to its stakeholders.

On 2 April 2020 Abu Dhabi Commercial Bank (ADCB), one of NMC's major creditors, filed an application for the appointment of administrators in respect of the company under paragraph 12(1)(c) of Schedule B1 to the Insolvency Act 1986. ADCB said that it was working with other lenders and that if appointed, the administrators would take immediate control and launch an investigation into suspected irregular activities and financial representations. The company announced that a hearing had been scheduled for 9 April 2020. It said that:

> The Board is in discussions with ADCB and other creditors to address creditors' concerns; to have the application withdrawn; and to avoid the appointment of administrators, which it does not believe would be in the interests of stakeholders as a whole. The resolution is likely to involve material changes to corporate governance of the Group and the composition of the Board itself.

Appointment of administrators

By 8 April 2020 the board had concluded that it would not be able to reach any agreement with its creditors outside of formal administration proceedings and announced that it had written to the court to that effect expecting the company to be placed into administration in due course.[21] NMC was placed into administration by order of the High Court of England and Wales following ADCB's application and Alvarez & Marsal (A&M) were appointed as administrators on 9 April 2020. Judge Sebastian Prentis in granting the application said that he was satisfied that NMC was cash-flow insolvent, and that something had gone very wrong with the management and oversight of the company.[22]

Commenting on the appointment Alvarez and Marsal said:

> NMC Health PLC is the holding company of the largest private healthcare Group in the UAE. The Administrators' primary objective is to ensure the continuity of patient care, stability for staff and suppliers, and immediate financial security for NMC PLC's operating companies. The operating entities are unaffected by the Administrators' appointment. NMC's hospitals, medical centres, care facilities and other operations in the Group will continue to operate, under existing management, with patients continuing to be treated as they are currently.[23]

On 14 April the administrators announced that they had removed all of the previous directors from the board and appointed four new non-executive directors "with broad international restructuring experience". Only two members of the senior management team were left in post, the interim CEO and chief operating officer, and the group company secretary.

Governance in disarray

On 15 April 2020 ADCB confirmed that it had initiated criminal legal proceedings "against a number of individuals in relation to NMC Health Group".[24] A statement by [the founder] reported in the Financial Times on 29 April 2020 blamed a small group of current and former executives for what he alleged was a "serious fraud" at NMC. According to the report, he said that he was pursuing legal action against those who had committed the alleged fraud and that the preliminary findings of his own investigations had found the use of fraudulent accounts and powers of attorney in his name of which he had no knowledge. He is also reported to have said that the alleged fraud and misconduct at NMC had shocked him "as much as anyone else".[25]

On 2 December 2020 the UK High Court held a private court hearing to consider an application by ADCB for an urgent worldwide freezing order and related disclosure order against six former principal owners and officers of NMC.[26] The judgment (para. 6) set out the bank's claim that it was seeking compensation for losses caused by fraudulent misrepresentations and conspiracy stating:

> It is said that the defendants colluded in a scheme by which false accounts were created to give a misleading impression as to, first, their accuracy and reliability and, second, the strength and robustness of NMC Plc's financial performance. The accounts were adopted as the basis for related certificates and/or financial models that were provided to the Bank to induce them, it is said, to enter into or renew six credit arrangements by which the Bank committed approximately US$1.2 billion to entities in the NMC Group ("the Core Facilities").

Paragraph 7 of the judgment stated that "It is said that a fraud on this scale will have entailed very close control over internal management and accounting information." The judgment (para. 7) also commented on the apparent use of two sets of inconsistent financial accounts. It referred to the roles of the defendants stating that "It is said by reason of the roles played and control exerted by each defendant over the operation of NMC Plc…that each of the defendants was party to this dishonest scheme which it is said operated for their mutual benefit."

The judgment discusses witness statements that demonstrated the potential extent of involvement across NMC in the potential fraud (para. 10). The judgment quoted one witness as follows:

> "The documentary evidence uncovered by the forensic team shows that the fraud was perpetrated against the applicants and other companies in the NMC Group by the principal shareholders" that is D1 to D3 "their vehicle companies and other family business," that is D4 "certain members of senior management of NMC Group including the former CFO team and various other institutions which conspired in the wrongdoing."

Paragraph 18 describes a key moment in the initial investigation into potential fraud when a witness reported that a series of documents represented as bank account balances were uploaded for review by the independent investigators in February 2020 by employees in the NMC Group Treasury Department. The employees were said to have accidentally uploaded two versions of the same bank statement, the true copy and a copy which they had fabricated. They were also said to have uploaded copies with typing errors in fields recording cash entries that should have been automatically populated by the finance system "which indicated that the statements had been tampered with".

Evidence given to the court made specific claims of different types of fraud that appear to have been perpetrated (para. 24). These included keeping two sets of financial accounts, theft of money from bank accounts, the procurement of loans from financial institutions that were not reported in NMC Group's financial accounts, many of which were regularly refinanced, and misappropriation of some of the proceeds of these loans. These were described in the evidence statement as part of a broader pattern of representations to ADCB designed to confirm to the bank the "Group's robust financial health and growth" (para. 26).

Making his judgment on the application Mr Justice Bryan noted that "given the nature of the fraud and its underlying sophistication, the financial manipulation and concealment, that the order would be just and convenient and it is appropriate for this court to make a worldwide freezing order" (para. 107). Justice Bryan noted that the first defendant had left for India and had been there since February 2020, also noting that he had said that he went there to visit an ailing relative, and despite attempting to do so he has not been allowed to return to the UAE to clear his name (para. 34). He also noted that the defendant had said that he was the victim of the actions of a number of subordinates, including three of those who had been included in the court proceedings, and that he had stated that he has made a written criminal complaint to a police station in Bangalore and also in a letter to the UAE Attorney General asking for an investigation. Justice Bryan also noted his (defendant's) claim in the Abu Dhabi local court that guarantees that were provided to the bank in relation to him were forged. Justice Bryan also noted evidence that around 24 February multiple employees in the NMC Treasury Department and the joint deputy CFOs suddenly without notice to the Group, boarded flights to India whilst the CFO had already left the country in January (para. 20).

NMC in administration

On 27 April 2020 the company requested that its ordinary shares be cancelled from listing on the London Stock Exchange to reduce costs and complexity. The Joint Administrators' initial review indicated that it would not be possible to rescue the company as a going concern (para. 3(1) (a) of the Insolvency Act) given the company's resources and level of guarantees that would be necessary, and therefore determined that the purpose of the administration would be to achieve a better result for the company's creditors as a whole than would be likely if the company were to be wound up (para. 3 (1) (b) of the Insolvency Act).[27]

On 31 July 2020 A&M presented the findings of the first stage of its work setting out its view of market prospects and a plan for the next three years covering core business activities (UAE and Oman) and International (non-core) options.[28] The plan outlined progress on financial restructuring and set out options for funding the process. Disposal of the company's trading business (importing, selling and distributing approximately 500 different brands across five business lines including pharmaceuticals, medical equipment and consumables) had been implemented and was seen as one critical element towards simplifying the focus of the business.

The plan also discussed the impact of revelations of the fraud on investor confidence which it believed had undermined the underlying strength of the business. One of the significant business strengths identified in the presentation was the market position that NMC had in healthcare provision in the region, which itself had strong growth potential (particularly in the demand for private hospital beds). The presentation described the intention to sell off the company's international businesses.

Its initial assessment of the HI 2019 accounts indicated that net revenue and EBITDA had been overstated by 24% and 178% respectively. Comparable audited figures for the full 2018 year were estimated to be overstated by 25% and 295% respectively. However, the presentation indicated that the company's underlying performance for 2019 was "solid", with real revenue and EBITDA growing at 25% and 30% respectively (despite the impact of Covid-19) in the early part of the year.

The process of administration would be conducted through the Abu Dhabi Global Market (ADGM) jurisdiction which A&M believed would be optimal since it was based largely on English law, allowing for a debt moratorium, super-priority of new money providers and flexibility when implementing balance sheet restructuring. It would also be faster and cheaper, according to the presentation than some other jurisdictions. Its presentation set out two alternative outcomes. The preferred outcome would be to exit from ADGM under a plan of reorganisation that it believed would be the best value for all stakeholders. The second less favoured alternative was to prepare for the marketing (sale) of the core assets of the business. It confirmed that A&M had secured an agreement with lenders to raise up to $300m to fund the business during administration and had begun the process of selling non-core assets.

A&M presented its progress to all lenders in an update on 10 February 2021.[29] The presentation stressed the underlying resilience of the company demonstrated in strong results for 2020 that had been "achieved in the face of adversity and a global pandemic". These results had "placed the company well to ride out whatever comes next, and have cemented our position as the leading private healthcare business in the UAE". A&M claimed that they were continuing to build a strong independent leadership team "that is capable of leading the company through the next stage of the restructuring and beyond". Finally, the presentation was optimistic about the chance of a plan of reorganisation being successful based on preliminary outcomes from the EPM (entity priority model) that indicated higher recovery expectations for creditors from a plan of reorganisation scenario.

Independent governance

The sudden collapse of NMC generated considerable debate relating to the role of independent directors and external auditors. An examination of the published report and accounts of the company indicates a high degree of compliance in terms of presentation and content with reporting rules for an LSE listed company. In its last completed annual report and accounts the section on governance begins with the following statement. "The Board and management team have strengthened internal controls and kept the approach to risk under review during the period of sustained growth and integration." The Board's audit committee reported that during financial year 2018 "it had been concerned to ensure that all new group financing arrangements are dealt with appropriately in the group's financial statements".

Ernst & Young were appointed as auditors at the time of the Company's IPO in April 2012. EY's audit statement that formed part of the 2018 report and accounts described how auditors checked for material misstatement "including how fraud might occur through individual transactions, transactions with related parties or transactions with a high degree of management judgement or estimate[. . .]. Our procedures included performing journal entry testing with a focus on [. . .] larger or one off transactions especially those impacting revenues." Nothing of major consequence was declared in the final audit report for that year. On 15 April 2020 the FRC opened an investigation into the audit by EY of the financial statements of NMC Health Plc for the year ended 31 December 2018 under the audit enforcement procedure.[30] On 6 November 2020 the Financial Times reported that A&M were preparing to sue EY for more than £1bn over claims that EY were negligent when signing off its accounts over the seven-year period since NMC's IPO in 2012.[31]

Notes

1 NMC Health Plc, (2012) *Annual Report 2012.* 31 December.
2 NMC Health Plc, (2019) *Continuing our strategic growth journey Annual Report and Accounts 2018.*
3 NMC Health Plc, (2019) *Financial Statements Period ended 30 November 2019.*
4 Muddy Waters Research, (2019) *MW is Short NMC Health Plc NMC.LN* [online]. December 17 Available at: https://www.muddywatersresearch.com/research/nmc/mw-is-short-nmc/ [Accessed 27 February 2021].
5 NMC Health Plc, (2019) *Response to Recent Report* [online]19 December. Available at: https://www.investegate.co.uk/nmc-health-Plc–nmc-/rns/response-to-recent-report/201912191725385592X/ [Accessed 27 February 2021].
6 O'Murchu, C. and Smith, R. (2019) NMC held talks to raise €200 m in off-balance sheet debt to fund growth. Healthcare Group under pressure from short-sellers over scale of borrowings. *Financial Times* [online] December 20 Available at: https://www.ft.com/content/c3469f08-2231-11ea-b8a1-584213ee7b2b [Accessed 27 February 2021].

7 NMC Health Plc, (2019) *Response to Financial Times article* [online]. 20 December. Available at: https://cf-cdn.nmc.ae/Uploads/InvestorRelations/denial-of-press-article-20-dec-2019-7778fc83-f2a5-4048-98b8-38e358af4c1f.pdf [Accessed 27 February 2021].

8 Kerr, S. (2019) NMC Health to launch independent review after Muddy Waters attack. *Financial Times* [online]. December 23 Available at: https://www.ft.com/content/96518e14-2596-11ea-9a4f-963f0ec7e134 [Accessed 27 February 2021].

9 NMC Health Plc, (2020) *NMC Health Independent Committee Retains Former FBI Director Louis Freeh to Conduct Independent Investigation* [online]. January 17 Available at: https://www.investe gate.co.uk/nmc-health-Plc–nmc-/rns/independent-review-investigators/202001170700051388A/ [Accessed 27 February 2021].

10 NMC Health Plc, (2020) *Statement regarding major shareholdings* [online].10 February. Available at: https://www.investegate.co.uk/nmc-health-Plc–nmc-/rns/statement-regarding-major-sharehold ings/202002100700074572C/ [Accessed 27 February 2021].

11 NMC Health Plc, (2020) *Director resignation* [online]. 14 February. Available at: https://www.in vestegate.co.uk/nmc-health-Plc–nmc-/rns/director-resignation/202002140807520455D/ [Accessed 27 February 2021].

12 NMC Health Plc, (2020) *Director resignation announcements* [online]. 17 February. Available at: https://www.investegate.co.uk/Index.aspx?searchtype=2&words=nmc [Accessed 27 February 2021].

13 NMC Health Plc, (2020) *Review Update, CEO removal and other matters* [online]. 26 February. Available at: https://www.investegate.co.uk/nmc-health-Plc–nmc-/rns/review-update–ceo-re moval-and-other-matters/202002261717282587E/ [Accessed 27 February 2021].

14 Smith, R. and O'Murchu, C. (2020) NMC Health pledged credit card payments to raise bank funds *Financial Times* [online]. 27 February. Available at: https://www.ft.com/content/ee823c48-5893-11ea-abe5-8e03987b7b20 [Accessed 27 February 2021].

15 NMC Health Plc, (2020) *Suspension of Shares* [online]. 27 February. Available at: https://www.in vestegate.co.uk/nmc-health-Plc–nmc-/rns/suspension-of-shares/202002270758143245E/ [Accessed 27 February 2021].

16 NMC Health Plc, (2020) *Appointment of financial advisors, financial stabilisation, change in major shareholders' holdings and change of control considerations* [online]. 2 March. Available at: https://www.investegate.co.uk/nmc-health-Plc–nmc-/rns/advisers–stabilisation–shareholders-and-control/202003020700066441E/ [Accessed 27 February 2021].

17 NMC Health Plc, (2020) *Update on Financial Position* [online]. 10 March. Available at: https://www.investegate.co.uk/nmc-health-Plc–nmc-/rns/update-on-financial-position/202003101611146635F/ [Accessed on 27 February 2021].

18 NMC Health Plc, (2020) *Update regarding independent review* [online]. 12 March. Available at: https://www.investegate.co.uk/nmc-health-Plc–nmc-/rns/update-regarding-independent-review/202003120831209023F/ [Accessed 27 February 2021].

19 NMC Health Plc, (2020) *Update on Financial Position* [online]. 24 March. Available at: https://www.investegate.co.uk/nmc-health-Plc–nmc-/rns/update-on-financial-position/202003240946273554H/ [Accessed 27 February 2021].

20 NMC Health Plc, (2020) *Board Changes* [online]. 26 March. Available at: https://www.investegate.co.uk/nmc-health-Plc–nmc-/rns/board-changes/202003261609437692H/ [Accessed 27 February 2021].

21 NMC Health Plc, (2020). *Statement regarding Abu Dhabi Commercial Bank* [online]. 6 April. Available at: https://www.investegate.co.uk/nmc-health-plc–nmc-/rns/statement-regarding-abu-dhabi-commercial-bank/202004060700118197I/ [Accessed 27 February 2021].

22 Croft, J., Smith, R. and Kerr, S. (2020) NMC Health goes into administration. *Financial Times* [online], 9 April. Available at: https://www.ft.com/content/dd71ea1c-92a7-4f88-81f4-c3602c0c65dd [Accessed 28 February 2021].

23 NMC Health Plc, (2020) *ALVAREZ & MARSAL APPOINTED ADMINISTRATORS TO NMC HEALTH PLC* [online]. 9 April Available at: https://www.investegate.co.uk/nmc-health-Plc–nmc-/rns/alvarez–marsal-appointed-as-administrators/202004091430124167J/ [Accessed 27 February 2020].

24 ADCB Group, (2020) *ADCB Statement on initiation of criminal proceedings in relation to NMC Health Group* [online]. 15 April. Available at: https://www.adcb.com/en/about-us/media-centre/news/2020/april/nmc-criminal-proceedings [Accessed 28 February 2020].

25 Kerr, S. (2020) NMC Founder blames executives for suspected fraud *Financial Times* [online]. 29 April. Available at: https://www.ft.com/content/58d582c8-4d30-4f52-b869-ce2ab8081a11 [Accessed 28 February 2021].

26 *Abu Dhabi Commercial Bank PJSC v Shetty and others* [2020] EWHC 3423 (Comm).

27 Alvarez and Marsal Europe LLP, (2020) *NMC Health in Administration, Joint Administrator's proposals* [online]. 28 May. Available at: https://cf-cdn.nmc.ae/Uploads/InvestorRelations/nmc-health-Plc-administrators-proposals-28-may-2020-9673ee7d-a034-43ae-8e3e-9275fe48993e.pdf [Accessed 28 February 2021].

28 NMC Health LLC, (2020) *CARE, COMMUNITY, COMPASSION 3-Year Business Plan Summary* [online]. July 31. Available at: https://cf-cdn.nmc.ae/Uploads/InvestorRelations/all-lender-call-presentation-19-aug-2020-e0436784-fae0-4d99-a9b6-2b2b24714448.pdf [Accessed 28 February 2021].

29 NMC Healthcare Ltd (in administration), (2021) *Care. Community. Compassion. All lender update call* [online]. February 10. Available at: https://cf-cdn.nmc.ae/Uploads/InvestorRelations/all-lender-call-presentation-10-february-2021-10-feb-2021-ade3ed0f-922c-4a95-aa7d-2088ac03b7b4.pdf [Accessed 28 February 2021].

30 Financial Reporting Council, (2020) *Investigation into the audit of NMC Health* [online]. 4 May Available at: https://www.frc.org.uk/news/may/investigation-into-the-audit-of-nmc-health [Accessed 28 February 2021].

31 Thomas, D. and Kinder T. (2020) EY faces £1bn lawsuit over audit work for NMC Health *Financial Times* [online]. 6 November. Available at: https://www.ft.com/content/6978e876-1fc2-4a1d-887c-30b0d9dd1c9a [Accessed 1 March 2021].

6 Business turnaround

"How did you go bankrupt?" Bill asked.
  "Two ways," Mike said. "Gradually and then suddenly." (Ernest Hemingway, 1927)

Gradually and then suddenly

In Chapter 1 we introduced the framework that guides the structure of this book. We reproduce the figure again here for ease of reference (Figure 6.1). Chapters 2 to 5 have discussed each of the areas associated with building business resilience and set out a series of areas for the board to consider (BFQ 1–6). The circular nature of the left-hand side of the figure reflects a balanced situation in an effectively managed company. As we discussed in the last chapter the board of such a company will constantly review its performance in each area and make changes where necessary to remedy perceived problems or improve performance.

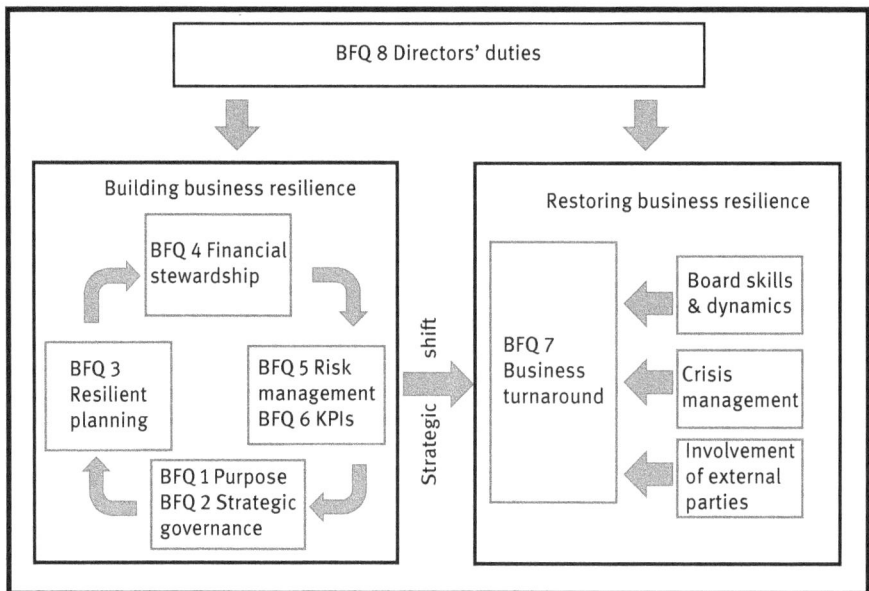

Figure 6.1: Building and restoring business resilience.

Ultimately however, even the best managed companies may need to make more fundamental changes to turn the business around – a strategic shift (BFQ 7). In such circumstances the degree to which a board is able to retain control of the business depends on a range of different factors, including board skills and dynamics,

https://doi.org/10.1515/9783110689495-010

the effectiveness of crisis management and the role played by a range of different external parties.

Chapter 6 considers the various steps that may be taken in response to a deteriorating business situation. Companies may be able to sustain a poor business model over an extended time frame through financial restructuring. Actions can include new finance raised through the issue of bonds and equity as well as restructuring of borrowings and the creation of new debt. Such restructuring may provide a temporary respite but will ultimately prove unsuccessful unless changes are also made in parallel to the business model. Such changes could include product/service rationalisation, cost-saving programmes and asset sale. At some point the CEO is also likely to be replaced. Each of the major case studies in this book illustrates how this process can take place over an extended time frame, with periods of recovery followed by periods of decline and ultimately business failure. For each of these companies business decline was a continuous process with a sudden final event that tipped the balance into formal insolvency procedures.

In the final part of this chapter we look at the steps which may be necessary when a gradually worsening business positions turns into a crisis. Our review covers the immediate priorities of cash preservation and providing reassurance to existing secured creditors as well as other stakeholders. We also discuss the process of developing a new sustainable business model to take the company forward.

The benchmarking questions that we have suggested for this area are set out in Table 6.1.

Again as with previous chapters readers may prefer to look ahead and read the case study at the end of this chapter before starting on the main content. The case study details how Thomas Cook Group plc struggled to operate with a business model that was difficult to change in a competitive environment that became increasingly challenging.

Strategic shift

BFQ 7.1 Is the board willing to accept that the business may face challenges to business continuity that require a step change in planning?

If it ain't broke fix it anyway

Change is built into the DNA of some companies. Such businesses react quickly when problems emerge. According to members of the Boston Consulting Group (BCG) such companies get ahead of business problems before they show up in the company's profit and loss account (Baeza, Fæsta, Lay, Seppä, Bartletta, Ganeriwalla, Moldenhauer and Webb, 2017). They describe the approach as follows "If it ain't broke, fix it anyway." Such businesses "redefine the company's

Table 6.1: BFQ 7 Business turnaround: How effectively does the board implement strategies to restore resilience where appropriate or deal with crisis situations as they emerge?

Benchmarking questions	Commentary (Evidence)	Score
Strategic shift BFQ 7.1 **Is the board willing to accept that the business may face challenges to business continuity that require a step change in planning?**	Willingness to acknowledge that change may be necessary to avoid negative impact as much as positive strategic development Previous history of making successful substantial changes in the past in response to business challenges Evidence of systematic review and learning from previous situations Realistic attempts to map alternative futures that include the possibility that the existing business model may longer be appropriate If it ain't broke fix it anyway attitude	
Restoring strategic resilience BFQ 7.2 **Does the company have the necessary knowledge, skills and experience (particularly at board level) to identify and address emerging strategic problems?**	Accepting that getting to OK may be a valid initial goal. Presence of board members with financial and industry expertise that relates directly to marketing, operations, and broader strategic issues addressed in table 5.3 (strategic resilience scorecard) Non-executive directors who are sufficiently qualified and empowered to play an active role in the process Effective use of external advisors as and where appropriate Acceptance that if it is broke and no one wants it anymore – don't bother trying to fix it – get out as quickly as possible	
Leadership qualities BFQ 7.3 *Does the business have the right leadership to take it through the changes that might be required?*	Risk management, cost reduction and restructuring experience Effective strategic governance systems where board members are regularly updated and involved in discussions Decisiveness in addressing immediate problems Willingness to engage specialist external assistance Willingness to change the CEO-senior team or re-evaluate their roles Effectiveness of internal and external communications	

Table 6.1 (continued)

Fixing the financial position *BFQ 7.4* *Is there a well thought through long-term plan to reset the financial position when it becomes evident that the current model is unsustainable?*	A realistic picture of the relative strengths and weaknesses of balance sheet and cash generation that the board is briefed on Key questions on financial resilience that the board includes as an integral part of its ongoing business agenda Regular strategic consideration of the pattern of borrowings and other financial decisions such as supply chain finance and the impact on key financial ratios Explicit strategies to address financial legacy problems ahead of potential financial crises that are implemented in a structured manner
Business failure - a sudden event *BFQ 7.5* **Is there a well-structured plan to deal with crisis situations?**	Willingness to take quick measures to stabilise cash flow Ownership of the problem at board level and an immediate explicit communications plan for employees Acceptance of the potential need to replace leadership positions quickly if necessary Use of skilled external advice where appropriate Immediate review of the business model to determine if there are any prospects for the long-term survival of parts of the business and identification of which elements might be closed or disposed of Effective engagement with key external partners including lenders, suppliers and investors

strategic focus, restructure to reduce costs and complexity, build the right culture and invest in digital". The BCG describes these companies as the "comeback kids".

Some businesses can survive in challenging situations for an extended period, renegotiating loans or accessing new sources of funding. Many companies in such circumstances will attempt to reduce costs, close or dispose of peripheral areas of the business and rationalise operations. Some may be able to attract further funding from shareholders or issue bonds. This cycle may repeat over time, with a temporary respite when new financing arrangements are put in place or costs savings realised. Ultimately the options for further financial restructuring or cost efficiencies disappear and more fundamental change is required, frequently in a crisis situation if the business is to avoid entry into formal insolvency proceedings.

On a more positive note a survey of over 500 corporate leaders, and financial and legal experts in April 2021 concluded that disruption had become the new business driver, in a future "dictated by pace, frequency, and unpredictability of change" where a "turnaround mindset will need to become the norm in order to respond to and ultimately harness the effect of multiple constant disruptive forces" (AlixPartners,

2021). Back in 1987 that same thought had also occurred to John Whitney who pointed out that business turnarounds were "superb management schools" where "everything needs fixing" and "nothing is sure except the need to recover".

Who makes the call that something needs to change?

The question "who makes the call?" can be interpreted in different ways. At any point in time a range of different parties have an interest in the performance of a business. Those who are directly involved in running the business are most aware of changes that might affect ongoing viability. Members of the board should be aware of emerging problems especially if they are regularly briefed on progress by executive directors. These internal stakeholders have a specific frame of reference which is informed by their experiences as they run the business on a day-to-day basis. Most managers spend most of their time solving immediate problems. They may be reluctant to acknowledge that problems which are emerging cannot be resolved by changes that they have already implemented. In such circumstances a new CEO may be necessary to put in place changes to the basic business model and turn the company around.

The possibility of creditor intervention is likely to be the first key external factor that makes a board think explicitly about the need to deal with emerging business problems, particularly when it seems likely that a business is in danger of breaching financial covenants. Most businesses would regard this as one of their most critical relationships which needs to be carefully managed to avoid an uncomfortable telephone call or email from the bank inviting them in for a discussion to discuss the business's current financial arrangements.

External stakeholders such as activist investors or other private equity investors frequently challenge the decisions of the board when they disagree with their actions. This may be an important precipitating factor that causes a board to consider a more extensive review of the business's position. This is evident in the Flybe, Carillion and NMC case studies in this book. In such circumstances it is reasonable to ask who is actually running the company and what is the overall purpose of interventions by such parties, especially if it appears that they are advocating short-term policies designed to extract value from the business at the expense of long-run commercial viability.

Other external parties (auditors and external consultants) may also influence the decision to make a more extensive review of the business situation. In Chapter 4 we considered the going concern statement that is an obligatory part of the annual reporting process. Part of the responsibility of an external auditor in the UK is to report on the extent to which they have any material concerns. Such a report should raise any questions about viability and make a call that action is required.

Restoring strategic resilience

BFQ 7.2 Does the company have the necessary knowledge, skills and experience (particularly at board level) to identify and address emerging strategic problems?

Poor strategic choices

Bradley, Hirt and Smit (2018) suggest that many directors seeking to transform the performance of their business focus on cost reduction without considering their broader strategic position. Their conclusions are based on a review of decision-making in 2,393 of the world's largest non-financial companies between 2004 and 2014. Their findings indicate that whilst cost savings can bring immediate tangible results to the bottom line, such actions are unlikely to bring long-term improvements unless businesses are also prepared to consider more fundamental changes.

Companies that made changes to their underlying strategies at the same time as implementing productivity improvements saw the greatest improvement in performance. Such strategic shifts included attempts to create differentiation through innovation in products or business models, changing the overall portfolio of products or services and ultimately mergers and acquisitions. Significantly companies operating in declining relatively mature industries are least likely to see the benefit of any change programmes (Bradley, de Jong and Walden, 2019). Although the authors did not explicitly consider business turnaround the findings are also directly applicable to situations of business distress. In such situations efforts need to be all-in if they are to stand any chance of success.

When demand goes into freefall due to a major event such as a global pandemic then the impact on sales, profitability and cash flow is obvious. Pandemics eventually recede and those businesses that survive can potentially restart. A slower pattern of decline may be less easy to detect but the effects could ultimately be more serious, as the Thomas Cook case study featured at the end of this chapter illustrates.

In Thomas Cook's case the original core product was built on a reputation for providing packages for a large number of travellers to well-known tourism destinations. Its vertical business model (retail outlets, airlines and hotels) provided an integrated system to meet the needs of those seeking to book traditional holiday breaks with a high degree of customer security and support. The scale of the operation also provided significant cost advantages to the company with overheads shared over a large number of individual customer transactions.

Over time this model became increasingly less competitive as new entrants emerged, frequently focused on specific niche markets (for example, weekend breaks) and unique destinations that were not offered by mainstream operators such as Thomas Cook. At the same time variations in demand such as those caused by acts of terrorism in specific resorts or natural events such as volcanic activity had a direct effect on profitability. The increasing use of online booking systems coupled with greater customer confidence in assembling their own unique packages steadily eroded the mainstream tourism market that Thomas Cook had served for many years. For more than ten years prior to its ultimate collapse Thomas Cook attempted to adjust its position to new market realities in a situation where many of its existing physical assets were dedicated to the original business model. It also had a legacy of high levels of debt associated with acquisitions that made increasing demands on cash flow over time.

Carillion by contrast, which features at the end of Chapter 4 attempted to build its position by acquiring other businesses in the same business areas. However, it proved difficult for the business to control the extensive mix of main contractors and sub-contractors that were added with each new business acquisition. As the business grew in size it became an increasingly large and cumbersome organisation that was widely criticised for its efficiency and effectiveness at the time of its closure. Each new acquisition was financed by increased borrowing which put considerable pressure on cash flow in a market where competition was largely price-based. It was widely criticised in subsequent enquiries for bidding for construction contracts at prices that would generate little or no net cash contribution.

Norton Motorcycles, which we also featured in Chapter 4 attempted to position itself in the "enthusiast" segment of the motorcycle industry but ultimately did not have access to the level of funding needed to invest in new technology and brand development and provide appropriate levels of customer service.

What are the options when the current strategy is no longer appropriate? Thomas Cook could not easily adopt many of the strategies of smaller tour operators that were operating online and taking away much of its profitable business in higher value-added markets. Carillion could not produce a differentiated solution for clients who simply wanted the lowest possible price. Norton Motorcycles was unlikely to ever grow to the size where it could challenge Honda in mainstream motorcycle markets.

The classic strategy for companies with a strong competitive position in markets that are slowly declining is "harvesting" – seeking to manage for cash but making no significant new investment. Companies in a weaker position in such markets are likely to try to rationalise products and services more rapidly with a view to exiting the market relatively quickly. Irrespective of whether the decline of a market is a long-drawn-out process or a sudden shock, the underlying message is clear. No amount of fine-tuning will turn the situation around. Sooner or later the company will need to get out of the market and apply its resources to new opportunities. To paraphrase an earlier comment "If it is broke and no-one wants it anymore – don't bother trying to fix it – get out as quickly as possible."

In practice many products/services may be offered long after the demand for them is no longer sufficient to sustain a positive return. These problems are illustrated in the Flybe case study at the end of Chapter 2. Flybe's strategic dilemma, which persisted through most of its existence was the choice between which routes to develop, which to retain and which to stop operating. The problem was compounded by the need to adjust the size and composition of its fleet of aircraft to match a new operating environment where improved surface transport and better online communications were rapidly replacing the need for regional air travel. We quoted CAPA's opinion on Flybe's position in 2017 in the case study. They said:

> In spite of operating a network that faces no competition from other airlines on the majority of its routes, and in spite of being comfortably Europe's largest regional airline – Flybe has regularly struggled to make a profit. Its thin/negative margins are evidence that, in fact, it faces significant competition, but from surface transport. They are also evidence that its unit cost is too high relative to the unit revenue that it is able to generate. This has been exacerbated by excess capacity growth, but also partly reflects the high unit cost that is inherent in the regional airline model.

Poor marketing competence

Marketing is often regarded as a tactical activity focused on managing the marketing mix. It has a broader strategic contribution to make. It is marketing's job to bring the customer's voice to the boardroom table. When this voice is muted the cumulative effect can be very damaging. Marketing can best be considered as the management of a long-term relationship between the company and its customers that is punctuated from time to time by specific purchases. This relationship is driven by different elements of the marketing programme that combine to give unique value to customers. When this relationship breaks down organisational resilience is diminished as we discussed in the Arcadia case at the end of Chapter 3.

Restoring customer focus in a business can be a difficult process. The first critical stage is to gain general acceptance that change is needed. The board may be broadly aware that there are problems with the current approach, particularly if some members have relevant industry or market experience. Specific performance indicators such as sales and profitability analysed by market segment, product return rates, customer satisfaction surveys including net promoter scores and competitive price surveys can provide evidence that problems are emerging. Numbers and graphs presented to a board are often less useful in communicating a sense that something is wrong and needs to be put right than direct interaction with customers and front-line employees. Effective boards find ways of bringing these experiences into the boardroom and raising consciousness about the customer journey.

In some turnaround situations companies may attempt to fix the problem by appointing a new head of marketing. If the main problem is the marketing programme rather than underlying problems in the market in which the company is operating then a new appointment may make a difference. Many small and medium-sized businesses do not have the luxury of even contemplating the appointment of someone to focus solely on marketing. They may be limited to trying to deal with specific problems themselves or use external consultants to address specific problem areas. Those owner-managers responsible for running every aspect of the business are particularly vulnerable when market conditions change making the original business model increasingly less relevant. The advantage they have is close interaction with customers that can at least provide good insight into emerging problems (providing they are prepared to listen and adjust!).

Improving operational efficiency

Attempts to reduce costs feature in most turnaround situations. All of our main cases studies contain examples of such approaches as successive management teams attempted to turn the business around. Such changes included substantial amounts of delayering, reduction of central overhead costs and elimination of marginal areas of business through sale or closure. The threat of financial distress is likely to focus attention on how far competitive advantage has eroded and how this position might be remedied. Detailed analysis of costs and revenue may lead to some surprises such as discovering that activities that were previously seen as major cash generators actually make a loss whilst other areas are significant contributors once the indirect costs of product or service support are taken into account.

Over the years a wide range of different approaches have been applied to improve business efficiency including business process re-engineering, total quality management, outsourcing, and organisational development. These are part of the tool-kit of the professional business turnaround consultant. Unfortunately for those who are directly affected, this process frequently begins with a reduction in the number of employees, often in areas that provide administrative support. Understandably perhaps, the debate about which areas of the business are essential and need to be retained and which areas are not crucial to business continuity can become an intense internal political exercise where different factions make the case for their own areas of activity to be retained.

Attempts to reduce cost can also be targeted at suppliers, many of whom may not be in a position to resist a call from a major customer to reduce prices or accept delayed payment of invoices. A relevant recent example of the latter is revealed in the pressure put on landlords during the Covid-19 pandemic when retailers were forced to close for extended periods of time and were unable to meet payments due under leasing agreements. In many cases this led to leases being renegotiated on terms that were more advantageous to the tenant. Finding a new tenant for a property that could not readily be converted to alternative uses was not an attractive option for many of these companies. The Arcadia case study at the end of Chapter 3 describes how one company used a formal legal process – a CVA (company voluntary arrangement) to achieve rent reductions from seven of its landlords.

There is a finite limit to the capacity of cost-based strategies to return a company to solvency. This is especially the case where previous cost reduction exercises have already stripped out much of the business's non-core activity. Despite conscious attempts to manage operational efficiency unexpected events can also disrupt plans placing considerable strain on business systems. We have already cited the impact of three major events between 2020 and 2022 (the Covid pandemic, UK exit from the EU and the war in the Ukraine) that have had such an impact. At the time of writing (2022) it is not clear what long-term effect these events will have on the viability of a wide range of businesses many of which will need to radically change their business model if they are to recover.

Leadership qualities

BFQ 7.3 Does the business have the right leadership to take it through the changes that might be required?

The recent pandemic has led to an increased focus on the role of business leaders in dealing with urgent crises and the concept of resilient leadership. Nichols, Hayden and Trendler (2020) identify four key leadership characteristics that appear to have a positive impact in crisis situations. These are to decide with speed over precision, adapt boldly, reliably deliver and engage (with others) for impact. In a similar vein, Renjen (2020) has proposed five qualities of resilient leadership particularly in responding to Covid-19. His analysis was based on a synthesis of the views of senior managers in Deloitte working with companies in different regions around the world. These qualities include an ability to "Design from the heart . . . and the head", reflecting "the need to be genuinely sincerely empathetic". "Putting the mission first" and "aiming for speed over elegance" are also seen as critical. Many of these qualities resonate with those put forward to describe effective leadership by Goffee and Jones (2006). We discussed this in more detail in Chapter 2. Whilst these comments are aimed at the CEO they are equally important benchmarks for the behaviour of the board as a whole.

An empirical study of CEO turnover of UK companies in the Russell 3000 Index in 2020 compared the turnover rate of CEOs in 2019 with corresponding data for 2020. The authors found that CEO replacement rates dropped during the second quarter of 2020 as boards sought to maintain business continuity and investor confidence during the challenging times created by the Covid-19 pandemic (Heidrick and Struggles, 2020). Their interpretation was that during the early stages of the pandemic traditional CEO skills such as risk management, achieving cost efficiencies and restructuring were crucial elements in maintaining business continuity. The survey concluded that CEO replacement was likely to accelerate again once the pandemic was at an end as companies revisited their objectives and concluded that a new leadership style was required.

In larger companies the CEO typically reports to the chair of the board, assuming that these two roles are separated. Any decision to replace the CEO will depend on a range of different factors, including the perceived style of the CEO, and the relationship between the CEO and the board, particularly the chair. Ultimately however the key determinant is the extent to which business performance continues to meet the expectations of investors. Much of the time of the chair can be spent in meetings with investors and other stakeholders to discuss business progress. Such meetings will frequently focus on the performance of the executive team. Negative feedback from key investors can be a major precipitating factor in decisions about CEO replacement. Boards that hold out against such pressures may find that external criticism becomes increasingly vocal and damaging.

Ultimately changing the CEO may be necessary to reassure shareholders and stakeholders – secured creditors in particular – that the company has recognised that the business has problems and is taking positive steps to address the situation. This is a judgement call for the board. The speed of the change and the nature of any new appointment may also depend on the extent to which key shareholders become involved in the process. If activist shareholders have identified an opportunity to unlock potential value, address underperforming areas of the business through divestment or ultimately put the company up for sale, they may seek to put the board under pressure to make changes to strategy and executive leadership.

Chief restructuring officer

As problems become more apparent a board may also recognise that it needs external support, potentially through the appointment of a chief restructuring officer. Such a role may sit alongside the existing senior team, or more frequently be an interim appointment between the departing CEO and any new incoming team. The Arcadia case study describes the circumstances in which two restructuring appointments were made to the board in April 2019 approximately 18 months before the company was placed into administration. The NMC case study describes a similar appointment made by the company's interim CEO in this case in the last few weeks before the company entered administration.

Business restructuring has become a major business in its own right. As with other areas of business consultancy each of the major firms has its own prescription for success as an examination of company websites quickly indicates. One description of the role indicates the scale of the issues that could be involved and the personal skills and character that might be needed (Gething, Hudson, Johnston, O'Neill and Wlodarz, 2020).

> CROs draw on an expansive financial tool kit but recognize that only certain tools will prove optimal in any given balance sheet restructuring and that each situation is unique. CROs know

how to stabilize the crisis and manage cash, when to raise equity, roll over debt, divest units, equitize debt, or work an insolvency process – and when not to.

Effective CROs are also exceptional people managers who strike a balance between challenging teams and offering support – leaders who both motivate people to change and hold them accountable, while rebuilding trust and consensus across multiple external stakeholder Groups with differing views and objectives.

But CROs bring another trait that's crucial to their success, and it would be folly to short-change its value: the ability to communicate the restructuring plan to the board, management, employees, secured lenders, shareholders, the pension regulator, the press, and any other key stakeholders.

In sum, a CRO is by nature rigorous, with a strong grip on numbers; a good negotiator; an empathetic leader; thick skinned – able to take the shots, deflect criticism, and reduce emotions; and gifted with the ability to connect with people. Of course, not all CROs are made the same – these success factors are markers of truly great CROs.

Fixing the financial position

BFQ 7.4 Is there a well thought through long-term plan to reset the financial position when it becomes evident that the current model is unsustainable?

Strategic financial restructuring problems

One turnaround practitioner has summarised the main signs of distress he has encountered into four main categories (Yakola, 2014). These include issues of working capital and liquidity, financial indicators such as declining stock price, inability to meet debt covenants and downgrades in debt ratings, profitability and industry outlook including the going concern opinion, and significant changes to employees including reductions in the workforce and changes to key management personnel. Each of these separately and cumulatively may be sufficient to indicate a serious potential problem.

When increases in debt have been used as a primary mechanism to fund business continuity then this can put excessive pressure on financial resources. An increase in cash flow is required from ongoing operations to fund debt repayments leaving potentially diminishing resources to finance other aspects of the company's business. This situation featured in all of the main cases studies described in this book at different stages in their development. As long as the costs of borrowing remain low then this strategy can provide an effective way of sustaining business activity. A long period of low interest rates and the ready availability of funding in many Western economies over a sustained period in the first two decades of the twenty-first century made this an attractive strategy, particularly for those companies seeking to bolster a marginally profitable business model or acquire other companies at apparently high prices. At some point however the costs of repaying debt may become increasingly problematic.

The balance sheet of many companies may also reflect legacy decisions that are no longer relevant to current trading conditions. For example, both Carillion and Thomas Cook acquired a range of different businesses over an extended period of time. Each of these purchases increased the value of intangible assets (goodwill) shown in the balance sheet. These indefinite life values were not reduced (impaired) significantly in successive years following acquisition up to the point where bankruptcy seemed unavoidable and carried unrealistically high values. When assets are suddenly impaired this can cause major shock waves when this is reported in trading updates.

Equally the balance sheet may not reflect other outstanding liabilities such as payments due to suppliers. Supply chain finance has been used effectively over an extended time frame by many companies to smooth out the effects of payments that are due to suppliers. Increasingly however it has become evident that this approach can also be used to disguise increasing amounts of debt which are not necessarily reported as part of standard reports. Such items may have been dealt with as "off-balance sheet" items which are not reported in the accounts produced for external use. This issue has been a critical feature of several recent business insolvency cases including Greensill Capital (Smith, 2021).

Financial restructuring processes

Financial restructuring in periods of business distress can take a variety of different forms. This book focuses on the stages before formal insolvency proceedings. Harmon (2020) identifies eight main out-of-court approaches, namely amendment/waiver, asset sale, debt-for-debt exchange, debt for equity swap, debt repurchase, new financing, sale and leaseback and finally sale of company. It is beyond the scope of this book to discuss each of these areas in detail. Each approach has advantages and disadvantages when applied to specific circumstances. The ability to control this process depends on the relative size of the company (larger companies are typically better placed to negotiate alternative positions with lenders), the urgency of the emerging problem and the willingness of shareholders and creditors to accept specific proposals that could potentially damage their interests. It can also extend over a considerable time frame with different initiatives at different times as successive boards attempt to resolve problems with the basic financial model. Each company will approach the problem in different ways. At this point readers may again want to skip forward to the Thomas Cook case study at the end of this chapter where we detail the steps that the company took in an attempt to resolve its financial situation in the months immediately prior to its formal liquidation.

Lender relationships in the early stages of distress: Small businesses

As the extent of financial distress becomes obvious to outsiders so possible options are reduced and become more costly. The ability to make progress with any of these alternatives ultimately depends on the viability of the business model and relationships with secured creditors. One of the authors has discussed this process in depth in a series of major case studies of businesses in financial distress (Parkinson, 2018). Most companies need specialist advice to explore viable alternatives, negotiate terms and conditions with lenders, secure new borrowings and raise funding. Small and medium-sized companies can face specific problems given the degree of control that such lenders may have over their business decisions.

Over 15 years ago Franks and Sussman looked at the management of business distress in 542 small and medium-sized companies that had been identified as needing support by three major UK clearing banks (Franks and Sussman, 2005). These companies ranged in size from a turnover of £20,000 to the largest with a turnover of £73m. Each of the banks operated a business rescue unit that had been set up to assist these companies. The reasons identified for sending a firm to the business rescue unit included "the failure to make payments of interest or repayments of the loan, the occurrence of business losses, frequent breaches of the borrowing limit, [and] a request for larger borrowing facilities accompanied by a deterioration in the business or concern over the company's business strategy".

For many small and medium-sized companies lending is typically secured by floating and fixed charges over the main assets, with personal guarantees by directors. This puts the lender in a strong position where it can control the process of debt resolution. Trade creditors, despite providing a significant percentage of most companies' overall financing have far less control over the process. Franks and Sussman's analysis indicated that if companies in their sample addressed their problems early enough there was greater likelihood of successful exit from distress. Typical solutions adopted by the companies that they looked at included management changes, the sale of assets and new finance or directors' guarantees. Over 33% of the companies banking with one of the major three clearing banks dealt with the problem by moving accounts to another competitor on different terms and conditions. Trade creditors appear to have fared less well in such circumstances. In the event of these businesses entering formal insolvency processes, very few of the trade creditors were able to recover any of the debt, with secured creditors managing to get 27% return. The authors contrast this result with the situation in the US where Chapter 11 provisions appear to make it easier for unsecured creditors to exert greater influence on debt recovery.

The report identified how companies in distress situations were compelled by the lender to make asset sales and refinance with third parties. The report also described how lenders sought to impose control by withdrawing or reducing working capital facilities, and replacing on-demand facilities with term loan facilities. Pricing increases were also part of many renegotiated borrowings. This was linked to additional requests for personal guarantees to provide security against borrowings, based on an assessment of the borrower's perceived level of financial difficulty.

Business failure: A sudden event

BFQ 7.5 Is there a well-structured plan to deal with crisis situations?

Business distress situations crystallise as an urgent priority when immediate financial problems emerge that cannot be easily resolved within a company's existing cash reserves or agreed borrowing facilities.

Examples of specific events could include:

- an over-optimistic forecast of cash flow that is identified following the appointment of new accounting staff
- the discovery of a major business fraud
- unexpected demands from a tax authority to make overdue tax payments
- an unsolicited phone call from the bank manager that asks for a meeting to discuss the company's current borrowing facility
- sudden and unexpected increases in energy costs such as those experienced by many businesses as a consequence of the war in Ukraine
- a phone call from one of the company's major lenders to the CFO saying that they are no longer able to offer supply chain financing because they (lender) are unable to obtain insurance for the transaction
- notification that a major customer has gone into administration and will not be making any immediate provision for payment of monies owed
- sudden withdrawal of financial support by external sponsors following disclosure of failure to act on cases of bullying and racial discrimination.

Each of the above is likely to precipitate follow-on actions including a detailed analysis of the problem and broader sharing of the issue amongst the management team. Suddenly a general problem that a business might have believed that it was dealing with could turn into a major crisis.

Wirecard Technologies GmbH: "Spurious balance confirmations"

The discovery of fraud in Wirecard, an apparently successful financial technology services company and a member of the Dax 30 Index in Germany in 2020 illustrates how financial problems can gradually and then suddenly overtake a company.

For several years preceding the collapse of the company concerns had been expressed about the company's financial performance (McCrum, 2020). These were linked to claims that profits were fraudulently inflated and customers listed by the company did not exist. On 18 June 2020 Wirecard announced that its auditor Ernst &

Young GmbH had informed the business that it could not find sufficient evidence of cash balances on trust accounts to be consolidated into the financial statements to the value of €1.9bn (approximately a quarter of the consolidated balance sheet total) (Wirecard AG, 2020-a). The announcement referred to "spurious balance confirmations" that had been provided to the auditor that were "intended to deceive the auditor and create a wrong perception of the existence of such cash balances". Publication of the annual financial statements would be delayed as a result.

Four days later on 22 June 2020 the Management Board of Wirecard acknowledged that there was a "prevailing likelihood" that the bank trust accounts did not exist. These accounts had been reported as an asset in its financial accounts. The company announced that it was withdrawing its assessment of its preliminary results and could not exclude the possibility that the annual results of previous years might also be affected. Its announcement referred to the possible impact that this might have on its continuing viability. The company stated:

> Wirecard continues to be in constructive discussions with its lending banks with regard to the continuation of credit lines and the further business relationship, including the continuation of the current drawing coming due at the end of June. Together with the renowned and internationally active investment bank Houlihan Lokey, Wirecard is assessing options for a sustainable financing strategy for the company.
>
> In addition, the Company is examining a broad range of possible further measures to ensure continuation of its business operations, including cost reductions as well as restructuring, disposal or termination of business units and product segments. (Wirecard AG, 2020-b)

On the same day the company announced that it had dismissed its chief operating officer from the management board and extraordinarily terminated his contract. Two days later the company's CEO was arrested. According to a Financial Times report, this was on suspicion of "artificially inflating the payment Group's balance sheet and revenues to make it more attractive to investors and clients" (Storbeck, McCrum, and Palma, 2020).

By 25 June 2020 the company had decided to file an application for the opening of insolvency proceedings, stating that the management board could no longer make a positive going concern forecast. The company would pursue possible chances of reorganisation in collaboration with the temporary insolvency administrator (Wirecard AG, 2020-c). Within 7 days the company had gone from apparently successful trading to entering insolvency with little chance to address the situation.

Sudden, unexpected events also occurred in two of the major case studies in this book. In Carillion at the end of Chapter 4, an initial concern expressed by a member of the finance team rapidly escalated into a detailed review of assumptions about revenue and cash flow, leading to a recognition that the company was rapidly approaching insolvency. In NMC comments by an investment analyst led to an immediate inquiry into the business's financial situation. Readers may want to compare events in both of these cases with the more gradual deterioration described in Thomas Cook, Arcadia and Flybe.

Dealing with a crisis

It is not within the scope of this book to consider the final stages of business distress in detail. Resolving immediate crises that threaten business continuity can be a complex task where commercial and legal considerations overlap. Professional advice is frequently required to resolve a range of different issues that can emerge in such situations. Slatter and Lovett (1991) have produced a step-by-step description of the typical turnaround process in such a situation, written from a practitioner's perspective. The authors set out key stages to resolve the situation, beginning with crisis stabilisation. At this stage the main aims are typically to address immediate cash flow problems to provide temporary respite, convince lenders that the business is serious about attempts to resolve the situation and win some breathing space to address immediate problems. The choice of who takes the business forward is also a crucial early decision.

In parallel the authors stress the importance of presenting a credible picture of how the business could be remodelled to convince different stakeholders that turnaround could plausibly be achieved. The success of any proposals will depend on being able to design a business model that builds on the business's existing capabilities and opportunities and perhaps equally importantly identifies areas that should be discarded. If it is agreed that there is still a viable part of the business that can be saved and there is some agreement on the nature and scale of the business that still remains, the next stage is to put in place appropriate actions to implement the new business survival and growth plan.

Slatter and Lovett comment on the value of conducting a quick overall analysis of the prospects of business survival before getting into a detailed investigation of cause and effect. They describe this process as a diagnostic review which is typically "quick and dirty" and designed to answer key questions including the ability of the firm to survive in the short term, assess the options open to the company and determine the best options for different stakeholders.

In the initial stage of crisis stabilisation only essential spending required to keep the business going in the short term would be authorised. In small companies this may be readily achieved with all purchases authorised by an owner-manager. When several members of a company can authorise expenditure the process may need careful monitoring and control. Accounts receivable and payable might be monitored on a weekly basis. Specific actions could include more stringent control and signing off of expenditure as well as attempting to change the terms of trade with suppliers to delay or make modifications to repayment terms. Costs could also be reduced quickly in areas such as advertising, training and recruitment.

At this point a new business plan to take the company forward is required. Such a plan will need to be credible to lenders, creditors and potential investors if they are to be convinced of the value of extending borrowings, changing loan conditions or investing in new equity or bonds. The challenges are considerable. Those leading the change must convince both internal and external stakeholders that the organisation has a sustainable future. This process can be difficult enough in normal times when there is no apparent financial threat hanging over the business. When such a turnaround is planned during a period of financial distress other parties with vested interest in the outcomes may play a greater role in the process and influence its outcome.

In such circumstances, where insolvency is a potential outcome if a solution is not found, directors' focus legitimately shifts from shareholder interests to creditor interests. Significant creditors are likely to take a direct interest in any proposals for changes to the existing business model. Up until the point that directors begin formal insolvency procedures creditors have no explicit right to get involved in the process of reorganisation, although their informal influence may be considerable. When the company breaches the terms of any borrowing covenant then a creditor may trigger a formal insolvency process by application to the court. The threat of such an action can be an important bargaining device for any lender seeking to gain an advantage from any proposed changes.

Thomas Cook Group plc

Thomas Cook is one of the world's best-recognised travel and tourism brands. The company's roots can be traced back almost two hundred years. The case study describes the period from Thomas Cook's launch as a PLC on the London Stock Exchange in 2007 to liquidation in 2019.

Some of the areas that you might want to focus on in the case could include:

- the relevance of the original business model to changes in the travel and tourism market over the period covered by the case and the growth of alternative forms of competition
- the financial legacy created by attempts to grow the business through acquisition including its impact on debt and cash flow
- attempts to improve the company's financial position through cost savings, asset sale, debt renegotiation, equity and bond issue
- changes in CEOs at critical points in the company's development
- the range of different stakeholder interests that had to be addressed in any workable long-term solution to the company's problems in the final days before compulsory liquidation.

Case study: Thomas Cook Group plc

"Celebrating 200 years"

The following case study examines the evolution of Thomas Cook Group plc from its formation in June 2007 by the merger of Thomas Cook AG and the Mytravel Group to the Group's ultimate liquidation in 2019.

The merger in 2007 created one of the largest travel companies in the world with sales of around £8bn, 19m customers annually, around 33,000 employees, 97 aircraft, over 3,000 owned or franchised stores and a number of hotels and resort properties.[1] In November 2007 at an investor strategy day the CEO referred to the merger with the Mytravel Group as an action that had "transformed both our business and the industry in general". The Group announced its intention to improve its performance in mainstream tour operating, make significant advances in independent travel and travel-related financial services, develop its position in emerging markets and grow overall revenue and profit.[2]

During 2008 the Group made a series of acquisitions including the licenses for the Thomas Cook brand in 15 Middle East countries, Elegant Resorts Ltd, TriWest Travel Holdings, a leading independent travel wholesaler in Canada and France-based Jet Tours. Financial results for 2007–2008 showed a revenue of £8,167m, profit from operations of £363m, a positive operating cash flow of £357m and a net debt of £292m.[3]

A new chair was appointed in March 2009. A new CFO was appointed with effect from 1 January 2009, with the previous finance director becoming group strategy director.

Results for 2010 show that revenue had declined by 4% compared to the same period in the previous year, which the board attributed to the general global recession following the major financial crisis of 2008. A volcanic eruption had also caused major disruption leading to losses estimated at over £80m. The company announced that it had lengthened the maturity period of current loans, creating a 3-year bank facility with the ability to extend for a further two years and raised further capital though the issue of two major bonds.[4]

In July 2011 a trading update confirmed that the company's performance for the first three quarters of the year had fallen behind expectations. This was blamed on ongoing political unrest in the Middle East and North Africa and the performance of the UK business ". . . as a result of the continued squeeze on UK consumers' disposable income".[5] Commenting on the company's cash flow position the CFO said: "As stated in our recent trading update, we continue to perform well on cash flow, with circa £900m of available cash and committed facilities. We are focused on reducing our debt and strengthening our balance sheet and we have a number of

https://doi.org/10.1515/9783110689495-011

initiatives underway to deliver progress on this including the disposal of certain hotel and surplus assets."[6]

External analysts at the time suggested that the Group had too many commodity holidays in "humdrum" resorts on its books and a brand that was too closely associated with the mass holiday market that did not attract better-off customers. A further threat was the move to online bookings that had fuelled intensive price competition.[7]

The group CEO stood down on 3 August 2011 with immediate effect with his deputy taking on the role on an interim basis. On 11 August the head of UK retail operations also departed. A statement by the chair commented on the Group's position as follows:

> The Board is focused on restoring market confidence in the Group, which has been impacted by concerns over debt levels and the poor performance of our UK business. We are taking actions to strengthen the balance sheet, including a disposal programme that we expect to realise up to £200m. In addition, (the new interim CEO's) extensive experience in the travel industry will be invaluable in guiding the UK [business] through its strategic and operational review.[8]

The chair's comments reflected an increasing amount of concern amongst investors about its banking covenants, fuelled by the Group's third profit warning of the calendar year and the announcement of a review of its UK operations.[9] The company successfully managed to renegotiate its bank debt in October 2011, agreeing to pay an extra 0.5% in interest payments on an existing total debt of £1bn.[10] A further deterioration in the company's trading position forced the company to renegotiate the repayment terms of its debt for the second time in a month in November 2011. A new £200m loan facility was secured, granting four banks the right to take a total of 5% of the business's shares. Interest charges on the loan were increased and covenants eased.[11]

Commenting on the Group's performance during the year the new incoming chair said:

> During the year the Board was disappointed that management performance in certain areas fell short of the standards that we demand. Decisive action was taken, with changes at the Group Executive Board level as well as placing new senior management teams into both the UK and French operations. . .Together we will take all the actions necessary to improve performance and embed the right culture, values and behaviours across the Group.[12]

"Taking action to strengthen our business"

A new financial deal with existing lenders was announced on 5 May 2012, extending the maturity of £1.4bn of finance facilities with more relaxed financial covenants. The interest margin over LIBOR on the facility (with the exception of a £200m liquidity facility) was increased to 3.5%.[13] On 9 May it was announced that a new group CFO had been appointed. The incoming CFO was described as someone who had played a key role in "implementing a business plan to reduce the risk in a highly levered business".[14]

In May 2012 the company sold its interest in Thomas Cook (India) for £94m, in a move described as part of the company's plans to reduce debt.[15] In the same month the company announced the appointment of a new Group CEO. The new CEO was described as someone capable of rising to the challenges facing the Group:

> [She has] extensive experience of driving business transformation and change programmes globally. At Premier Farnell she has overseen a period of significant strategic change, driving industry leading returns and creating a cost-effective multi-channel operation where the majority of business is now transacted through ecommerce channels.[16]

An initial statement from the incoming CEO described her main priorities as follows:

> My initial focus is to review our businesses, quickly establish priorities and develop a clear plan to reinvigorate Thomas Cook, which I expect to be able to present to you next Spring. The Group has been through a difficult period, but much has been achieved which has strengthened the balance sheet and improved liquidity. The strength of the Group's brands and the quality of its businesses and people provides a foundation from which to bring the business back to full strength.[17]

"Energise–focus–rebuild"

On 13 March 2013 the company presented what it described as a UK business transformation update. The announcement detailed a reduction of 2,500 in the Group's UK workforce, mostly in back-office functions and its retail network. This announcement was followed one week later by the publication of a new growth strategy and updated profit improvement plan. The group CEO described the plans as follows:

> Our Business Transformation plans are ahead of schedule and already delivering substantially improved performance, which resulted in our recent return to the FTSE 250. We have exceeded our initial commitments and today announced a further £50m of cost out actions, bringing the total profit improvement actions identified already to £350m, £290m of which is still to come. Stabilising the business has been our priority through addressing our cost and cash challenges, and strengthening the leadership team to create a more effective, aligned organisation focused on rigorous execution.[18]

One week later the Group announced the sale of the North American business "to enable the company to focus on our core segments and future growth". Further sales occurred in November when the Group sold its specialist tour operator Neilson Active Holidays Ltd and its interests in the Airline Group. The group CEO described the sale as a result of the continued rationalisation of the business that would allow

the company "to focus on those key brands, propositions and products that will deliver our strategy for profitable growth".[19]

In May 2013 the company announced a capital refinancing plan.[20] The plan included raising approximately £425m from a rights issue and €525m from the issue of
new bonds maturing in 2020. The objectives of the plan were described as follows:

> The Capital Refinancing Plan will:
> – significantly reduce the proportion of debt funding of the Group's balance sheet;
> – extend the maturity profile of the Group's financing arrangements;
> – facilitate the implementation of the Group's Business Transformation which is expected to
>   increase the generation of surplus cash flow with a view to deleveraging the Group, while
>   providing a platform for the Group to resume dividends payments in the future; and
> – deliver a strengthened capital base and financial position which is expected to improve
>   the credit perception of Thomas Cook with suppliers and trading counterparties.

In February 2014 the Group sold another of its businesses, Gold Medal, a UK-based
distributor of long-haul scheduled flights for a total consideration of £45m to
dnata, a Dubai-based travel company. It also sold Elegant Resorts, a luxury travel
operator to Al Tayyar, a Saudi Arabian global travel group for gross cash proceedings of £14.3m. The group CEO described the sale as being "consistent with our
strategy of rationalising our UK business [. . .] allowing us to further focus on our
key brands and products to drive our profitable growth strategy".[21]

On 26 November 2014 the Group announced that the group CEO would be leaving
the business with immediate effect. On the same day audited results for the year
ended 30 September 2014 announced that the company had delivered strong profit
growth, driven by cost out and profit improvement programmes and business disposals. Net debt had been reduced by £95m to £326m.[22]

In March 2015 the Group announced that it had entered into a strategic partnership with Fosun International Limited to "build international collaboration across a
number of business areas".[23]

In May 2015 an inquest jury found that two children who had died from carbon
monoxide poisoning caused by a faulty boiler at a hotel in Corfu in 2006 had been
"unlawfully killed", and that Thomas Cook had "breached its duty of care" to the
children. The company was widely criticised in the media for the way in which it
handled the case and its apparent insensitivity to the situation that the family had
found itself in, leading to serious reputational damage.[24] An independent review of
the way in which the company handled the crisis, by the former CEO of Sainsbury's,
Justin King was particularly damaging saying that parts of the company "have a
tendency to protect cost rather than maximise the customer experience".

"Customer at our heart: continuing the transformation"

Thomas Cook's traditional offer to its core markets was based on a standardised inflexible package, typically sold through high street outlets well ahead of customer travel time. This business model was under increasing pressure from a rapid growth in more flexible and potentially cheaper alternatives from companies such as Expedia and Airbnb. Thomas Cook's business model also required a substantial upfront financial commitment by the company to the purchase of in-resort accommodation from local providers well ahead of the holiday season. This accommodation was then sold on to the final customer as part of the package, making the business vulnerable to downturns in customer demand or new alternatives offered by more flexible competitors.

Audited results for the year ended 30 September 2015 showed that profit from operations had improved from the previous year to £211m and net debt had reduced to £139m. The announcement of results also stated that the company had made its first profit after tax in five years (£19m based on like-for-like comparisons). The Group cited investment in customer service, including introducing customer satisfaction as a key performance indicator, focusing on growing sales of differentiated holidays, building the appeal of own-brand hotels and improving online and retail experience as key performance drivers.[25] Analysts commented on the company's continuing debt problems, citing the fact that a large percentage of the company's operating profit had been used to cover annual finance costs (£179m) associated with £1.4bn of gross debt.[26]

Audited results for the year ended 30 September 2016 showed profit from operations at £205m with profit after tax of £9m and net debt of £129m. Commenting on the results the group CEO pointed to the impact of a difficult year for tourism linked to a series of terrorist attacks in Paris, Brussels, Ankara and Istanbul, Tunisia and Egypt as well as the mitigating effects that he believed the company had put in place. He said:

> Right across our business we're making customers' experience of our holidays better. By focusing on fewer hotels, we can have a bigger influence on quality and service, whether that's a promise to fix any issues within 24 hours or the reassurance of regular checks on health and safety standards.
>
> [. . .]
>
> We're also building a stronger portfolio of own-brand hotels, with the aim of increasing the proportion that we manage ourselves. This will enable us to offer holidays that are unique to Thomas Cook and to attract a new generation who might have thought a package holiday wasn't for them. We're building momentum with 14 new hotels in the pipeline to open in the next two years, including the roll-out of Casa Cook into Kos and Mallorca and a new Ocean Beach Club in Cyprus.
>
> Our renewed focus on the customer has breathed new energy into the business and I'm proud of the way that our people, in our markets and in resort, have embraced the challenge. It is these efforts to create lifelong advocates for Thomas Cook that will generate greatest value in the future.[27]

Shareholders expressed their opinion about the performance of the board at the company's AGM in February 2017 where approximately one third of the investors voted against approval of the company's strategic share incentive plan and 22.5% voted against approval of the directors' remuneration report.

On 14 September 2017, the Group announced a major strategic alliance with Expedia Inc in which Expedia would become the preferred supplier of hotels for Thomas Cook city break and hotel-only sales across Europe. In return Thomas Cook was given the option to offer its core sun and beach packages on Expedia sites globally.[28] Twelve days later the company announced a strategic partnership with LMEY Investments, a Swiss-based hotel property development company to develop and grow the Group's own-brand hotel portfolio.

On 26 September 2017 the group CFO announced his plans to retire, following five years in the role. Results for the year ended 30 September 2017 showed profit from operations of £231m with £12m profit after tax. Net debt was £40m.

By comparison end of year results for 2017–2018 showed a reduction in profit from operations to £97m and a loss after tax of £163m. Net debt had increased from £40m to £389m.[29] Thomas Cook's business had faced a series of challenges including an unusually hot summer in the UK which deterred many holidaymakers from travelling abroad and the relative weakness of the pound. The annual report set out four main priorities for 2019 onwards. These were:

- Address performance in our UK tour operator business
- Better capacity management and improved operational flexibility
- Drive increased focus on cash and cost discipline across Group
- Improve selling of higher-margin own-brand hotels and differentiated holidays.

On 22 March 2019 the Group announced that it was streamlining its UK retail network as part of an ongoing programme to drive greater efficiencies across the whole business and address changing customer behaviour. It acknowledged that more and more holidaymakers were switching to online bookings (64% in the UK in 2018). Twenty-one stores would be closed across the country.[30]

Financial challenges

On 3 May 2019 the Group announced that it was engaged in discussions with its major financers about the company's overall financial position.[31]

The Group described the situation as follows:

As stated in our first quarter trading announcement of 7 February 2019, Thomas Cook kept a healthy level of liquidity headroom through the last winter cash low period, maintaining a minimum liquidity buffer within our targeted range of £150 million to £200 million.

Since that update, the business has moved into its key summer booking period where the Group's liquidity position continues to strengthen. Looking ahead to Winter 2019/20, we have taken the proactive step of engaging in discussions with our lending banks now to ensure we have both the financial flexibility necessary to maintain an appropriate liquidity buffer through the winter, and also the ability to continue to invest in our strategy of growth.

The group CEO said: "We have taken a number of prudent early steps to de-risk our business by taking out capacity in a challenging consumer environment. We have also taken the proactive step to approach our financing partners and are engaged in constructive discussions to ensure we have the flexibility and resources to continue investing behind our plans over the long-term."

Results for the first six months of the financial year 2018–2019 showed a loss from operations of £1,386m including £1,104m goodwill and brand name impairment and a loss before tax of £1,456m. Net debt was shown as £1,247m. Comparable figures for the corresponding 6 months of the previous year were £215m loss from operations, £303m loss before tax, and a net debt of £886m. Most of the company's losses were as the result of the impairment charge related to the 2007 merger with MyTravel. The Group said that it had had to revalue the deal "in light of the weak trading environment".[32]

By July 2019 the board had concluded that a major recapitalisation of the Group was required. It announced that it was in advanced discussions with the Group's largest shareholder, Fosun Tourism Group and Thomas Cook's core lending banks.[33] The Group was seeking an injection of £750m new money to provide it with sufficient liquidity to take it over the winter season and flexibility to invest in the future. Fosun would acquire a significant controlling stake in the group tour operator and a minority interest in the group airline. A significant amount of external bank and bond debt would be converted into equity.

An interim announcement on 28 August 2019 indicated that there was substantial agreement on commercial terms between the Group, Fosun, the company's core lending banks and a majority of the company's senior note holders.[34] This agreement would be subject to Fosun agreeing to contribute £450m of new money to the Group and acquiring at least 75% of the equity of the group tour operator and 25% of the group airline. The Group's core lending banks and noteholders would be required to provide a total of £450m new money and convert their existing debt into 75% of the equity of the group airline and up to 25% of new equity in the group tour operator. The announcement acknowledged that under the terms of this agreement existing shareholder interests would be significantly diluted and that any agreement would be subject to the approval of creditors, new money providers and other stakeholders.

Any agreement was subject to a range of different requirements being met. The statement set out a range of key considerations that would influence the chances of reaching a final agreement. The list, reproduced in full below, illustrates the complexity of the decisions facing the Group as it attempted to restructure its financial position.

The proposed recapitalisation remains subject to certain matters, including credit approvals, investment approvals, agreement on Group performance conditions, due diligence, agreement as to risk allocation amongst Fosun and Group creditors with respect to the bridge financing during transaction implementation, agreement between Fosun and the Group's core lending banks and noteholders on the separation of the Group into Airline and Tour Operator and timely execution of the separation, reaching agreement with a range of the Company's stakeholders (including fuel and foreign exchange hedging counterparties, the pension fund trustees, noteholders, other financial creditors and approval of Fosun's shareholders), licence renewals and receipt of regulatory and antitrust clearances and approvals.

In a final comment the board acknowledged that although their intention was to maintain the Company's listing, in certain circumstances the listing might be cancelled.

In September plans to rescue the Group were thrown into disarray when lenders asked for an additional £200m to be put in place to cover the costs of the coming winter period, when cash flow was traditionally stretched, significantly adding to the original business plan put forward by the Group that had shown it required £900m in financing to carry it over this period.[35]

Compulsory liquidation

Despite apparent goodwill between the different parties it proved impossible to reach a satisfactory agreement. On 23 September 2019 the company's board concluded that it had no choice but to enter compulsory liquidation with immediate effect. The group CEO confirmed that the company was cash flow and balance sheet insolvent.[36] A separate statement by him confirmed that the company was closing with immediate effect. He said:

> We have worked exhaustively in the past few days to resolve the outstanding issues on an agreement to secure Thomas Cook's future for its employees, customers and suppliers. Although a deal had been largely agreed, an additional facility requested in the last few days of negotiations presented a challenge that ultimately proved insurmountable.
>
> It is a matter of profound regret to me and the rest of the board that we were not successful. I would like to apologise to our millions of customers, and thousands of employees, suppliers and partners who have supported us for many years. Despite huge uncertainty over recent weeks, our teams continued to put customers first, showing why Thomas Cook is one of the best-loved brands in travel.
>
> Generations of customers entrusted their family holiday to Thomas Cook because our people kept our customers at the heart of the business and maintained our founder's spirit of innovation.
>
> This marks a deeply sad day for the company which pioneered package holidays and made travel possible for millions of people around the world.[37]

Notes

1 Thomas Cook Group plc, (2007) *UK Integration Proposals* [online], 26 June. Available at: https://www.investegate.co.uk/thomas-cook-Group–tcg-/rns/uk-integration-proposals/200706261519000585Z/ [Accessed 23 September 2021].

2 Thomas Cook Group plc, (2007) *Thomas Cook Group Investor Strategy Day* [online], 21 November. Available at: https://www.investegate.co.uk/thomas-cook-Group–tcg-/rns/investor-strategy-day/200711210702071659I/ [Accessed 23 September 2021].

3 Thomas Cook Group plc, (2008) *Unaudited results for the eleven month period ended 30 September 2008* [online] 2 December Available at: https://www.investegate.co.uk/thomas-cook-group–tcg-/rns/final-results/200812020700143363J/ [Accessed 29 April 2022].

4 Thomas Cook Group plc, (2010) *Interim Management Statement* [Online] 11 August. Available at: https://www.investegate.co.uk/thomas-cook-group–tcg-/rns/interim-management-statement/201008110700118719Q/ [Accessed 29 April 2022].

5 Thomas Cook Group plc, (2011) *Trading Update* [online] 12 July. Available at: https://www.investegate.co.uk/thomas-cook-group–tcg-/rns/trading-update/201107120700081937K/ Accessed 29 April 2022.

6 Thomas Cook Group plc, (2011) *Bank facilities extended and interest rate margin reduced* [online]. 18 July. Available at: https://www.investegate.co.uk/thomas-cook-Group–tcg-/rns/bank-facilities-extended—interest-margin-reduced/201107180746235509K/ [Accessed 23 September 2021].

7 Guthrie, J. (2011) Thomas Cook's problems are close to home. *Financial Times* [online], 12 July. Available at: https://www.ft.com/content/9c543b44-ac56-11e0-bac9-00144feabdc0 [Accessed 24 September 2021].

8 Thomas Cook Group plc, (2011) *Interim Management Statement*. 3 August. Available at: https://www.investegate.co.uk/thomas-cook-Group–tcg-/rns/interim-management-statement/201108030711296407L/ [Accessed 23 September 2021].

9 Blitz, R. (2011) Thomas Cook seeks to ease debt pressures. *Financial Times* [online], 18 July. Available at: https://www.ft.com/content/8d6f0762-b142-11e0-a43e-00144feab49a [Accessed 24 September 2021].

10 Thomas Cook Group plc, (2011) *Amendment to bank facilities*. 21 October. Available at: https://www.investegate.co.uk/thomas-cook-Group–tcg-/rns/amendment-to-bank-facilities/201110210700176012Q/ [Accessed 6 December 2021].

11 Thomas Cook Group plc, (2011) *Amendment to existing bank facilities and new £200 m bank facility secured*.[online] 25 November. Available at: https://www.investegate.co.uk/thomas-cook-Group–tcg-/rns/new-200m-bank-facility/201111280700318646S/ [Accessed 6 December 2021].

12 Thomas Cook Group plc, (2011) *Annual report and Accounts 2011*. 13 December. 2.

13 Thomas Cook Group plc, (2012) *New Longer Term Financing Agreed*. [online] 5 May. Available at: https://www.investegate.co.uk/thomas-cook-Group–tcg-/rns/new-longer-term-financing-agreed/201205080700488177C/ [Accessed 6 December 2021].

14 Thomas Cook Group plc, (2012) *Michael Healey appointed as Group CFO to succeed Paul Hollingwood*. [online]. 9 May. Available at: https://www.investegate.co.uk/thomas-cook-Group–tcg-/rns/michael-healy-appointed-as-Group-cfo/201205090700199343C/ [Accessed 6 December 2021].

15 Thomas Cook Group plc, (2012) *Disposal of Thomas Cook India*. [online]. 21 May. Available at: https://www.investegate.co.uk/thomas-cook-Group–tcg-/rns/disposal-of-thomas-cook-india/201205220700138039D/ [Accessed 6 December 2021].

16 Thomas Cook Group plc, (2012*) Harriet Green appointed as Group CEO*. [online] 24 May. Available at: https://www.investegate.co.uk/thomas-cook-Group–tcg-/rns/harriet-green-appointed-as-Group-ceo/201205240700209896D/ [Accessed 23 September 2021].

17 Thomas Cook Group plc, (2012) *Improved booking trend despite challenges*. [online] 2 August. Available at: https://www.investegate.co.uk/thomas-cook-Group–tcg-/rns/improved-booking-trend-despite-challenges/201208020700111098J/ [Accessed 23 September 2021].

18 Thomas Cook Group plc, (2013) *New growth Strategy and Updated Profit Improvement Plan.* [online] 13 March Available at: https://www.investegate.co.uk/thomas-cook-Group–tcg-/rns/growth-strategy—updated-profit-improvement-plans/201303130700228816Z/ [Accessed 23 September 2021].

19 Thomas Cook Group plc, (2013) *Sale of Neilson Active Holidays.* [online] 25 November. Available at: https://www.investegate.co.uk/thomas-cook-Group–tcg-/rns/sale-of-neilson-active-holidays/201311250930017894T/ [Accessed 23 September 2021].

20 Thomas Cook Group plc, (2013) *Thomas Cook Group £1.6 Billion Capital Refinancing Plan.* [online] 16 May. Available at: https://www.investegate.co.uk/thomas-cook-Group–tcg-/rns/capital-reorganisation/201305160700138578E/ [Accessed 23 September 2021].

21 Thomas Cook Group plc, (2014) *Thomas Cook Group Plc announces sale of Elegant Resorts.* [online] 6 February Available at: https://www.investegate.co.uk/thomas-cook-Group–tcg-/rns/tcg-Plc-announces-sale-of-elegant-resorts/201402061502325026Z/ [Accessed 6 December 2021].

22 Thomas Cook Group plc, (2014) *Thomas Cook delivers further strong profit growth.* [online] 26 November. Available at: https://www.investegate.co.uk/thomas-cook-Group–tcg-/rns/final-results/201411260700120010Y/ [Accessed 6 December 2021].

23 Thomas Cook Group plc, (2015) *Thomas Cook and Fosun announce a strategic partnership* [online]Available at https://www.investegate.co.uk/thomas-cook-group–tcg-/rns/thomas-cook-and-fosun-strategic-partnership/201503060700137138G/ [accessed 29th April 2022].

24 Hill, A. (2015) Brands need to shore up their flimsy pledges on safety. *Financial Times* [online], 25 May. Available at: https://www.ft.com/content/8ceb71aa-ff08-11e4-84b2-00144feabdc0 [Accessed September 2021].

25 Thomas Cook Group plc, (2015) *Full year results 2015, Return to profit and well positioned for growth.* [online] 25 November https://www.investegate.co.uk/thomas-cook-Group–tcg-/rns/thomas-cook-Group-full-year-results-2015/201511250700068520G/ [Accessed 6 December 2021].

26 Opinion Lex, (2015) Thomas Cook: after the internet. *Financial Times* [online], 25 November. Available at: https://www.ft.com/content/8efb493c-9366-11e5-bd82-c1fb87bef7af [Accessed 24 September 2021].

27 Thomas Cook Group plc, (2016) *Proactively managed through tough market, resumption of dividend.*[online] 23 November. Available at: https://www.investegate.co.uk/thomas-cook-Group–tcg-/rns/full-year-results-2016/201611230700078862P/ [Accessed 23 September 2021].

28 Thomas Cook Group plc, (2017) *Thomas Cook and Expedia announce strategic alliance* 14 September. Available at: https://www.investegate.co.uk/thomas-cook-Group–tcg-/rns/thomas-cook—expedia-announce-strategic-alliance/201709140700026857Q/ [Accessed 6 December 2021].

29 Thomas Cook Group plc, (2018) *Full year results announcement for the year ended 30 September 2018.* [online] 29 November. Available at: https://www.investegate.co.uk/thomas-cook-Group–tcg-/rns/full-year-results-for-year-ended-30-september-2018/201811290700108754I/ [Accessed 23 September 2021].

30 Thomas Cook Group plc, (2019) *Thomas Cook accelerates UK efficiency programme.* [online] 22 March. Available at: https://www.investegate.co.uk/thomas-cook-Group–tcg-/rns/thomas-cook-accelerates-uk-efficiency-programme/201903220900017064T/ [Accessed 28 September 2021].

31 Thomas Cook Group plc, (2019) *Statement re bank financing.* [online] 3 May. Available at: https://www.investegate.co.uk/thomas-cook-Group–tcg-/rns/statement-re-bank-financing/201905031516500829Y/ [Accessed 6 December 2021].

32 Thomas Cook Group plc, (2019) *Results for the six months ended 31 March 2019.* [online] 16 May. Available at: https://www.investegate.co.uk/thomas-cook-Group–tcg-/rns/results-for-the-six-months-ended-31-march-2019/201905160700053322Z/ [Accessed 6 December 2021].

33 Thomas Cook Group plc, (2019) *Proposed recapitalisation of Thomas Cook Group.* [online] 12 July. Available at: https://www.investegate.co.uk/thomas-cook-Group–tcg-/rns/proposed-recapitalisation-of-thomas-cook-Group/201907120700043094F/ [Accessed 23 September 2021].

34 Thomas Cook Group plc, (2019) *Update on Proposed Recapitalisation Plan*.[online] 28 August Available at: https://www.investegate.co.uk/thomas-cook-Group–tcg-/rns/update-on-proposed-re capitalisation-plan/201908280700043318K/ [Accessed 28 September 2021].
35 Hancock, A. (2019) Thomas Cook lenders seek £200 m to add to rescue. *Financial Times* [online], 19 September. Available at: https://www.ft.com/content/24ca06c2-db04-11e9-8f9b-77216ebe1f17 [Accessed 28 September 2021].
36 Dr Peter Fankhauser, 22 September 2019, "Witness statement", IN THE HIGH COURT OF JUSTICE BUSINESS AND PROPERTY COURTS OF ENGLAND AND WALES INSOLVENCY AND COMPANIES LIST (ChD) IN THE MATTER OF THOMAS COOK GROUP PLC AND IN THE MATTER OF THE INSOLVEN-CYACT 1986 [online]. Available at: https://www.tcuk-information.co.uk/matterhorn_court_file_case_cr-2019-006326/witness_statement_of_dr_peter_fankhauser.PDF [Accessed 23 September 2021].
37 Thomas Cook Group plc, (2019) *Compulsory liquidation of Thomas Cook Group plc.* [online] 23 September. Available at: https://www.investegate.co.uk/thomas-cook-Group–tcg-/rns/compul sory-liquidation-of-thomas-cook-Group-Plc/201909230700112443N/ [Accessed 23 September 2021].

7 Directors' duties

In Chapter 1 we introduced the overall framework that sets out the main themes of this book. This was presented as a series of key benchmarking questions for boards to consider. Previous chapters have covered 7 key areas (BFQs 1–7). All of these decisions need to be considered within the context of directors' legal duties to the company (BFQ 8). Table 7.1 sets out two benchmarking questions related to the fiduciary role of directors and directors' personal liabilities in situations of business distress.

We have reserved our discussion of this area until last, although we could have begun our discussion in Chapter 2 with this area. Ultimately we decided to begin with commercial aspects and discuss legal elements as the final part of the model. This sequence reflects the typical agenda for most boards, which tends to focus on essentially business-related topics, without giving much consideration to legal issues until they become critical. This perspective changes rapidly as companies experience periods of financial uncertainty that generate a wide range of questions about directors' responsibilities and challenge the relationships between the company and a wide range of different stakeholders.

The question that is addressed in this chapter is as follows:

BFQ 8 Directors' duties: To what extent do directors have an effective and relevant understanding of their general duties in situations of business distress?

Disclaimer
The discussion that follows presents an overview of key legal issues that directors might expect to face when facing problems of business distress. It is a general discussion of these areas and cannot be relied upon to inform decisions in specific situations. Any reader who is currently facing specific problems in any of these areas should take independent legal advice as appropriate.

Shareholders and members
In this chapter we use the terms shareholder and member interchangeably. The term "shareholders" refers to ordinary shareholders.

The fiduciary role of directors

BFQ 8.1 To what extent are directors aware of and meet their formal legal obligations (duties) to shareholders, lenders and other stakeholders?
Whilst the previous chapters have focused on the functional roles of directors, this chapter provides an overview of directors' general legal duties. In common law jurisdictions a company per se is considered as having no capacity to think or make decisions on its own. It is completely reliant on company directors who make decisions on its behalf acting as fiduciaries. One core element that has driven much of this

https://doi.org/10.1515/9783110689495-012

Table 7.1: BFQ 8 Directors' duties: To what extent do directors have an effective and relevant understanding of their general duties in situations of business distress?.

Benchmarking questions	Commentary (Evidence)	Score
The fiduciary role of directors **BFQ 8.1 To what extent are directors aware of and meet their formal legal obligations (duties) to shareholders, lenders and other stakeholders?**	Awareness and knowledge of director duties and an explicit regular review of performance in relevant areas Systematic evaluation of prospective decisions against formal director duties including responsibility to consider the impact of decisions on other stakeholders and the exercise of independent judgement Regular in-house training and director development programmes specifically relating to the exercise of reasonable care, skill and diligence	
Directors' personal liabilities **BFQ 8.2 How does the board monitor and safeguard itself against possible wrongful or fraudulent trading, misfeasance and preferential treatment?**	Stress testing of different financial assumptions about the future Use of specialist independent advisors Effective record keeping and use of key financial ratios including cash flow and balance sheet performance [See the discussion of evidence in Tables 4.1, 5.1 and 5.2. All of these are relevant to BFQ 8.2] Rapid response to any emerging doubts about the business situation or decisions taken by the business Effective corporate governance systems that monitor and report on executive and board decision-making	

discussion is the concept of the company as an independent entity.[1] This concept is a legal fiction that creates a clear distinction between the company as a separate entity, those who invest money in the company and those who manage its affairs. This principle has evolved over time as a result of different judicial interpretations.

All members of the board who are formally included in the register of directors have a range of general responsibilities to the company by virtue of their appointment. These responsibilities exist irrespective of the size or nature of the business. In the smallest of companies with only one registered director running the business that director still has the same general responsibilities that apply to the directors of the largest companies. Non-executive directors have the same general responsibilities, as do those who may not be registered as directors but may be exercising control or influence over the business (shadow directors).

Directors do not have an obligation to take a formal oath when they take on their fiduciary role. They are not required to show any knowledge or understanding of their legal obligations leading to the criticism that they are frequently ill-trained or ill-prepared. This criticism was reflected in a UK government consultation on insolvency and corporate governance in 2018. The consultation sought views on a range of different matters including whether "when commissioning and using professional advice, company directors did so with an adequate awareness of their legal duties under the Companies Act 2006, specifically the duties in sections 172–177 which include the requirement to exercise independent judgement". The report stated that the majority of respondents expressed confidence that "directors had a good awareness of their legal duties, including the need to apply an independent mind when making decisions on behalf of the company, taking into account any professional advice they may have commissioned". However, the report also recognised the need for more guidance and training for directors "particularly newly appointed directors in charge of large complex firms managing significant numbers of employees and contracts and having to comply with regulatory regimes".

Fiduciary duties are interrelated and extend beyond the relationship between directors and the company to include third parties. Common law jurisdictions provide an evolving perspective on these duties which in the UK are described as "simple, strict and salutary".[2] The Companies Act 2006 has codified such duties whilst also highlighting the need to consider the common law rules and equitable principles associated with each duty. In the US directors' duties include duty of care, duty of loyalty, duty of good faith, duty of confidentiality, duty of disclosure, duty of prudence and duty of disclosure. In some civil law jurisdictions company directors may also be subject to similar duties although they are not always characterised as fiduciaries. For example, in Germany company directors owe duties of care and loyalty to their companies. In France, directors' general duties include a duty of prudence and diligence (Thomson Reuters, 2022). In each of these jurisdictions breach of these duties may expose directors to temporary or permanent disqualification from future roles as directors.

Duty to promote the success of the company

Under English law, directors have an obligation to place their primary focus on the interests of the company. The same obligation applies in a range of other jurisdictions including Germany, France, Hong Kong and China. This exclusive focus is unilateral in the sense that it does not impose any reciprocal responsibility on the part of the company towards directors. It explicitly rules out the inclusion of alternative beneficiaries whether internal, such as other fellow directors and individual members, or external such as creditors regardless of the length of their contractual relationship with the company.

Under the Companies Act 2006, directors must pay attention to shareholders' collective interests as part of a specific duty that requires directors to promote the success of the company. The duty requires directors to fulfil this obligation in good faith.

Directors are encouraged to actively consider the opportunities and the threats that lie ahead of their beneficiary and take an entrepreneurial approach (McNicholas, 2020).

The UK Parliament took the first step towards explicitly recognising responsibility to stakeholders by introducing a provision in the Companies Act 2006 that creates a loose obligation for company directors to have regard for the interests of a wider range of stakeholders. Stakeholders identified in the legislation include employees, suppliers of goods and services and the community. Companies are also tasked with having due regard to the impact of their actions on the environment. Some stakeholders may have formal contractual relationships with the company. Others including the community do not have such relationships.

Duty to exercise independent judgement

The previous 5 chapters have covered a wide range of different decisions that directors can be faced with when building a resilient company or attempting to turn a company with problems around. In each area we suggested that directors might use their judgement to assess how well they are performing and identify areas for improvement. Whilst director judgement might feature implicitly or explicitly in any commercial decisions that directors make on behalf of a company, it also has a very specific and much more narrowly defined meaning from a legal perspective.

The responsibility of directors to exercise independent judgement focuses on the restriction of director discretion under certain contractual conditions. In principle this duty protects a company director from undue pressure or limitations on decisions, unless such restrictions form part of the company's constitution or are included in previously agreed contracts between the company and third parties. The evolution of this duty and its potential impact on decision-making is described in detail by Parkinson (2017). This duty applies the concept of good faith to director decisions, requiring them to ensure that all of the company's interests are thought through before they enter into contracts with third parties that commit the company to specific obligations in return for certain rights. In the UK section 173 of the Companies Act 2006 which addresses this duty does not impose specific restrictions on how directors should exercise independent judgement, implying its recognition of the complexity of corporate decision-making and the range of different issues that may be involved. Directors have the freedom to enter into any lawful agreement whether it is of commercial or non-commercial nature.

In some cases, company directors may not be happy with the implementation of contracts that have already been agreed, as unforeseen problems emerge that were not evident when the contract was signed, for instance when a change of circumstances means that the projected profits from a specific venture turn into a projected loss. To resolve such problems, directors may attempt to breach the terms and conditions of such contracts arguing that the implementation of the contract will not be in the best interests of the company. However, the duty to exercise independent judgement prevents directors from making such U-turns. This applies provided that it can be demonstrated that directors have taken into account the company's best interests prior to the point at which the contract is signed and becomes legally enforceable.

Duty to exercise reasonable care, skill and diligence

Directors differ widely in terms of the relevant skills and experience that they bring to their role. Whilst they may be comfortable with their role as entrepreneur or as a member of the executive team, they may be less likely to be aware of the broader skills and competences that their role may require. It is not uncommon for directors to be in breach of a continuing equitable duty that lawmakers have formulated as "exercising reasonable care, skill and diligence".

In general, this duty means that directors should be actively involved in fulfilment of their functions and responsibilities and ensure that they have applied their knowledge, skills and experience reasonably.[3] It is necessary for directors to be aware of the minimum standards of competence that a reasonable diligent person should have in that role. Further, they should also be able to evidence their deployment of their qualities. They may be held in breach of this general duty if they fail to meet these two tests.

At first glance this duty may sound irrelevant to many company directors, particularly those who manage small family owned companies. After all their appointment as a director was not dependent on being able to demonstrate their mastery of specific skills. Entrepreneurs who have set up new start-up companies may question the validity of needing to demonstrate such qualities. They may legitimately argue that they are passionate about their company and spend all of their time on building the business. They can also argue that they use external advisors for specialist support as and when needed. Directors who are appointed to the boards of large and medium-sized companies will point to the fact that many specific aspects of the job are delegated to others within the organisation and that they have access to specialist internal assistance and external professional service companies to support the decisions they make. The law does not challenge directors' decisions to delegate responsibilities to competent and qualified people as appropriate. In such circumstances directors are still expected to retain a supervisory role and ensure that the delegated functions have been carried out properly.

On the other hand, courts have been critical of those company directors who have specialist knowledge but fail to act appropriately when they recognise there is a problem. Such directors have an obligation to intervene when they become aware that the company's affairs are being managed in an ineffective or improper way. They cannot avoid this responsibility. For example, taking no action when they realise that misleading information has been released to investors about the company's business prospects or true indebtedness may be a breach of this general duty. Giving way to the proposals of other senior executives at a board meeting when it is clear that such decisions are illegal or go against established governance principles is also a breach of this general duty. Directors should also not allow other directors to engage in a wide range of fraudulent activities including producing backdated documents, or the forgery of someone else's signature.

Directors' conflict of interests, gifts and personal transactions with the company

The law weaves two principles into the relationship between directors and companies that reflect the company's primacy position. These two principles, the "no-conflict" rule and the "no-secrecy" rule specify how directors must deal with any potential conflict between their fiduciary duties to the company and personal interests. Under the no-conflict rule directors may not access or benefit from any opportunity, property or information that compromises their duty to the company and puts it in a secondary position in their assessment of priorities and the decisions that they make. Directors may be entitled to benefit personally from decisions agreed by the board as whole, provided that the nature and type of interest is disclosed and declared to the other directors. Typically such decisions are ratified by the board through a voting process where the relevant director loses the right to vote on the subject matter. The same director is not barred from lobbying other directors prior to the actual vote.

The purpose of the duty is to protect the company from any potential loss that may be created by undisclosed benefits gained by that director at the expense of the company. All potential gains must be disclosed ahead of any decision on whether those involved may take advantage of such opportunities. The negligible or nominal value of any personal advantage and the period of time that it has been enjoyed cannot be used as an excuse to justify non-disclosure. In large companies directors may be suspended or removed from their position for failing to declare such interests. The "no-conflict/no-secrecy" rules may be treated differently if the relevant director is the sole owner and manager of company. For instance, directors of small companies or family-owned businesses where decisions are often made by owner-managers typically have few if any problems in getting formal approval for decisions that may provide personal benefit.

Directors' personal liabilities

BFQ 8.2 How does the board monitor and safeguard itself against possible wrongful or fraudulent trading, misfeasance and preferential treatment?

Wrongful trading

When company directors become aware that their company has encountered severe financial problems that threaten its viability and there is no reasonable prospect of avoiding insolvent liquidation or administration, they are expected to take reasonable steps to minimise potential losses to creditors.[4] Failure to do so may mean that they could face personal liability for wrongful trading, requiring them to make a financial contribution to the pool of assets available to creditors for any losses that are incurred. Directors are legally bound to take action when they know or should have known that insolvent liquidation or administration was inevitable. Their actions will be compared with those of a hypothetical director applying reasonable prudence in taking such decisions, based on assumptions about their general knowledge, skills and experience. Their performance will be subject to both objective and subjective tests. There is no immediate obligation for directors in such circumstances to terminate the company's trading. There is also no assumption that directors should be able to see into the future and act as a "clairvoyant".[5] Their decisions should reflect a reasonable standard of care rather than "a cavalier attitude" towards creditors' interests.

In successful court cases instigated by administrators or liquidators on behalf of insolvent companies, the financial contribution of former directors is determined by the court and depends on the circumstances of each case. The calculation is generally based on the increase in company debt and depletion of assets during the specific period of time that exposed the company to irreversible risk. In principle, the logic behind such a compensatory remedy is that directors ignored one basic question: "could the company properly continue to trade?" Directors are financially penalised for an irresponsible approach in keeping their insolvent company operating.

Directors have been able to avoid liability for wrongful trading when they can demonstrate that they have made an effort to address financial problems. This can include stopping the payment of personal salaries or providing a substantial loan to the company. Evidence of the possibility of outside funding, retaining a qualified accountant to prepare regular financial reports, reliance on professional advice (even erroneous) and reduction in the number of employees have also been deemed to be evidence that directors can use to avoid such liability.[6] Directors have been held liable when they have failed to keep true, original and proper records, where there are no records detailing payments to directors and relatives, or there has been unjustified use of the company's money for personal purposes including the purchase of a car. Regular payment of director salaries in such circumstances has also been seen to be inappropriate. Directors will also be held liable where it can be shown that they have entered into agreements with new creditors despite having insufficient capital or inadequate future funds to implement such agreements.[7]

Fraudulent trading

Many company directors are more likely to be concerned about the potential of being accused of fraudulent trading. Accusations of fraudulent trading impugn directors' credibility and their trustworthiness. A detailed investigation may be carried by an administrator or a liquidator if there is potential evidence of company directors' continuing to operate the company as a going concern whilst insolvent with an intention to defraud creditors.[8]

Evidence of one significant fraudulent transaction may provide sufficient justification to establish directors' involvement in a criminal offence.[9] The challenge for an insolvency practitioner is to provide evidence to the satisfaction of the court that the company, its directors or a third person had the requisite actual knowledge or belief of the facts relating to the fraudulent nature of activities.[10] This requirement forms the first part of a test of liability and is assessed on a subjective basis. Further, the scope of knowledge has been narrowed down to exclude those cases where the defendant failed to recognise the existence of fraud, regardless of how obvious it was.[11]

There is no requirement to show evidence that the company through its directors or employees "knew every detail of the fraud or the precise mechanics of how it would be carried out, but [this] requires proof that clearly shows they did have to know, either from their own observation of what was being done or from what they were told, that the company was intent on a fraud".[12] Moreover, courts have not absolved civil liability where a defendant deliberately ignores the obvious ongoing fraud because she was "consciously" concerned that should she seek further information or clarification, her suspicion would be confirmed by the facts.[13] The defendant's knowledge with the benefit of hindsight is not sufficient.[14] Whilst there is no apparent statutory requirement to require proof of dishonesty, courts are required to use an objective test to examine the element of dishonesty based on the standards of ordinary decent people.[15]

Misfeasance

Misfeasance covers a broad range of misconducts carried out by any director who has held office in an insolvent company at any stage of its life cycle from formation to entry into a formal insolvency procedure and ultimately liquidation. Promoters and insolvency practitioners acting as a liquidator or administrative officer are also subject to the same potential liability.[16] Each of these may ultimately be held individually liable for any wrongful act that has led to a reduction in the assets available to unsecured creditors at the point of liquidation. Evidence of misfeasance may be provided to the court by a creditor, a liquidator or the official receiver of an insolvent company to show that on the balance of probabilities the relevant party has "misapplied, retained or become accountable for any money or property or breach of fiduciary duty".[17] Where this has been determined to be the case this may increase the pool of assets available for distribution by compelling the relevant company director (s) and/or other individuals to compensate the company for the loss.

Preferential treatment

Directors (predominantly in small businesses) frequently provide financial support in the form of a personal guarantee or a director's loan. Issues with a director's personal liability can arise when such directors make decisions to protect their personal interests and ignore the interests of creditors, with no credible commercial reason for their decisions. One example is the transfer of funds from one company to another. This may happen when a director is seeking to avoid personal liability for a potential default on loan repayments by the second company. If this then creates problems for the first company, particularly if that first company is also potentially insolvent, then this would be deemed to be inappropriate behaviour. Another example is a director's authorisation of payments to himself to settle debts agreed under any previous lending agreement.

Insolvency tests

When a company cannot meet the terms and conditions of an existing borrowing agreement it potentially becomes exposed to the threat of legal action by its creditors. Such problems may become apparent following an external creditor's initiation of legal proceedings for recovery of a debt or as part of an ongoing review of the company's circumstances by a lender. In such circumstances one or more creditors may obtain a court order that effectively forces the company to close following receipt of relevant statutory notices.

A company may need to enter a formal insolvency procedure if it becomes apparent that it is no longer able to meet either a cash flow test or balance sheet test. In the UK statutory law relating to the cash flow test focuses on the company's ability to meet its current liabilities as they fall due. The balance sheet test broadens the range of relevant liabilities to include the company's contingent and prospective liabilities valued against its assets.

Cash flow problems can occur from time to time in most businesses, for a range of different reasons and in many situations such problems are resolved. Cash flow can also be a problem when companies that are new to the market are experiencing rapid growth and realise that they need immediate injections of new capital to fund their development. The UK judicial interpretation of the cash flow test takes account of temporary illiquidity and the actions that management may have taken to resolve the situation. A range of options are open to companies in each of these different circumstances including an extension of overdraft facilities, new loans from their current lender or new lenders, director loans or further cash injection from members.

The cash flow test covers both present debts and those liabilities that are due in the reasonably near future. The test is "flexible" and relies heavily on the facts of each case.[18] The test does not identify situations where a company may carry on with payment of liabilities for some time but is actually insolvent due to "a fatal shortage of working capital" that ultimately results in its failure.[19] Long-term creditors have criticised the value of the cash flow test as the only measure of insolvency because of the priority that it gives to the repayment of debt owed to short-term creditors (Goode, 2011).

The balance sheet test addresses some of these concerns, providing a more comprehensive picture of the company's overall solvency based on a full assessment of the company's liabilities and assets. Applying this test present and future liabilities are compared with the company's total assets.[20] The balance sheet test is not an "exact" test[21] because it takes the timing and maturity of all liabilities into account; therefore, as the maturity date for such liabilities extends further into the future, it becomes increasingly difficult to establish balance sheet insolvency. Some assets will also be excluded from the calculation. Generally future income streams are only included if there is "credible evidence" of their positive impact.[22]

The outcome of the test depends on the judgment of the court and each case is evaluated on its own specific circumstances. The test is not considered to be "mechanistic".[23] Other non-financial factors may be taken into account leading to a range of different possible outcomes. For example, courts are often reluctant to regard start-up companies as balance sheet insolvent because they are typically supported by investors who hope to benefit from the ultimate success of their investment.[24] Some investors may provide loans to the company with no specific deadline on when their loan should be paid so long as the company does not incur losses in the meantime.[25] In such circumstances, it would be very difficult to conclude that such companies were balance sheet insolvent.

Insolvency and directors' fiduciary duty

The directors of solvent companies are free to commit the company to a range of agreements with creditors under different contractual terms and conditions. Creditors can be classified in different ways according to the nature of their business with the company. Different categories include suppliers, employees, lenders/

banks, the tax authorities and customers. Contracts with creditors can be classified as secured or unsecured depending on whether or not the transactions have been guaranteed by security interests granted over the company's assets including premises and machinery. Mortgage, lien, fixed and floating charges are the most common forms of such securities.

The relationship between directors and each of these third parties changes when it becomes apparent that a company is no longer able to meet its financial obligations and the company is likely to enter a formal insolvency procedure unless directors take appropriate action. In such circumstances directors have a fiduciary duty to creditors that overrides their duty to members. Common law jurisdictions including the UK and the USA have established a priority ranking that governs the relative position of creditors in such situations. Secured creditors have the most significant influence.

A range of different frameworks have been introduced in different countries to provide temporary relief from creditor claims whilst directors attempt to restructure the company's existing debt structure. These frameworks provide temporary respite from creditors' claims at the point when companies are subject to formal insolvency procedures. They have been designed to maximise the chances of business recovery by giving directors the time to discuss and implement alternative ways to resolve financial problems. The main feature of these frameworks is the way in which they allow company directors to remain in control of the company's business and contribute to the development of any restructuring plan (termed debtor in possession or DIP).

Once a formal procedure has been implemented directors' powers are greatly limited in terms of their discretion to sell the company's assets or use such assets to obtain secured loans. Any decisions are subject to review and modification by an officer of the court who is appointed to provide a realistic overview of the company's prospects of rescue and monitor the company's compliance with mandatory requirements.[26] Such appointees are required to take an independent view of the company's position based on their review of the company's financial information including assets, liabilities and the specific rating and prioritisation of the company's different creditors, classified by the nature of their claims.

A distinctive feature of the DIP restructuring framework in both the US and the UK is the requirement for creditor and shareholder approval of proposals that might impact their interests. Such approval is based on voting by class which is an essential requirement of any restructuring plan. A plan is deemed to have been approved if the majority of creditors vote in favour, taking account of the relative scale of individual claims. In the UK, a majority is defined as 75% of the majority voting in favour. Given the possibility of creditors of one class rejecting the proposed changes, the court retains its discretion to approve a restructuring plan under a provision known as cross-class cram-down that binds all creditors to the proposed plan. The cram-down power allows the court to balance the interests of one group of creditors with those of creditors as a whole if it can be demonstrated that any class of creditors that are dissenting to the plan will be better off under the plan than under any other option.

A formal insolvency procedure puts a temporary freeze on the standing of the company as a going concern. This freeze may become permanent depending on the outcome of negotiations between the company and its creditors. Once the company enters formal processes the roles and obligations of directors are subject to different statutory provisions and creditors' claims are subject to different priorities, depending on their standing. In such circumstances directors may also have personal liabilities and have to contribute to the pool of assets distributed among creditors.

The multiple roles and functions of insolvency practitioners in UK insolvency law

Formal insolvency frameworks in the UK have been designed to hand over control of the business to an independent practitioner to manage its affairs. In the most commonly used framework known as administration, the previous directors are no longer involved in the management of the company although some may be retained in the short term to assist the work of the practitioner. However, in a Company Voluntary Arrangement (CVA), insolvency practitioners are involved in different stages of formulation, approval and implementation of a rescue plan in various capacities. All insolvency practitioners are qualified professionals who act as officers of the court and agents of the company. Their role, powers, rights and liabilities are determined by the type of insolvency procedure that they oversee and their independence from company directors or creditors.

The UK Insolvency Act 1986 sets out three alternative scenarios when a company enters administration. The first and most desirable outcome is that the company is able to continue as a going concern. Alternatively, the process may be used to ensure that when a company is formally declared insolvent creditors receive a better financial return than if the company were to be wound up. The least preferred option would be to realise assets with a view to making a distribution among one or more secured creditors or preferential creditors, potentially leaving unsecured creditors empty-handed. The evaluation of the relative benefits and disadvantages of each of these options is a matter of judgement for the insolvency practitioner.

Insolvency practitioners may often be actively involved in evaluating a company's financial and economic viability prior to any decision being taken about the company's potential entry into a formal insolvency process. Appointment of an administrator ends the direct control of directors over the affairs of the business. This appointment may be made by the directors themselves, the company, a court order or holders of a qualifying floating charge over the company's assets. In the UK the appointment of administrators should be registered at Companies House and notice of their appointment filed with the court. Typically such appointments are also widely reported in the appropriate financial media.

The primary role of an administrator is to ensure that a company's debts to its various creditors are resolved in a prescribed way. An administrator has wide discretionary powers to maximise the pool of assets available for distribution among creditors with non-disputed claims. An administrator has general powers to dispose of assets that are not subject to any security interests. In the case of those assets that have been used as security the administrator has to consider the type of security and consult all secured creditors before any proposed sale of such assets. Assets subject to a floating charge may be disposed of without prior consultation or consent from the charge holder or court permission. An administrator does not have this authority when it comes to assets that are subject to a fixed charge. In these circumstances the administrator is obliged to seek the informed consent of the fixed charge holder or seek a court order. Asset disposal cannot be made before the asset has been subject to independent valuation.

In a pre-packaged administration, an administrator may facilitate the sale of part of the business, including its assets to company directors or an independent third party. This may result in the transfer of assets, employees and secured loan obligations to a new company set up by or on behalf of the purchasers. In such cases, an agreement is reached immediately before or soon after entry into administration with the likelihood that the consent of lenders has also been obtained.

An administrator has no obligation to ensure that the company continues as a going concern. In practice some companies may continue to trade to realise any potential return on assets on a temporary basis. For example, a retailer in administration may continue to trade for a temporary period to clear stock. In such circumstances an administrator may authorise the continuation of existing contracts with creditors or enter into new contracts with the proviso that payments due under such contracts will be given priority over existing debt and made as part of the expenses of administration.

Company Voluntary Arrangement (CVA)

A Company Voluntary Arrangement (CVA) is a formal insolvency procedure that allows the company to make new payment arrangements with one or more groups of its unsecured creditors. The CVA process is available to all companies in appropriate circumstances under the Insolvency Act 1986. The potential benefit to the company is a reduction in ongoing financial liabilities, potentially with less disruption to day-to-day business operations. The downside for unsecured creditors is that they are forced to accept a reduction in the amount owed to them by the company. Such agreements are likely to be accepted when such creditors perceive little or no likelihood of recovering the amounts owed to them by the company if the existing agreements remain in place. The Arcadia case study at the end of Chapter 3 discusses how Arcadia Group Ltd used CVAs as part of its attempts to restructure finances in the year before the business was placed into administration. A CVA may create a temporary pause to winding-up petitions but if ultimately unsuccessful it can be followed by administration or liquidation. This was the pattern with Arcadia.

In a CVA company directors retain their control powers over the affairs of the company. An insolvency practitioner will work with the company to lead the formulation of proposals, creditor voting on proposals and the implementation of the debt repayment schedule. The rights and interests of preferential creditors and secured creditors remain unchanged and they have no vote on the process; however, secured creditors may frequently require company directors to implement a CVA in appropriate circumstances as part of a broader restructuring plan for refinancing the company through further secured borrowing.

The role of an insolvency practitioner varies as the CVA evolves. As a nominee the practitioner is expected to file a report with the court presenting his expert opinion on the reasonable prospect of creditor approval of the proposed rescue plan and the likelihood of its successful implementation. The report should include recommendations about holding creditor meetings and shareholder meetings including a timetable for voting on proposals. Any proposal should be based on detailed information about the company's overall financial position. Such nominees, particularly where they are appointed relatively early on in the process can help company directors to explore "the funding opportunities and assess insolvency options, review the company's cashflow forecasting and assist with developing working capital improvement opportunities".

The court filing is followed by creditor and shareholder meetings to vote on the plan. Creditors have the right to raise questions about the proposal, seek modifications and ultimately vote on proposals at a formal meeting. The meeting is chaired by the insolvency practitioner. The creditors' meeting also votes on proposals for the remuneration for supervisors of the fund. The outcome of the meeting is filed with the court. All unsecured creditors are ultimately bound by the outcome of the vote. A proposed debt payment plan is approved if it receives a majority of 75% of votes by value. Rejection of the plan by creditors is likely to result in the company being placed into administration or liquidation. Creditors who do not agree to any formal proposals that have been approved at such a meeting may challenge the outcome in court. The responsibility for the subsequent implementation of a CVA proposal lies with the insolvency practitioner who becomes the supervisor of a fund to be distributed amongst eligible creditors under the CVA plan.

Shareholder influence

Members are legally distanced from day to day management of the company. This exclusion relates to any explicit or implicit involvement in the negotiation, execution and completion of contracts between the company and its creditors. In situations of financial distress members' powers are limited in scope and enforcement. Any influence on the company's affairs is determined by the grant of statutory rights attached to the ownership of shares that are exercisable under certain circumstances. Individual shareholders cannot be held liable for voting in favour or against a resolution as they owe no fiduciary duty to the company.

Shareholders may be involved in voting on specific corporate rescue procedures such as a CVA or US Chapter 11 bankruptcy. Shareholder approval is also likely to be necessary for decisions about the closure of a company prior to entry into formal insolvency procedures or the acceptance of a takeover bid from a third party. In such circumstances the majority view will prevail. In exceptional circumstances, minority shareholders can seek the intervention of the courts to pursue a derivative claim on behalf of the company based on the potential harm that a decision might bring although there is no assurance that the claim will succeed.

Members seeking to have a more proactive role are likely to have higher levels of share ownership. Such members including institutional shareholders will seek informal avenues to engage with directors on the future direction of the company. In reality where a small number of shareholders hold a significant proportion of the shares with voting rights, formal voting processes are often confirmation of decisions that have already been agreed with such major shareholders. Managing the expectations of such large investors is an important element of the role of many directors in distress situations as the Carillion case study at the end of Chapter 4 illustrates.

Formal shareholder meetings, with formal resolutions may not be required to endorse some board decisions in distress situations. For example, the employment of new directors does not require prior approval by shareholders although public disclosure of their employment is mandatory. Listing rules also exempt those public companies that are financially distressed from seeking shareholder approval for asset sale,[27] although disclosure of information is again mandatory.

Shareholder endorsement does become critical when the board adopts other rescue strategies, including the issue of new equity or loan renegotiation particularly when major institutional shareholders are involved (Short and Keasey, 1999). The Thomas Cook case study at the end of the last chapter illustrates how this process can become complicated with a range of different factors influencing the final outcome.

Reflection

The principle of the independent nature of a limited liability company encouraged personal investment in new business ventures, whilst at the same time sheltering investors from the possible personal financial consequences of business failure. Subsequent cases and statutes over the last
120 years have focused on the role of those who manage the funds of investors as custodians of
their wealth. We have looked at this role briefly in this chapter, focusing on directors' duties and
how they impact on decision-making in times of business distress and insolvency.

In many countries including the UK, corporate governance codes sit alongside statutory legislation. Such codes are intended to ensure that boards meet explicit performance standards in areas
such as leadership and direction, composition and responsibilities, internal audit processes and
the development and remuneration of board members. We have touched on specific elements of
such codes in the discussion in previous chapters. Such codes are a form of "soft law" that sits
alongside more formal legal considerations.

Corporate governance in its classical form is about reassuring others that the board is doing a
good job and meeting its duties to shareholders, creditors and other interested parties. Whilst this
is an important focus we believe that there is another form of governance – strategic governance.
Strategic governance is the process by which the board checks for itself how well it is performing
in critical areas and makes improvements where appropriate. Whilst outcomes are important and
will continue to dominate the agenda of most boards, developing an understanding of the relative
effectiveness of decision-making and identification of areas for improvement is also critical to effective board performance.

Building and restoring a resilient business has become a priority for many boards. This book
has set out a benchmarking framework that we hope will be useful for those seeking to improve
their performance in this critical area as well as adding to the debate about the future development
and usefulness of governance models. In the next and final chapter we discuss how this framework
might be applied in practice.

Notes

1 The focus of this chapter is on companies limited by shares rather than other types of business
organisations.

2 *Tower v Premier Waste Management* [2011] EWCA Civ 923.

3 Companies Act 2006, s 174.

4 Insolvency Act 1986, s 214.

5 *Re Hawkes Hill Publishing Co Ltd* [2007] BCC 937;.

6 See for instance, *Re Hawkes Hill Publishing Co Ltd (in liquidation); Ward v Perks* [2007] EWHC
3073(Ch).

7 See for instance *Singla v Hedman* [2010] 2 BCLC 61;.

8 See Insolvency Act 1986, s213.

9 See Westlaw Practical Law Business Crime and Investigations, "Note for the board on fraudulent
trading".

10 See Insolvency Act 1986, s213. See also *Morris v Bank of India*.

11 *Morris v Bank of India* [2004] BCC 404, 419.

12 *Morris v Bank of India* [2004] BCC 404, 419.

13 *Morris v Bank of India* [2004] BCC 404, 419. See Also *Pantiles Investments Ltd (In liquidation)*
[2019] BCC 1003, 1014.

14 *Morris v Bank of India* [2004] BCC 404, 419.

15 *Re Pantiles Investments Ltd (in Liquidation)* [2019] BCC 1003, 1004.

16 See Insolvency Act 1986, s 212.

17 Insolvency Act 1986, s 212.

18 *Bucci v Carman (Liquidator of Casa Estates (UK) Limited)* [2014] BCC 269, [34] per Lewison LJ.

19 *Re Cheyne* [2008] BCC 182 at [51] per Briggs J.

20 *BNY v Eurosail* [2013] 1 BCLC 613 [37] per Lord Walker.

21 *BNY v Eurosail* [2013] 1 BCLC 613, 631 [37] per Lord Walker.

22 *Carman (Liquidator of Casa Estates (UK) Ltd) v Bucci* [2013] EWHC 2371 (Ch) [70] per Warren J.; *Bucci v Carman (Liquidator of Casa Estates (UK) Limited)* [2014] BCC 269, [38] per Lewison LJ;.

23 *Carman (Liquidator of Casa Estates (UK) Ltd) v Bucci* [2013] EWHC 2371 (Ch) [72] per Warren J.

24 *Carman (Liquidator of Casa Estates (UK) Ltd) v Bucci* [2013] EWHC 2371 (Ch) [82] per Warren J.

25 *Carman (Liquidator of Casa Estates (UK) Ltd) v Bucci* [2013] EWHC 2371 (Ch) [82] per Warren J.

26 In the US, such a qualified person is called trustee in bankruptcy and in the UK a monitor who is actually a licensed insolvency practitioner.

27 Under rule 10.8 of the *Financial Conduct Authority Handbook*, a financially distressed company may obtain a waiver with regards to seeking shareholder approval when asset sale is initiated.

8 Benchmarking strategic governance

Ways to use the framework

Initial scoping exercise

One effective way to begin is to use the eight main benchmarking questions set out in Table 1.1 to focus on the overall picture first before exploring each area in depth. An initial review could be used to determine if there are significant problem areas and identify aspects of the framework for specific focus in any further more detailed follow-up. This review could be done by one or more members of the board as a quick exercise to see if a broader more extensive process is worth pursuing. If such a review generates specific areas of interest then a second stage could be to involve the whole board in reviewing the generic list. At the same time other significant stakeholders such as a representative group of employees could be asked to review the same questions.

By way of illustration Table 8.1 uses the main benchmarking questions (BFQ 1 to BFQ 8) to review the history of Flybe Group plc, our first extended case discussed at the end of Chapter 2. It is important to state again at the outset that we are making no comment on the quality of executive decisions that were made by successive boards over the period that the case covers. From an outsider's point of view it is difficult when looking into an organisation to determine what the motives of the board may have been when they made specific decisions.

The purpose of the presentation in Table 8.1 is to illustrate how each of the main generic benchmarking questions could be used to structure a general discussion of business resilience and identify areas for improvement. This review has been written by someone looking into the business. By definition we were not party to the range of different influences on the decisions that were made nor all of the potential consequences. Readers will note that we have made no comment on directors' duties (BFQ 8). Such information is not readily available in this case to the external observer.

https://doi.org/10.1515/9783110689495-013

Table 8.1: Flybe Group Plc: Generic benchmarking framework.

Benchmarking Questions	Commentary	Score
	Building business resilience	
BFQ 1 Purpose Does the board actively consider business purpose and update to reflect changing stakeholder expectations and the external environment?	Flybe's business model appears to have been driven by the desire to be the leading regional operator in the UK, building an extensive route network connecting regional destinations across the UK and providing a series of hubs where passengers could connect with flights to international destinations using partnership agreements with major international carriers. Ultimately the consortium that agreed to buy Flybe was unwilling to continue to support the operation of the company across a large number of unprofitable routes, with increasing competition from road and rail and ultimately a switch to online rather than face-to-face meetings for many commercial and social purposes.	
BFQ 2 Strategic governance Does the board regularly and systematically review its own competences and performance?	Flybe's original board was evenly split with 5 executive and five non-executive directors following its official listing on 15 December 2010. The role of the CEO and chairman of the board were combined. This pattern changed in 2013 with the separation of the roles and the appointment of a new CEO. The number of executive directors on the board was also reduced to two. Over nine years the Flybe Group had four different CEOs and three different CFOs.	
BFQ 3 Resilient planning How effective is the board in setting the overall direction of the business and monitoring how well plans are implemented?	For the first three years following its IPO in 2010 Flybe sought to differentiate itself from the competition by increasing the number of routes it offered. This strategy was followed by a period of aggressive cost reduction in an attempt to improve the relative thin margins that were available in the markets in which it operated, resulting in some minor improvements in profitability. In the third phase the company focused more explicitly on customer experience and reducing the scale of operations to more profitable (less costly) largely UK-based routes with a scaled down turbo-prop based fleet.	

Table 8.1 (continued)

BFQ 4 Financial Stewardship To what extent do directors give careful long-term consideration to the financial and broader commercial resilience of the company?	Reviewing Flybe's annual reports over a nine-year period it is evident that management of cash flow is a critical concern. In six of the eight years following its initial public offering the company reported a pre-tax loss, albeit marginal. Cash drained consistently out of the company over all nine years between its IPO in 2010 and its sale in 2019, being topped up in 2013-14 by a rights issue.
BFQ 5 Risk management How well does the board assess and manage potential risks to the business?	Flybe operated in a rapidly changing external environment where business operations were subject to fluctuations in patterns of weather that impacted on the public's willingness to travel, changes to exchange rates and the cost of fuel. In addition natural events such as the volcanic eruption in 2010 caused major unexpected problems. Most of these potential risk factors were recognised in successive annual reports, with mitigating strategies for some areas – for example hedging fuel prices by advance purchase agreements. Other uncertainties were created by the company's own early business decisions—for example the forward commitment to buy/lease aircraft that may have been more suited to longer European travel than regional UK destinations and the continued operation of a number of marginally profitable domestic flight routes.
BFQ 6 Performance Indicators How effectively does the board monitor key performance dimensions?	Flybe used a range of key performance indicators and monitored its performance against a range of such indicators. The new CEO in 2017 introduced a new planning mechanism linking KPIs to individual roles across the business.
BFQ 7 Business Turnaround How effectively does the board implement strategies to restore resilience where appropriate and deal with crisis situations as they emerge?	**Restoring business resilience** During its relatively brief history Flybe Group Plc renegotiated debts with its principal lenders and implemented a significant cost reduction programme, including staff redundancies and rationalisation of some of its routes, including curtailment of a major strategic partnership with Finnair. It also sold major assets including its rights to operate out of Gatwick airport and pledged other assets as securities for borrowing.

Table 8.1 (continued)

BFQ 8 Directors' duties To what extent do directors have an effective and relevant understanding of their general duties in situations of financial distress?	No information available to the outside observer.

A focused review

The most immediate and obvious follow-up application of this framework would be to conduct a one-off review, perhaps as part of an "awayday" session where a specific group of managers (ideally executive and non-executive members of the board) are invited to address each of the different questions in the framework and form a view about strengths and weaknesses on each component. An alternative approach might be to initiate an internal review with a lead manager who is tasked with forming a subgroup to address the evidence and produce a summary report and conclusions that could then be addressed by the main board. Such a lead manager could ultimately be given the responsibility of extending and developing the application of this process across the company over time. This second approach would allow time for more attention to detail and an opportunity to identify key issues for a subsequent higher-level discussion and review. The major problem with such an approach is that once this form of "management by delegation" has occurred then the rest of the company may perceive that the problem has been addressed and move on to areas perceived to be of greater concern.

An internal review could be facilitated by an external advisor who combines an assessment of background evidence including company history and procedures with a series of interviews with key members of the company. This might be supported by meetings with different representative groups of employees to discuss each element of the framework. This process will have its biggest impact where there are clear objectives for the exercise that have senior-level endorsement and there is an underlying evidence base that is sufficiently strong, credible and compelling to get the attention of those involved. The ultimate success of any face-to-face meetings will depend on the extent to which the necessary level of "pre-selling" has taken place to bring together a group of key individuals who have been well briefed in advance on the aims and objectives of the process and are prepared to participate fully.

Problems to avoid

Practical problems to avoid include:

Lack of leadership – where the senior managers responsible for initiating the exercise have not determined in advance what the specific purpose is and how it could add value – typically because they did not put sufficient time into thinking about the structure and content, and the follow-up actions that it may generate ahead of implementation.

Lack of information – where many participants are not comfortable with the lack of information that they believe is necessary to reach any concrete conclusions.

Overly complex – which could be summarised by the comment "can't understand what this is about or how practical it is", and perhaps most critically.

No responsibility for follow-through – typically summarised most clearly several weeks or months later by the statement "I thought you were going to do that".

Resilience scorecard: bringing strategic governance to life

Whilst workshops, presentations and external reviews may have an important role ultimately if such activities are to have any long-term value they need to be integrated into the overall planning and control process with identifiable responsibilities for action. One way of achieving this is through a resilience scorecard.

Table 8.2 sets out an example of such a scorecard. The scorecard focuses on purpose, the first element of the benchmarking framework. Similar scorecards could be used to capture the results of reviews of each of the other seven elements of the framework. Ahead of any review those involved might choose to look back at the discussion of each of the elements of the framework in earlier chapters to inform the main areas that could be assessed. Following a review those involved could then consider what actions are required and who should take the lead on implementation. An overall summary resilience scorecard could then establish a series of key resilience indicators. Responsibilities for each area could be allocated to specific members of the business and monitored by the board alongside other more traditional indicators.

Scoring indicators

Scoring is a subjective process. Asking someone to put a score on a particular area is designed to provoke debate and establish a general sense of priorities. The final score although indicative of the overall position is far less important than the process of analysis, reflection and discussion that scoring can enhance. Rather than a

Table 8.2: Resilience scorecard: Application.

Framework questions	Evidence	Score
Purpose		
BFQ 1.1 What are the assumptions about why we are in business? How do we define business success?		
BFQ 1.2 Have we got an explicit statement of purpose and do we communicate this to relevant stakeholders?		
BFQ 1.3 When did we last check these assumptions about purpose? How did we do this? How do others see us?		
BFQ 1.4 Is purpose evident in brands and broader corporate reputation?		
Review date	Agreed actions	
Reviewer		

generalised discussion about a specific area those involved are asked to make a more systematic evaluation based on more specific criteria.

One way to summarise this process is to produce a score for individual areas based on relative effectiveness (for example from 0 to 5, where 0 is given when there is little or no evidence that the area is being addressed and 5 if participants consider that the area is being managed very effectively).

Table 8.3 sets out some examples from specific questions in the overall benchmarking framework to illustrate how such a process could be implemented. It would not be appropriate here to set out a scoring framework for all of the 25 indicators across the 8 different benchmark framework questions.

Table 8.3: Scoring scheme for a sample of indicators.

Framework question	0	1	3	5
BFQ 4.1 Is there a conscious and strategic recognition of accountancy and finance roles, and the impact of effective performance on business outcomes?	Little attempt to disseminate reports on company performance on critical factors internally or to key outsiders with an interest in company activities	Basic accounting systems in place that are compliant with external requirements – does not go beyond annual presentation and review required by regulation	Regular production of financial statements and forecasts to appropriate internal and external audiences – consistent review programme in place to assess performance and adapt behaviour appropriately	Active benchmarking of financial performance against key competitors and industry standards – performance goals set as a result of analysis
BFQ 6.1 **Is there an effective internal system that provides up-to-date information for the board on performance against financial and strategic objectives?**	No evidence of the use of performance indicators	Performance indicators are used on a limited basis to monitor some basic performance statistics but are not widely distributed within the organisation	There is a conscious awareness of the importance of using internal performance indicators which are collected on key areas and regularly discussed at board level	Competitive performance measures are also used to evaluate and modify performance, supplemented by customer and market feedback
BFQ 8.1 To what extent are directors aware of and meet their formal legal obligations (duties) to shareholders, lenders and other stakeholders?	Little or attempt is made to review director actions in terms of responsibilities under relevant legislation	Awareness of director responsibilities and annual review and reporting of compliance on a reactive basis –responsibility of company secretary	Directors recruited and evaluated against performance of formal responsibilities as well as strategic objectives – periodic internal review by non-executive directors as part of formal accountabilitiies	Regular in-house training and director development programmes relating to director duties – systematic evaluation of past, current and prospective strategic decisions against formal director responsibilities

Scores could be added together to produce a score for each of the framework questions and for the framework as a whole. Multi-divisional companies might choose to ask those responsible for each of the divisions to produce a score for their respective division and compare the overall pattern of results. They might choose to invite an external advisor to conduct such a review for each division and report on the overall pattern. There are a range of different options that could be used for different purposes.

Setting priorities for action

The broad scope of this framework means that there are many different areas that could potentially be worth further analysis and ultimately actioned. Setting priorities for areas of attention is a critical part of any implementation plan. Some of these actions will be relatively straightforward and within the scope of existing processes, such as improvement in financial forecasting or identification and reporting of performance on business drivers. Some may require new business structures or frameworks such as more effective strategies to manage cash flow and build up cash reserves. Some elements of the framework may require more fundamental work such as revisiting vision or purpose and branding strategies. Each of the areas for improvement will need to be prioritised and appropriate leadership identified. This may then lead to regular periodic reviews to identify new areas for focus and monitor progress on existing priority areas.

The overall process would then bring strategic governance to life making it a very practical and applied exercise.

References

ACCA, (2012) *Going Concern–Who is responsible?* [online]. March. Available at: https://www.acca global.com/ie/en/technical-activities/technical-resources-search/2012/march/going-concern-responsible.html [Accessed 30 October 2020].

Airbus SE, (2020) *Airbus reports First Quarter (Q1) 2020 results*[online]. Available at: https://www.investegate.co.uk/airbus-se/eqs/airbus-reports-first-quarter–q1–2020-results/20200429052953ERHAN/ [Accessed 10 December 2021].

Al-Hadi, A., Chatterjee, B., Yaftian, A., Taylor, G. and Hasan, M.M. (2019) Corporate social responsibility performance, financial distress and firm life cycle: Evidence from Australia. *Accounting and Finance, 59*(2), 961–989.

AlixPartners. (2021) *ALIXPARTNERS' 16TH ANNUAL TURNAROUND AND TRANSFORMATION SURVEY WHERE NEXT?* [online]. Available at: https://www.alixpartners.com/insights-impact/insights/alixpartners-16th-annual-turnaround-and-transformation-survey/ [Accessed 11 October 2021].

Allianz Group, (2021) *Allianz Risk Barometer 2021, Top Business Risk for 2021* [online]. (ND) Available at: https://www.agcs.allianz.com/content/dam/onemarketing/agcs/agcs/reports/Allianz-Risk-Barometer-2021-Presentation.pdf [Accessed 31 October 2021].

Association of Corporate Treasurers (ACT), (2021) *The Business of Treasury 2021* [online]. Available at: https://www.treasurers.org/system/files/ACT%20Business%20of%20Treasury%202021.pdf [accessed 13 December 2021]

Aston Martin Lagonda Global Holdings plc, (2019) Annual Report.

Aston Martin Lagonda Global Holdings plc, (2021), *Preliminary results for the 12 months to 31 December 2020*. Available at: https://www.investegate.co.uk/aston-martin-lagonda–aml-/rns/final-results/202102250700052656Q/ [accessed 3 May 2021]

Baeza, R., Fæsta, L., Lay, C., Seppä, T., Bartletta, S., Ganeriwalla, A., Moldenhauer, R. and Webb, D. (2017) *The Comeback Kids-Lessons from Successful Turnarounds [Online]*. Boston: Boston Consulting Group, Henderson Institute. Available at https://www.bcg.com/publications/collections/comeback-kids-successful-turnarounds.

Barker, A. (2020) Netflix to take crown for spending on films and television, *Financial Times* [online].14 September, Available at: https://www.ft.com/content/7d66dd4c-440c-44d3-a234-39346fb69a91 [Accessed 14 September 2020].

Beazley Group, (2021) *Beazley-risk-&-resilience-client-report* [online]. (ND). Available at: https://reports.beazley.com/2021/rr/index.html [Accessed 31 October 2021].

Berman, K. and Knight, J. (2009) Are Your People Financially Literate?. *Harvard Business Review, 87*(10), 28–38.

Birshan, M., Gerken, A., Kemmer, S., Petrov, A. and Polyakov, Y. (2020) *The secret to unlocking hidden value in the balance sheet* [online]. McKinsey & Company. 18 March. Available at: https://www.mckinsey.com/business-functions/risk/our-insights/the-secret-to-unlocking-hidden-value-in-the-balance-sheet [Accessed 9 October, 2020].

Boubaker, S., Cellier, A., Manita, R. and Saeed, A. (2020) Does corporate social responsibility reduce financial distress risk?. *Economic Modelling, 91*, 835–851.

Bradley, C., de Jong, M. and Walden, W. (2019) Why your next transformation should be 'all in. *McKinsey Quarterly* October 10, https://www.mckinsey.com/business-functions/strategy-and-corporate-finance/our-insights/why-your-next-transformation-should-be-all-in%26%23x0023 [Accessed 20 May 2021].

Bradley, C., Hirt, M. and Smit, S. (2018) *Strategy beyond the Hockey Stick: People, Probabilities, and Big Moves to Beat the Odds*. New Jersey: Wiley.

https://doi.org/10.1515/9783110689495-014

Brown, P. (2020) *Impossible Impact Report 2020 A Letter from Pat Brown*. 4 December [online]. Available at: https://impossiblefoods.com/impact-report-2020/letter-from-the-ceo [Accessed 10 December 2021]

Burberry Group plc, (2020) *Annual Report 2019/20* [online]. 22 May: 7, 15–17. Available at: https://www.burberryPlc.com/content/dam/burberry/corporate/oar/2020/pdf/Burberry_Annual_Report_2019-20.pdf [Accessed 13 December 2021].

Burgess, K. (2019) The names bond . . . perilously expensive Aston Martin bond, *Financial Times* [online]. 25 September, Available at: https://www.ft.com/content/1ad7f2a0-df82-11e9-9743-db5a370481bc [acccessed 14 March 2021]

Bushey, C. (2020) Airbus is "bleeding cash", says chief executive [online]. *Financial Times*, 27 April. Available at: https://www.ft.com/content/230a0b31-77ef-4ebd-b85e-dfee7ba33eb7 [Accessed 5 November, 2020].

Business Roundtable, (2019) *Business Roundtable Redefines the Purpose of a Corporation to Promote 'An Economy That Serves All Americans'* [online] 19 August. Available at: https://www.businessroundtable.org/business-roundtable-redefines-the-purpose-of-a-corporation-to-promote-an-economy-that-serves-all-americans [Accessed 28 May 2020]

Campbell, M. for UK Commission for Employment and Skills (2013) *Management Matters: key findings from the UKCES Surveys* Briefing Paper (online). March 2013. Available at https://assets.publishing.service.gov.uk/government/uploads/system/uploads/attachment_data/file/305797/briefing-paper-management-matters.pdf Accessed 10 February 2022

CAPA, (2017) *Flybe plans post peak fleet profit progress; new CEO introduces a business improvement plan*[online]. 20 June. Available at: https://centreforaviation.com/analysis/reports/flybe-plans-post-peak-fleet-profit-progress-new-ceo-introduces-a-business-improvement-plan-349670 [Accessed 10 December 2021.]

Chocolats Camille Bloch SA, (ND) *Camille Bloch: About us* [online]. Berne Switzerland: Available at: https://camillebloch.ch/en/about-us/#values [Accessed 2 March 2021].

Citrin, J.M., Hildebrand, C.A. and Stark, R.J. (2019) The CEO Life Cycle. *Harvard Business Review*, *97*(6), 56–60.

Companies Act 2006, ss170–177. Available at: https://www.legislation.gov.uk/ukpga/2006/46/part/10/chapter/2/enacted

Companies Act 2006, s414A. Available at: https://www.legislation.gov.uk/ukpga/2006/46/part/15/chapter/4A

Coyne, K. (2008) Enduring Ideas: The GE-McKinsey nine-box matrix. *McKinsey Quarterly*, 1 September. https://www.mckinsey.com/business-functions/strategy-and-corporate-finance/our-insights/enduring-ideas-the-ge-and-mckinsey-nine-box-matrix [Accessed 25 June 2021].

Cross, J. and Lawrence, S. (2021) *The Good Governance Guide to Board Dynamics*. UK and Ireland: Chartered Governance Institute.

Davidson, J. (2020) *Transforming culture in financial services – Driving purposeful cultures, Discussion Paper, DP20* [online]. 5 March. Available at: https://www.fca.org.uk/publications/discussion-papers/dp20-1-transforming-culture-financial-services-driving-purposeful-cultures [accessed 22 December 2021]

Department for Business, Energy & Industrial Strategy, (2020) *National Statistics Business populations estimates for the UK and regions 2020: statistical release* [online]. October 8. Available at: https://www.gov.uk/government/publications/business-population-estimates-2020/business-population-estimates-for-the-uk-and-regions-2020-statistical-release-html#composition-of-the-2020-business-population [Accessed 11 November, 2020].

Donaldson, G. (1969) Strategy for financial emergencies. *Harvard Business Review*, 47(6), 67–80.

Financial Accounting Standards Board, (2014) *Presentation of Financial Statements – Going Concern (Subtopic 205-40), Disclosure of Uncertainties about an Entity's Ability to Continue as*

a Going Concern, No. 2014-15 [online]. August. Available at: https://www.fasb.org/jsp/FASB/
Document_C/DocumentPage?cid=1176164329772&acceptedDisclaimer=true [Accessed
10 November 2020].

Financial Reporting Council, (2009) *Going Concern and Liquidity Risk Guidance for Directors of UK
Companies* [online]. October. Available at: https://www.frc.org.uk/getattachment/079e9ca2-
7153-4831-8248-5de419041f6c/Going-concern-and-liquidity-risk-guidance-for-directors-of-uk-
companies-093.pdf [Accessed 11 November, 2020].

Financial Reporting Council, (2012) *The Sharman Inquiry Going Concern and Liquidity Risks:
Lessons for Companies and Auditors, Final Report and Recommendations of the Panel of
Enquiry* [online]. June. Available at: https://www.frc.org.uk/getattachment/4a7f9880-0158-
4cf0-b41e-b9e1bf006bd7/Sharman-Inquiry-final-report-FINAL.pdf [Accessed
2 November 2020].

Financial Reporting Council (2014) *Guidance on Risk Management, Internal Control and Related
Business Reporting*. September: 21. Available at: https://www.frc.org.uk/getattachment/
d672c107-b1fb-4051-84b0-f5b83a1b93f6/Guidance-on-Risk-Management-Internal-Control-and-
Related-Reporting.pdf

Financial Reporting Council, (2018-a) *The UK Corporate Governance Code* [online]. July. Available
at: https://www.frc.org.uk/getattachment/88bd8c45-50ea-4841-95b0-d2f4f48069a2/2018-uk
-corporate-governance-code-final.pdf [accessed 23 December 2021].

Financial Reporting Council, (2018-b) *Guidance on Board Effectiveness* [online]. *July. 3*. Available at:
https://www.frc.org.uk/getattachment/61232f60-a338-471b-ba5a-bfed25219147/2018-
guidance-on-board-effectiveness-final.pdf [accessed 23 December 2021].

Financial Reporting Council (2018-c) *Reporting of performance metrics*, [online]. June. Available at:
https://www.frc.org.uk/getattachment/e94631d1-69c1-4349-8ce5-780d4eca455f/LAB_Report
ing-of-performance-metrics_June-2018.PDF [Accessed 14 December 2021]

Financial Reporting Council (2018-d) *Performance metrics: Principles and Practice* [online].
November. Available at https://www.frc.org.uk/getattachment/cd978ef7-72ad-4785-81ee-
e08bb7b7f152/LAB-Performance-metrics-FINAL.pdf [Accessed 17 March 2021].

Financial Reporting Council, (2019-a) *ISA (UK) 570 (REVISED SEPTEMBER 2019) Going Concern*
[online]. September: 15-16. Available at: https://www.frc.org.uk/getattachment/13b19e6c-
4d2c-425e-84f9-da8b6c1a19c9/ISA-UK-570-revised-September-2019-Full-Covers.pdf [Accessed
8 November 2020].

Financial Reporting Council, (2019-b) *Disclosures on the sources and uses of cash* [online].
September. Available at: https://www.frc.org.uk/getattachment/0689ba0c-2a23-4850-b0b9
-8bec52938cce/Disclosures-on-the-sources-and-uses-of-cash-Final.pdf [Accessed
5 November 2020].

Fiskars Corporation (ND) *Our heritage From 1649 to the present.* [online] Available at: https://www.
fiskars.eu/About-Us/Our-Heritage [Accessed 10 December 2021].

Franks, J. and Sussman, O. (2005) Financial Distress and Bank Restructuring of Small to Medium
Size UK Companies. *Review of Finance, 9*, 65–96.

Freeman, R.E. (1984) *Strategic Management: A Stakeholder Approach*. 4th Edition Pitman: London.

Friedman, M., (1970) The Social Responsibility of Business is to Increase its Profits. *The New York
Times Magazine*, September 13.

Garratt, B. (2010) *The Fish Rots from the Head. Developing Effective Board Directors*. 3rd Edition
London: Profile Books Ltd.

Gast, A., Illanes, P., Probst, N., Schaninger, B. and Simpson, B., (2020) Purpose: Shifting from Why
to How. *McKinsey Quarterly* April [online]. Available at: https://www.mckinsey.com/business-
functions/organization/our-insights/purpose-shifting-from-why-to-how [Accessed
28 May 2020].

George, P., (2016) The scary truth about corporate survival: Companies are really failing faster. *Harvard Business Review*, Vol. 94 (12), 24–25 citing Vijay Govindarajan and Anup Srivastava (2016) Strategy When Creative Destruction Accelerates, (*Tuck School of Business Working paper* No. 2836135) Available at: https://papers.ssrn.com/sol3/papers.cfm?abstract_id= 2836135 [Accessed 21 September 21 2020].

Gething, J., Hudson, R., Johnston, M., O'Neill, D. and Wlodarz, M. (2020) When do you need a chief restructuring officer?. *McKinsey & Company*, 13 November. Available at: https://www.mckin sey.com/business-functions/transformation/our-insights/when-do-you-need-a-chief-restructuring-officer [Accessed 8 October 2021].

Goffee, R. and Jones, G. (2006) *Why Should Anyone Be Led by You? What It Takes to Be an Authentic Leader*. Harvard: Harvard Business School Press.

Goode, R.M. (2011) *Principles of Corporate Insolvency Law*. 4th Ed Sweet & Maxwell: London.

Grimes, C. and Nicolaou, A. (2022), Are you still watching? Netflix and the future of streaming. Financial Times [online] 22 April. Available at https://www.ft.com/content/fd376c16-f8d7 -49fd-9b13-9ed2f001eaa1 accessed 26 April 2022

Grube, C., Park, S. and Rüden, J.. (2020) *Moving from cash preservation to cash excellence for the next normal* [online]. McKinsey & Company. 29 September. Available at: https://www.mckin sey.com/business-functions/strategy-and-corporate-finance/our-insights/moving-from-cash-preservation-to-cash-excellence-for-the-next-normal [Accessed 9 October, 2020].

Hall, L.A. and Davis, G. (2017) The board's new innovation imperative. Directors need to rethink their roles and attitudes to risk. *Harvard Business Review*, *95*(6), 102–109.

Hamel, G. and Prahalad, C.K. (1989) Strategic Intent. *Harvard Business Review*, *67*(3), 63–78.

Harmon, M. (2020) 'A primer on restructuring your company's finances', HBR.org (June) Reprint H05N2J Available at https://hbr.org/2020/06/a-primer-on-restructuring-your-companys-finances [Accessed 22 February 2022]

Hastings, R. and Meyer, E. (2020) *No Rules Rules: Netflixand the Culture of Reinvention*. London: Penguin.

Heidrick & Struggles, The Conference Board (2020) CEO Succession Practices In The Russell 3000 and S&P 500 [online]. Available at: https://conference-board.org/pdfdownload.cfm?masterPro ductID=23423 [Accessed 11 October 2021].

Hemingway, E. (1927) *Fiesta: The Sun Also Rises*. London: Johnathon Cape.

HM Government: Department for Business, Energy & Industrial Strategy (2018) *Insolvency and Corporate Governance, Government response August:* Available at: https://assets.publishing. service.gov.uk/government/uploads/system/uploads/attachment_data/file/736163/ICG_-_ Government_response_doc_-_24_Aug_clean_version__with_Minister_s_photo_and_signa ture__AC.pdf [accessed 15 April 2022]

HM Government (2021) *Covid-19 Response- Spring 2021*. CP 398. 53. [online]. Available at: https://assets.publishing.service.gov.uk/government/uploads/system/uploads/attachment_ data/file/963491/COVID-19_Response_-_Spring_2021.pdf [Accessed 7 August 2021].

ICAEW, (2011) *Reporting Business Risks: Meeting Expectations Information for Better Markets Initiative*. London:

ICAEW, (2014) *The 99.9%: Small and Medium Sized Businesses: Who are They and What Do They Need?*. London.

Intuit Inc. (ND) Available at: https://quickbooks.intuit.com/uk/ [Accessed 10 December 2021].

Jashan, E. (2019) Sir Philip Green appoints restructuring experts to Arcadia board. *Retail Gazette* [online], 11 April. Available at: https://www.retailgazette.co.uk/blog/2019/04/sir-philip-green-appoints-restructuring-experts-to-arcadia-board/ [Accessed 16 February 2021].

Jolly, J., (2021) Losses at Aston Martin almost quadruple as Covid cuts sales, *The Guardian* [online] 25 February. Available at: https://www.theguardian.com/business/2021/feb/25/losses-at-aston-martin-almost-quadruple-as-covid-cuts-sales [accessed 14 March 2021].

Kaplan, R.S. and Mikes, A. (2012) Managing risks: A new framework. *Harvard Business Review*, *90*(6), 48–60.

Kaplan, R.S. and Norton, D.P. (1996) *The Balanced Scorecard*. Boston: Harvard Business School Press.

Kaplan, R.S., Leonard, H.B. and Milkes, A. (2020) The risks you can't foresee- What to do when there's no playbook. *Harvard Business Review*, *98*(6), 40–46.

Kay, J. (2011) Don't blame luck when your models misfire. *Financial Times* [online], 1 March, Available at https://www.ft.com/content/77bf5f98-4441-11e0-931d-00144feab49a [Accessed 15 March 2021].

Kensuke, K. (2017) *Lessons of the 1997 financial crisis in Japan*. Nippon.com, [online]. Available at: https://www.nippon.com/en/currents/d00360/lessons-of-the-1997-financial-crisis-in-japan.html [Accessed 28 December 2021].

Kipling, R. (1910) *IF*. New York: Doubleday Page & Company.

Kiyosaki, R. (2011) *Rich Dad Poor Dad: What the Rich Teach Their Kids about Money that the Poor and Middle Class Do Not!*. UK: Plata Publishing/Simon & Schuster.

Kollewe, J. (2009) Waterford Wedgwood 250 years of history. *Guardian* [online], 5 January. Available at: https://www.theguardian.com/business/2009/jan/05/waterford-wedgwood-history [Accessed 28 February 2020].

Kongo-Gumi (2013-a) [online]. Available at: https://www.kongogumi.co.jp/idea.html [Accessed 28 December 2021].

Kongo-Gumi (2013-b) [online]. Available at: https://www.kongogumi.co.jp/posture.html [Accessed 28 December 2021].

KPMG, Dumble, K.. (ed) (2014) *The KPMG Survey of Business Reporting* [online]. Available at: https://assets.kpmg/content/dam/kpmg/pdf/2014/06/kpmg-survey-business-reporting.pdf [Accessed 10 December 2021].

KPMG, (2020-a) 'Spain: Government and institution measures in response to COVID-19' [online]. Available at: https://home.kpmg/xx/en/home/insights/2020/04/spain-government-and-institution-measures-in-response-to-Covid.html [Accessed 7 August 2021].

KPMG, (2020-b) 'Canada: Government and institution measures in response to COVID-19', [online]. Available at: https://home.kpmg/xx/en/home/insights/2020/04/canada-government-and-institution-measures-in-response-to-Covid.html [Accessed 7 August 7 2021].

KPS Capital Partners, LP, (2015) *KPS Capital Partners to Sell WWRD to Fiskars Corporation* [online]. 11 May. Available at: https://www.kpsfund.com/news/press-releases/2015/05/11/kps-capital-partners-to-sell-wwrd-to-fiskars-corporation [Accessed 2 March 2021].

Lemerle, M., Allianz Research. (2020). *Close to 150 large companies went bust in Q2 2020* [online]. Available at: https://www.eulerhermes.com/content/dam/onemarketing/ehndbx/euler hermes_com/en_gl/erd/publications/pdf/FINAL2020_07_29_Majorinsolvencies.pdf [Accessed 16 August 2021].

Levitt, T. (1960) Marketing Myopia. *Harvard Business Review*, *38*(4), 45–56.

McCrum, D. (2020) Wirecard:timeline.*Financial Times* [online], 25 June. Available at: https://www.ft.com/content/284fb1ad-ddc0-45df-a075-0709b36868db [Accessed 12 May 2021].

McDonalds Corporation, (2020) *Annual Report for the Fiscal Year ended December 31, 2020* 29–35

McNicholas, G. (2020) Beyond Wrongful Trading: Remaining Risks and Responsibilities. *Journal of International Banking and Financial Law*, *6*, 391–393.

Mintzberg, H. (1975) The Manager's Job: Folklore and Fact. *Harvard Business Review*, *53*(4), 49–61.

Mintzberg, H. (1994) *The Rise and Fall of Strategic Planning*. New York: The Free Press.

Mintzberg, H. and Lampel, J. (1999) Reflecting on the Strategy Process. *Sloan Management Review*, *40*(3), 21–30.

Moats, M.C., DeNicola, P. and Malone, L. (2021) *Behavioural psychology might explain what's holding boards back*. [online] Harvard Law School Forum on Corporate Governance, March 25. Available at: https://corpgov.law.harvard.edu/2021/03/25/behavioral-psychology-might-explain-whats-holding-boards-back/#1 [accessed 23 March 2022)

Nestlé Group, (2016) *Nestlé Timeline 1866-today*. [online]. 4 January. Available at: https://www.nestle.co.uk/en-gb/media/newsfeatures/nestle-150-years-timeline [Accessed 10 May 2020].

Nestlé Group (2020) *153 Annual General Meeting. Speech by Chairman Paul Bulcke*. [online]. Available at: https://www.nestle.com/media/mediaeventscalendar/allevents/agm-2020 [Acccessed 10 December 2021]

Netflix Inc, (2020) 10-K ANNUAL REPORT PURSUANT TO SECTION 13 OR 15 (D) OF THE SECURITIES EXCHANGE ACT OF 1934, Fiscal year ended Dec 31, 2019 [online]. Available at: https://www.sec.gov/ix?doc=/Archives/edgar/data/1065280/000106528020000040/form10kq419.htm#s517E775B678B52C58A8FA48A874CF4DA [Accessed 15 October 2020].

Netflix Inc, (2022) *Netflix Culture* [online]. Available at: https://jobs.netflix.com/culture [accessed 2 January 2021]

Next Plc, (2019) *Annual Report and Accounts* 26 January. 14.

Niven, P.R. (2006) *Balanced Scorecard, Step by Step*. 2nd edition New Jersey: JohnWiley and Sons Inc.

Nichols, C., Hayden, C.S. and Trendler, C.. (2020) 4 behaviors that help leaders manage a crisis. *Harvard Business Review* [online], 2 April. Available at: https://hbr.org/2020/04/4-behaviors-that-help-leaders-manage-a-crisis [Accessed 5 May 2020]

NMUL Realisations Ltd, (2020) *Statement of administrator's proposals April 7 2020 and administrator's progress report September 17 2020*. Both available at https://find-and-update.company-information.service.gov.uk/company/06718623/filing-history [Accessed 8 March 2021].

Norton Motorcycles (UK) Limited, (2019) *Strategic Report, Report of the Directors and Audited Financial Statements for the Year Ended 31 March 2018*.

OECD (2021), "OECD Corporate Governance Factbook 2021". Available at https://www.oecd.org/corporate/corporategovernance-factbook.htm [accessed 10 December 2021].

Online Etymology Dictionary [online], (2021) *Director (n)*. Available at: https://www.etymonline.com/word/director [accessed 29 June 2021].

Parkinson, M.M. (2017) Directors' duties to exercise independent judgement: The path to s.173 of the Companies Act 2006 and beyond. *The Company Lawyer, 38*(9), 271–277.

Parkinson, M.M. (2018) *Corporate Governance in Transition: Dealing with Financial Distress and Insolvency in UK Companies*. Cham Switzerland: Springer Nature Switzerland AG.

Parkinson, S.T. (1990) Management development's strategic role. *Journal of General Management*, *16*(2), 63–74.

Parkinson, S.T. and Saren, M.A. (1981) *Offshore Technology: A Forecast and Review*. London: Financial Times Business Publications Division.

Portas, M. (2020) Covid didn't kill Topshop: A lack of creativity did. *Financial Times*, December 8. Available at: https://www.ft.com/content/f8bd6c9e-7b91-4fe3-af3a-d35d7fc617b5 [Accessed 16 February 2021].

Porter, M.E. (1979) How Competitive Forces Shape Strategy. *Harvard Business Review*, *57*(2), 137–145.

Porter, M.E. (1980) *Competitive Strategy: Techniques for Analysing Industries and Competitors*. New York: Free Press.

Porter, M.E. (1985) *Competitive Advantage: Creating and Sustaining Superior Performance*. NY: Free Press.

Power, M. (2009) The risk management of nothing. *Accounting, Organizations and Society*, *34*(6–7), 849–855.

Renjen, P. (2020) The heart of Resilient leadership: Responding to COVID-19 A guide for senior executives. *Deloitte Insights*, 16 March. Available at: https://www2.deloitte.com/us/en/in sights/economy/Covid-19/heart-of-resilient-leadership-responding-to-Covid-19.html?id= us:2el:3dp:wsjspon:awa:WSJCMO:2020:WSJFY20 [Accessed 26 April 2020]

Reuters London, (2020) *British Airways boss says burning through cash, urges unions to engage* [online]. 4 June. Available at: https://www.reuters.com/article/us-health-coronavirus-british-airways-idUSKBN23B1FJ [Accessed 5 November, 2020].

Rolls-Royce Holdings Plc, 'Trading and Trent 1000 update', 7 November 2019. Available at: https://investegate.co.uk/rolls-royce-holdings--rr.-/rns/trading-and-trent-1000-update /201911070700105611S/ [Accessed 3 December 2021].

Rolls-Royce Holdings Plc, (2020) *Rolls-Royce Proposes Major Reorganisation to Address Medium-Term Impact of Covid-19* [online]. 20 May. Available at: https://investegate.co.uk/rolls-royce-holdings--rr.-/rns/rolls-royce-proposes-major-reorganisation/202005200700034045N/ [Accessed 10 December 2021].

Rolls-Royce Holdings Plc (2020) *Annual Report 2019, Strategic Report*. 8 July. 50.

Sage Group plc, (ND). Available at: https://www.sage.com/en-gb/sage-business-cloud/account ing/ [Accessed 10 December 2021].

Schoeffler, S., Buzzell, R.D. and Heany, D.F. (1974) Impact of Strategic Planning on Profit Performance. *Harvard Business Review*, *52*(2), 137–145.

Schweizer, L. and Nienhaus, A. (2017) Corporate distress and turnaround: Integrating the literature and directing future research. *Business Research*, *10*(1), 3–47.

Schumpeter, J.A. (1942) *Capitalism, Socialism and Democracy*. First edition. New York; Harper & Brothers.

Short, H. and Keasey, K. (1999), Managerial Ownership and the Performance of Firms: Evidence from the UK. *Journal of Corporate Finance*, 5 (1), 79–101.

Sisodia, R., Sheth, J.N. and Wolfe, D. (2014) *Firms of Endearment: How World-Class Companies Profit from Passion and Purpose*. 2nd edition. Upper Saddle River, NJ: Pearson Education.

Slatter, S. and Lovett, D. (1999) *Corporate Turnaround*. London: Penguin Books.

Smith, R. (2021) 'Greensill and supply-chain finance: How a contentious funding tool works'. *Financial Times* (online) 2 March. Available at: https://www.ft.com/content/1bbbe94c-9c3d-43d1-bcdd-8add6557c5a7 [Accessed 22 February 2022]

Storbeck, O., McCrum, D. and Palma, S. (2020) Ex-Wirecard chief Markus Braun arrested. *Financial Times* [online], June 23. Available at: https://www.ft.com/content/30dd3df6-1db3-430a-b4d3-e4a114568410 [Accessed 3 May 2021].

Takamatsu Construction Group, (ND) Kongo-Gumi Co., Ltd [online]. Available at: https://www.taka matsu-cg.co.jp/eng/about/Group/takamatsu/kongogumi.html [Accessed 28 December 2021].

Tepper, T. (2022) 'Impossible Foods IPO: What You Need to Know'. *Forbes Advisor* [online] February 2. Available at https://www.forbes.com/advisor/investing/impossible-foods-ipo/ Accessed 4 April 2022

Terazono, E. (2021) Alt-protein start-ups cut prices for bigger slice of meat market. *Financial Times* [online] 20 March. Available at: https://www.ft.com/content/20ae8314-e1fa-4bcb-b2c0 -99e58df6bfb7 [Accessed 28 June 2021].

The Super league (2021), *Leading European Clubs Announce New Super League Competition* [online]. Available at: https://thesuperleague.com/press.html [Accessed 3 January 2022].

Reuters, T. (2022), *Practical Law: Corporate Governance and Directors' Duties Global Guide*. Available at: https://uk.practicallaw.thomsonreuters.com/Browse/Home/International/Corpo rateGovernanceandDirectorsDutiesGlobalGuide?__lrTS=20220414160103173&transitionType= Default&contextData=%28sc.Default%29 [Accessed 14 April 2022].

Thoreau, H.D. (1854) *Walden*. Published 2004 in paperback edition. New Jersey: Princeton University.

Trimm, P. (2013) *Entrepreneur Handbook. How to do accounts for small businesses* [online]. May 12. Available at: https://entrepreneurhandbook.co.uk/small-business-accounting/ [Accessed 10 December 2021].

TVS Motor Company (2020), *TVS Motor Company Completes Acquisition of Norton* [online]. 17 April. Available at https://www.tvsmotor.com/Media/Press-Release/tvs-motor-company-completes-acquisition-of-norton [Accessed 12 May 2020].

UK Banking (Special Provisions) Act 2008, [online]. Available at: https://www.legislation.gov.uk/ ukpga/2008/2/contents [Accessed 10 December 2021].

US Department of the Treasury, (ND) Troubled Asset Relief Program (TARP) [online]. Available at: https://home.treasury.gov/data/troubled-assets-relief-program/about-tarp [Accessed 10 December 2021].

Virgin Galactic Holdings Inc, (2019) *Form 10-K for the fiscal year ended December 31, 2019* [online]. Available at: https://www.sec.gov/ix?doc=/Archives/edgar/data/1706946/ 000162828020002471/spce-20191231.htm#i921cdb623e764b869653cf7eb86f9f89_1187 [Accessed 14 March 2021].

Whitney, J.O. (1987) Turnaround management every day. *Harvard Business Review*, 65(5), 49–55.

Wirecard, A.G., (2020-a) *Date for publication of annual and consolidated financial statements 2019 delayed due to indications of presentation of spurious balance confirmations*.[online] 18 June. Available at: https://www.investegate.co.uk/wirecard-ag/eqs/date-for-publication-of-annual-and-consolidated-financial-statements-2019-delayed-due-to-indications-of-presentation-of-spurious-balance-confirmations/20200618094336EMQST/ [Accessed 3 May 2021].

Wirecard, A.G., (2020-b) *Statement of the Management Board about the current situation of the Company*. [online] 22 June. Available at: https://www.investegate.co.uk/wirecard-ag/eqs/ statement-of-the-management-board-about-the-current-situation-of-the-company /20200622014858EHXEL/ [Accessed 3 May 2021].

Wirecard, A.G., (2020-c) *Company statement regarding filing for insolvency* [online]. 25 June. Available at: https://www.investegate.co.uk/wirecard-ag/eqs/company-statement-regarding-filing-for-insolvency/20200625123940EFAWS/ [Accessed 3 May 2021].

Yakola, D. (2014) Leading Companies out of a crisis: Ten tips from a veteran turnaround artist. *McKinsey on Finance: Perspectives on Corporate Finance and Strategy* [online], Number 49, Winter. Available at: https://www.mckinsey.com/Client_Service/Corporate_Finance/Latest_ thinking/McKinsey_on_Finance/~/media/DD440FCC4F7F4F04B28CE1DBBD82EAE6.ashx [Accessed 26 Aug 2020].

List of tables

https://doi.org/10.1515/9783110689495-015

List of figures

https://doi.org/10.1515/9783110689495-016

Index

https://doi.org/10.1515/9783110689495-017

www.ingramcontent.com/pod-product-compliance
Lightning Source LLC
Chambersburg PA
CBHW081103220326
41598CB00038B/7209